Trauma, Abandonme Privilege

A guide to therapeutic work with boarding school survivors

Nick Duffell and Thurstine Basset

Routledge
Taylor & Francis Group

LONDON AND NEW YORK

First published 2016
by Routledge
2 Park Square, Milton Park, Abingdon, Oxon OX14 4RN

and by Routledge
711 Third Avenue, New York, NY 10017

Routledge is an imprint of the Taylor & Francis Group, an informa business

© 2016 Nick Duffell and Thurstine Basset

The right of Nick Duffell and Thurstine Basset to be identified as authors of this work has been asserted by them in accordance with sections 77 and 78 of the Copyright, Designs and Patents Act 1988.

British Library Cataloguing in Publication Data
A catalogue record for this book is available from the British Library

Library of Congress Cataloguing in Publication Data
Names: Duffell, Nick, author. | Basset, Thurstine, author.
Title: Trauma, Abandonment and Privilege: a guide to therapeutic work with boarding school survivors / Nick Duffell & Thurstine Basset.
Description: Abingdon, Oxon: New York, NY: Routledge, 2016. |
Includes bibliographical references.
Identifiers: LCCN 2015039191 | ISBN 9781138788701 (hbk) |
ISBN 9781138788718 (pbk.) | ISBN 9781315760582 (ebk)
Subjects: | MESH: Psychotherapy–methods. | Adult Survivors of Child Abuse–psychology. | Anxiety, Separation. | Child, Institutionalized–psychology. | Stress, Psychological. | Students–psychology.
Classification: LCC RC480.5 | NLM WM 420 | DDC 616.89/14–dc23
LC record available at http://lccn.loc.gov/2015039191

ISBN: 978-1-138-78870-1 (hbk)
ISBN: 978-1-138-78871-8 (pbk)
ISBN: 978-1-315-76058-2 (ebk)

Extracts from 'A Perfect Spy' by John Le Carré, © 1986 Authors Workshop AG, are reproduced by permission of Hodder and Stoughton Limited

Illustrations/cartoons from 'Depresso: or How I Learned To Stop Worrying And Embrace Being Bonkers by Brick, ©) 2010 John Stuart Clark (Brick), are reproduced by permission of Knockabout Limited

Illustration 'Survival Personality Types' (Figure 4.1) is reproduced by permission of Emma Basset

Typeset in Times New Roman
by Out of House Publishing
Printed and bound by CPI Group (UK) Ltd, Croydon, CR0 4YY

Trauma, Abandonment and Privilege

Trauma, Abandonment and Privilege discusses how ex-boarders can be amongst the most challenging clients for therapists; even experienced therapists may unwittingly struggle to skilfully address the needs of this client group. It looks at the effect on adults of being sent away to board in childhood and the problems associated with boarding, which have only recently been acknowledged by mainstream mental health professionals.

This practice-based book is illustrated by case studies, diagrams and exercises and is divided into three parts: Recognition, Acceptance and Change. It aims to help readers understand the emotional processes of boarding and the psychological aspects of survival, outlining the steps toward recovery and the repercussions of survival. The book also explores how ex-boarders frequently struggle with intimate relationships with spouses and partners and offers interventions and strategies for those working with ex-boarder clients.

Trauma, Abandonment and Privilege will be of interest to therapists, counsellors and mental health workers across the UK. It will also be relevant to those who are well acquainted with boarding schools based on the UK model, for example in Canada, Australia, New Zealand and India.

Nick Duffell is a psychotherapist and trainer in private practice who pioneered therapeutic work with ex-boarders and specialist training for psychotherapists. He is the author of *The Making of Them: The British Attitude to Children and the Boarding School System* and *Wounded Leaders: British Elitism and the Entitlement Illusion: A Psychohistory*.

Thurstine Basset worked as a social worker, mostly in the mental health field, before entering the world of training and education in the 1980s. He has subsequently written and produced a variety of training packages, articles, book chapters and books on mental health. Early in the twenty-first century, he attended a Boarding School Survivors workshop and was a director of Boarding Concern, an organisation that supports boarding school survivors.

Contents

Preface

Since 1990, when Nick Duffell launched Boarding School Survivors, a handful of dedicated practitioners have been pioneering specialised psychotherapy with ex-boarders in individual and group formats. In 2000, the first account of the psychology of boarding, *The Making of Them: The British Attitude to Children and the Boarding School System*, appeared. It was always the intention to follow up that book with an in-depth account of therapy with boarding school survivors. The current volume attempts to share 25 years of experience of therapeutic work with ex-boarders for the benefit of psychotherapists, counsellors and other mental health workers, who may not be aware of the complications of this little-known syndrome. Also included are several exercises in each chapter for working with clients, both individually and in groups.

Although the number of informed practitioners has substantially grown, we do not – at the time of writing – have the results of any formal quantitative research into this topic. Nevertheless, this book is based on many hours of work with many hundreds of ex-boarders, and we hope it can inspire other therapists to intervene creatively with this difficult client group.

As mental health professionals who are also ex-boarders, our learnings and observations accompany the case material that illustrates this book. Over the years, countless unsolicited questions, comments and letters, describing the difficulties of boarding and the effect on later life, have come our way. We have drawn on this rich material throughout the book, sometimes naming the correspondent and sometimes leaving them anonymous, depending on the wishes of the person involved.

We are indebted to a number of people who supplied material for this book and to some who read parts of it and advised. They are Robert Arnold, Jane Barclay, Christopher Cox, Sarah Feldman, Sally Fraser, Marcus Gottlieb, Darrel Hunneybell, Olya Khaleelee, Zuzana Kucerova, Margaret Laughton, Rovianne Matovu, Nicola Miller, Andrew Morrison, Simon Partridge, Emilce Rees, Anni Townend, Jon Wallwork and Joy Warren-Adamson. Thanks are due to them.

Thanks also to the anonymous contributors, and to Sue Gerhard, Joy Schaverien, Stephen Porges and Felicity de Zuleta.

Thanks to the political cartoonist, Brick (John Stuart Clark), and to his publishers Knockabout for letting us use his illustrations.

Thurstine would like to extend special thanks to Frances Basset for both her thoughtful expertise and loving support; Nick would like to acknowledge Helena Løvendal-Duffell's pivotal role in identifying the issues and consequences of the boarding culture as well as the treatment approaches described in this book.

Part I

Recognition

Chapter 1

Introduction

I fell into conversation with a Frenchman I sat next to last night at dinner, and I just couldn't resist getting onto education, because the French have *such* different views on education – they cannot understand how we can possibly do what we do – how we can *bear* to send our children away: they should be coming in to us every night and talking to us every night, how we mustn't lose touch with them, and how vital it is to see them every day. I totally disagree – I think it's *the making of them*, this sending them away. And, you know, I can see what happens, I can see them every three weeks – it's not a *drama*, really.
(A mother of one of the 8-year-old new boarders talking to camera in Colin Luke's 1994 film *The Making of Them*)

Key points of chapter

- Psychology professionals have been slow to acknowledge that the British culture of sending young children to boarding school has an impact on psychological wellbeing.
- Although unsupported by any theory of child development, the practice is still seen in some quarters as a desirable way to educate children.
- A body of literature on this important topic has been built up over the last 20 years.

Setting the scene

This book aims to help psychotherapists, counsellors and other mental health workers to develop a therapeutic approach to adult clients who were sent to boarding school as young children. This first chapter gives background information to set the scene for these therapeutic interventions.

We are writing early on in the twenty-first century. Over the previous century enormous strides were made in the field of children's rights; psychology grew from small beginnings to become a major influence in society. Many theories of child development evolved from a number of perspectives – educational, cognitive, humanistic, maturational, behavioural, psychodynamic and so on. But nowhere can we find a single theory of child development that underpins or backs up the British practice of sending young children – aged 8 or sometimes younger – away from their families to reside in educational institutions for approximately 75 percent of each year.

Most people would accept that the fundamental role of parents is to love and protect their children while gradually nurturing their independence, so that by the time they reach adulthood, they can begin to make their own way in the world. This normally involves a step-by-step and very gradual process towards increasing maturity and appropriate autonomy.

And yet there is – in a manner of speaking – a tribe of people, living mostly in deepest Britain, who see things differently and have strange customs. They adhere to a socialisation doctrine perfected in mid-Victorian England, whereby the normal process of child development is interrupted by a dramatic and drastic change in which family attachments are deliberately broken. The practice appears cruel to those outside this tribe, as it does at the time to the children of the tribe, and it can leave deep emotional scars. Unlike such abhorrent practices as female genital mutilation, its scars are not obvious to the human eye and do not normally involve – anymore – bodily harm. But they are real scars nevertheless which can have a profoundly negative effect in adult life.

The tragedy is compounded because this wounding has been overlooked, denied and powerfully normalised. Huge financial lobbies support the business of boarding schools, to which the UK government grants special charity status. Moreover, the tribe that supports the practice is influential and vocal, consisting of those who can afford the fees – at the time of writing some £30,000 per annum per child. It includes the traditional upper classes, the wealthy middle classes as well as the less well off but aspirant socially mobile, supplemented by rich foreign families investing in the social status such an education affords.

Their children, typically 8 year olds, discover that from day one (and for the next 10 years) they will spend 9 out of every 12 months living in a boarding school and only 3 months at home with their family. They have neither the choice, nor the right to object, and soon an internal self-monitoring process kicks in to assist the child in surviving and adapting to the inevitable. The habit of sending the children away, the process of survival and accompanying trauma are disguised and compensated by the privilege afforded by the social elitism that accompanies this form of education. Hence the title of this book.

To most modern European observers and to psychologically minded people, this antiquated practice seems like a form of child neglect – even abuse. For example, the journalist George Monbiot suggested that 'Britain's most overt form of child abuse is mysteriously ignored' (Monbiot, 1998). But the educational system that lies at the heart of it is a well-trodden path to privilege, power and what can appear to be a successful life. It leads from prep school (from the age of 7) to public school (from 13) and then usually to Oxbridge. This path has been travelled by countless public luminaries, including, at the time of writing, the current UK Prime Minister, the Mayor of London, the Archbishop of Canterbury and Lord Layard, the champion of successive governments' strategies to 'improve access to psychological therapies'.

Herein lies one key reason why this practice is overlooked: private boarding has an almost unassailable position in the world and parents invest huge sums for their children to be part of it. It brings money into the UK, is looked up to and aspired to; insiders think it the envy of the world. A secondary vicious cycle enhances its position: the influential parents who support private boarding simultaneously opt out of the state system, which suffers in comparison and cannot compete in terms of resources. A Cinderella state system then helps further rationalise the parents' choice for the private system, which instead of seeming outdated, presents itself as the only option for parents who 'want to do the best for their children'.

And it does turn out many people who are 'success stories' – at least in the world of outer achievements. Yet, since 1990, in workshops run by the organisation Boarding School Survivors for both men and women ex-boarders seeking psychological help as adults, the overall boarding school experience has been frequently described in the following terms:

> neglect – betrayal – abandonment – grief – rage – abuse – confusion – sadness – helplessness – loneliness – motherless – missing daddy – sent away – neediness – anger – suppression – denial – tears – survival.
> (Selection of participants' initial impressions on the first morning of a four-day Boarding School Survivors workshop)

It is this gap between outer and inner reality with which ex-boarders and practitioners have to engage.

The early years

How has the boarding habit escaped serious attention for so long? The first traceable mention of any problems associated with boarding education comes from the renowned Scottish economist and philosopher Adam Smith:

> The education of boys at distant great schools, of young men at distant colleges, of young ladies in distant nunneries and boarding schools, seems in the higher ranks of society to have done crucial harm to domestic morals and thus to domestic happiness, both in France and in England ...

> From their parents' house they may, with propriety and advantage, go out
> every day to attend public schools: but let them continue to live at home.
>
> (Smith, 1759, V1.11.13)

It was not until the First World War that the first serious psychological hypothesis about ex-boarders was made. William Halse Rivers, the 'shell-shock' psychiatrist, noted that many wounded officers expressed their sickness differently to the enlisted men because they were already trained to withhold their personal responses through their public school education: 'The public schoolboy enters the army with a long course of training behind him which enables him successfully to repress, not only the expression of fear, but also the emotion itself' (Rivers, 1918).

The next serious attempt to examine the effects of boarding from a scientific viewpoint came from post-Second World War sociology. Royston Lambert and his colleagues collected data from 12,000 boys and girls in over 60 different boarding schools – public, prep, 'progressive', independent and state run. Their extraordinary piece of research has more a feel of *Tom Brown's Schooldays* than *Harry Potter* and has been widely read (Lambert and Millham, 1968). Amongst his data, Lambert reported anonymous comments from a huge number of pupils about teachers who were sexually abusing pupils, for example:

> Mr Tomkins is a house master and I think he is a vulgar man ... he does rude things to people ... please publish this to show everybody that a schoolmaster is not good at all.
>
> He has had a warning from the headmaster about being sexy. Nobody likes him.
>
> Keep your legs crossed if you go to coffee with Oscar, he is as bent as a clockwork orange and a right queer.
>
> When I was trying on a uniform, this bum bandit pressed his tool right up against me.
>
> (Lambert and Millham, 1968, pp. 272–3)

Lambert makes it clear that there were numerous similar statements and that many more disturbing comments were not published but were kept in the research files. He mentions that these revelations put pressure on research workers and made their task difficult. But there is no sense of any crime being committed or any outrage at the behaviour of the teachers for the damage that they were doing to the children in their care. The sexual abuse (not named as such) is glossed over, which probably accurately represents the prevailing attitude of the times.

Boarding on the couch

The topic was not properly discussed in a psychological perspective until 1990, when psychotherapist Nick Duffell aired the issue in an article in the *Independent* newspaper (Duffell, 1990) and received hundreds of confirmative letters from readers. In 1995, Duffell introduced the term 'boarding school survivor' to the therapy world in an article in *Self and Society* (Duffell, 1995). Drawing on his experience of his first decade of psychotherapy and group workshops for ex-boarders, Duffell published the first psychological exploration of the phenomenon of boarding with *The Making of Them* (Duffell, 2000).

As the first examination of boarding through a psychological lens, *The Making of Them* summarised the processes that boarding children go through and the subsequent problems encountered as adults, while proposing some avenues for therapeutic help. It was widely acclaimed, including an endorsement from the *BMJ* (BMJ, 2001), and enabled many ex-boarders to feel a sense of recognition. Indeed, reading the book has often been the first stage in an ongoing healing pathway for many ex-boarders.

Himself an ex-boarder and former boarding school teacher, Duffell enumerates the psychological tensions that are in force when children first leave their families to board and how they learn to survive at boarding school. He shows how this involves constructing what he calls a 'Strategic Survival Personality (SSP)'. Once in place, this may not be so helpful when, as adults, ex-boarders attempt to navigate the waters of sexual relationships, family and particularly parenthood. The survival personality, constructed by a child, is very durable; crucially, it is very difficult for the bearer to recognise or shed, because it is so close to the identity of the self.

The book's follow-up, *Wounded Leaders* (Duffell, 2014a), takes a broader societal view of the boarding school system by questioning the ability of the British ex-boarding elite to govern. He argues that:

> Ex-boarders hide their emotional and relational dysfunction behind a facade that usually projects confident functioning and resembles a classic national character ideal. The character ideal is one that is well known and regularly celebrated in our letters, theatre and film. Mostly, it appears as the self-effacing, conflict-avoiding, intimacy-shy, gentlemanly type so classically represented in the late 20th century by the actor Hugh Grant.
>
> (2014a, p. 71)

This is only one facet of an SSP, however, for there is also another side to it, writes Duffell, 'the hostile, sarcastic bullying type' akin to *Flashman* and not the sort of character that anybody wants to identify with.

Duffell (2014b) believes that British politics is awash with privileged men who hide their lack of emotional maturity behind a facade of confidence that is inevitably very brittle: 'There is, I believe, a direct link between the problems caused by boarding school experience and our domination by men who do not provide good leadership because of unacknowledged psychodynamics.'

Coming at the issue independently, Joy Schaverien, Jungian analyst and professor of art psychotherapy, building on an article in the *Journal of Analytical Psychology* (Schaverien, 2004), coined the term 'Boarding School Syndrome' (Schaverien, 2011a). Schaverien observed that in the disbelief that people want to hear about their institutionalised childhoods (2011b), ex-boarders may be 'lost for words', and that many famous names in the psychotherapy profession found that their boarding experiences did not interest their own analysts. In her latest book on the psychological trauma of the 'privileged' child (Schaverien 2015), she uses her experience as an analyst with ex-boarders to illustrate how ex-boarders can make extremely difficult clients. In particular, they tend to terminate therapy at the very point when they are starting to recognise how their boarding experience is still shaping how they make decisions and run their lives.

Increasingly, ex-boarders are beginning to write about their experiences. Some of these have been inspired by participating in Boarding School Survivor workshops, others from going to conferences organised by the survivor organisation, Boarding Concern, founded in 2001. Bob Arnold and Thurstine Basset (2005) attest to the healing nature of the group workshops in sharing often very emotional experiences with people in the same boat. They talk of escaping from the restrictions of the 'stiff upper lip' and introduce the term 'emotional courage' as being important for facing up to and exploring feelings rather than just burying them. Basset (2006) elaborates on this through recounting his plan to revisit his prep school 50 years on from his first arrival there.

Simon Partridge (2007) reflects that issues relating to his time at boarding school had not been dealt with in his individual psychoanalysis sessions but he has found the workshop a safe place to express his anger at his mother for abandoning him, followed by his empathy for her feeling of powerlessness in believing that she had to do it: 'It's something our sort of people just have to do – it happened to me.' Indeed, one can only wonder where all those feelings from mothers over many years go as they make what must be the hardest decision of their lives.

Ex-boarders who are themselves therapists have published articles in recent times. Jane Barclay considers the work that an ex-boarder needs to do, facilitated by their therapist, is: 'to escape the trauma "Freeze" position held in place by behaviour patterns that are only an illusion of reactivated Fight/ Flight energy (e.g. control over eating, power-seeking at work/at home) whilst driven by long-forgotten helpless rage and distress' (Barclay, 2011).

Jane Palmer discusses whether boarding school is a place of privilege or of sanctioned persecution. Unhappy at her school, but effectively silenced, she finds that on re-reading her letters to her mother many years after she sent them, she is only able to find one reference to unhappiness in seven years of weekly letters to home. Her aim was to protect her mother, and indeed herself, from the truth. Palmer finds healing from therapy: 'The relief at finding a space that has over time gradually allowed the silence and loneliness of all those years to dissipate has been enormous' (Palmer, 2006).

Marcus Gottlieb (2005) expands the knowledge base in writing about working as a therapist with gay boarding school survivors. In workshops that he runs, participants have experienced their boarding schools as:

> profoundly homophobic environments. Their parents, in some cases disappointed by their failure to align with male gender norms, had sometimes sent them away, in part, to 'make a man of them'. They went to a place where silence around gayness suggested a real sense of dread.
>
> (Gottlieb, 2005)

Gottlieb also comments on the broken attachment that co-exists with boarding:

> This breach of relationships has implications, for example, when a gay ex-boarder comes out to his family; the healthy connection, which might support a person in this process, has already been radically broken. Not surprisingly, 'nesting' and the security of a home can feel important and healing, and many of us have found new communities and 'families of choice' which have gone some way to filling the gap left by the rupture in our childhood.
>
> (Gottlieb, 2005)

The journal *Therapy Today* has helped to highlight the issues. David Mair, himself an ex-boarder, explains that he had been looking forward to boarding: 'But my almost instantaneous reaction, from which I never fully recovered in the five years I was at the school, was a kind of emotional paralysis and hyper-vigilance that I could not switch off' (Mair, 2005). Mair talks of his work as a therapist. He has attended a group workshop and wonders about adapting some of the techniques (imagery work, writing letters and drawing pictures) for work with individual clients. Some of his aims may be realised by this book.

The April 2011 edition of *Therapy Today* specifically featured the boarding issue, with the editor Sarah Browne commenting:

> I have several close relatives who were sent away to boarding school at a young age and at least two of them felt significantly damaged by it. I have

tried to imagine sending my own children away and how hard that would be. I remember how upset I sometimes felt even leaving them at primary school when they first started in reception. I have a friend who feels that her boarding school experience was in many ways 'the making of her', partly because it limited her exposure to her highly dysfunctional family.

(Browne, 2011)

Browne makes the important point here that, for some, boarding may be a better option than remaining at home in a dysfunctional family. Clearly this may occasionally be the case where the school can offer a more solid base than a very chaotic and unloving home, but it can hardly be a principle upon which to build an education system.

The same edition also contains an article by Duffell, in which he states:

Having spent more than two decades studying and working therapeutically with ex-boarders, and being one myself, I am unfortunately no longer astonished how resistant our nation is to acknowledging the problems inevitably associated with this uniquely British habit of sending children away from home to be brought up in residential institutions. To imagine that they will turn out fully-fledged human beings without any psychological harm, able to function within loving families that they themselves barely experienced, manifestly denies logic. Yes, as a nation we seem reluctant to recognise, let alone shed, this addiction.

(Duffell, 2011)

He reflects on why the world of therapy also finds this issue hard to engage with and makes the important point that the 'over-masculinised' nature of boarding for both boys and girls results in misogyny that may be unconscious in nature.

In the same edition Schaverien speaks about the need for words and terms to describe behaviours, and hence her description of Boarding School Syndrome as:

a cluster of learned behaviours and discontents that follow growing up in a boarding school. I was led to seek a definition because there is a need for theory to help in recognising and validating this as a particular form of psychological trauma.

(Schaverien, 2011a)

Boarding problems in general literature

Looking more broadly at the world of literature, there is significant reference to boarding school in autobiographies, biographies and novels. Here, we look at just a few from the recent era.

A biography of the comedian Peter Cook recounts:

> Peter's first year or so at Radley was utterly, miserably unhappy. He intensely disliked the authority the school exercised over him and those who applied it. A slight, asthmatic figure, always dressed in the same shabby, ill-fitting gown or blue sports jacket on Sundays – his parents' salary did not run to an extensive wardrobe – he was easy meat for bullies, of whom there were many.
> ... 'I hated the first two years' he explained, 'because of being bullied. And I was as cowardly as the next man. I didn't enjoy getting beaten up, and I disliked being away from home – that part was horrid. But it started a sort of defence mechanism in me, trying to make people laugh so that they wouldn't hit me.'
>
> (Thompson, 1997, p. 18)

Celebrity chef Antony Worrall-Thompson began boarding when he was only 3. But here he remembers his first night at prep school, aged 8:

> That night, in my new bed, I just cried. I wasn't the only one. Muffled sobs could be heard from beneath other bedclothes. I wished now I had brought Fred, my scruffy teddy bear, but when mum had tried to pack him, I had thrown him back, saying that I couldn't possibly be seen with a teddy bear at my new grown-up school. But I counted at least six other boys who had bears, and nobody was taking any notice of them. However, it was only a matter of days before I knew I had made the right decision. Once confidence was built, the boys started to turn on their teddies. Arms went missing, ears were cut off, there were bears blocking the loo and one was even ceremoniously burned.
>
> (Worrall-Thompson, 2003, p. 61)

The fate of these transitional objects for the boys stands next to Worrall-Thompson's graphic accounts of canings and his complaints about a paedophile teacher, who was dismissed but not prosecuted:

> Since my mother was not informed, neither, I guess, were the parents of the boys he had raped. Nothing was said to me on the matter by the headmaster, though if he had offered any kind of commiseration, it would have been so out of character that I would probably only have been disgusted anyway. No further action whatsoever was to be taken against the teacher. Instead he was free to walk the streets. God knows how many children he abused after he left the school. But that was how things were: scandal was to be avoided at all costs, and everything was just swept under the carpet.
>
> (2003, p. 117)

In a memoir of childhood, author Frederic Raphael recounts exchanging a family life in New York for becoming an English public schoolboy at Charterhouse, where he met much anti-Semitism:

> Anti-Semitism was at once the regimental tie and the crease in the trousers of genteel uniformity: it gave mundane flannel its edge. The young did not merely inherit the prejudices of their elders; they were admitted to them.
>
> (Raphael, 2007, p. 183)

In a letter to his father, he writes:

> Here I do not exist. For days no one has spoken to me. I am the Yid ... All my friends, or those I thought my friends, have turned against me. I have no one. They mimic Jews all day and mimic me too. I sit here and shiver. I am powerless.
>
> (Raphael, 2007, p. 234)

The full version of this letter was in fact published in the *Evening Standard* after his father passed it on to a journalist who was, in the late 1940s, writing a series of articles about Oswald Mosley and post-war fascism.

In her award winning novel *The Orchard* Drusilla Modjeska portrays a girls boarding school she calls 'Carn', though it is clearly based on her own school experience. Carn is a patriarchal place where femininity is frowned upon, where the mind must be encouraged and enlightened, but the body and its needs and desires should be suppressed. On Valentine's Day, a housemistress, 'The Asp', ceremoniously calls in girls so she can feed any cards they received, still in their envelopes, to the flames of her open fire. The cards are 'A vulgar habit, not befitting a Carn girl'. A former pupil decides to visit Carn with a friend who says: 'I can suddenly see what you mean about being English being a bit like being a man. That awesome certainty that your view of the world is the view of the world' (Modjeska, 1995, p. 203). The former pupil then reflects on Carn, while visiting the Freud Museum with two other friends:

> The gain is a discipline of mind that should not be undervalued. The loss, it seemed to us that afternoon, was represented by the figures of sirens and sphinxes that filled Freud's room: the repressed feminine that our culture denies. Our un-English, feminine waywardness.
>
> (1995, p. 235)

In a similar vein, Angela Lambert's novel *No Talking after Lights* is based on her own experience of a claustrophobic girls' boarding school in the 1950s. The book ably portrays the powerlessness of young Constance. On a visit to see the school, her parents say how much they love it, but Constance herself feels silenced and unable to give her views while in the intimidating atmosphere of the school (Lambert, 1990, p. 7). When Constance subsequently pleads with her parents not to send her to the school, her father tells her to control herself and stop being ridiculous and ungrateful. Sending her to the school will require many sacrifices, mostly financial, on the part of him and her mother. Her mother says they will bear her wishes in mind, but, overhearing her parents' discussion from the top of the stairs, no mention is made of her wishes and Constance realises that she has no say in the matter (Lambert, 1990, p. 13).

In essence, all the literature confirms that the combination of broken attachments, powerlessness and institutional life is psychologically toxic but normalised by the wider society.

Boarding in the media

Boarding is a topic that features in the media on a regular, if rather haphazard, basis. Coverage of the issues in the newspapers occurs from time to time, but occasionally an investigative journalist will take it up.

Guardian columnist Monbiot wonders why the British are keen to condemn global injustices against children but consistently fail to examine their own practice of early boarding:

> Those on the right will not defend these children as they will not criticise private schools. Those on the left won't defend them, as they see them as privileged and therefore undeserving of concern. But children's needs are universal; they know no such distinctions.
>
> (Monbiot, 2012)

Alex Renton takes the brave step of spotlighting sexual abuse at boarding school, which he reports as being part and parcel of the everyday cruelty that he and others experienced (Renton 2014a). As long-standing cases against paedophile teachers have only recently come to court, Renton questions whether the talk of a paedophile ring of teachers operating in the 1970s and 1980s can be dismissed as conjecture. In a subsequent article, he recounts harrowing stories emerging from the many emails he receives from people who have read his feature (Renton 2014b).

Three important television documentaries have specifically examined boarding. *The Making of Them*, a BBC *40 Minutes* documentary made by Colin Luke, was broadcast in 1994. It looks at two prep schools that take boys from the age of 8, following the experience from the boys' perspectives, while also featuring comments from teachers, parents and boarding school survivors. The film documents the boys from their first arrival and shows their struggle to cope in a strange environment; the impetus on them to adjust and 'grow up' very quickly is evident.

Leaving Home at 8, a 2010 Channel 4 *Cutting Edge* documentary, follows four 8-year-old girls through their first term at boarding school. The girls suffer upset and homesickness to different degrees, but all appear settled and relatively happy by the end of term. The parents, particularly the mothers, see this as a success while still musing whether it has been the right decision in the longer term.

In 2013, *A Very English Education*, director Hannah Berryman followed up on a handful of boys filmed 35 years earlier in a BBC documentary series that had featured the boarding school Radley College. The film provoked the following review from blogger Sally Fraser, whose husband boarded:

> One ex-boarder, sitting with his ex-boarder mother, quietly explains that he would not send his own children to boarding school. His mother nervously points out that this is mainly because he can't afford it. There is a pause, before he gently and courageously asserts that no, even if he had the money he would not send them. The look on his mother's face is one of pure cold fear, and one I recognise from being on my mother-in-law's face ninety percent of the time since I came into her life. It says please don't let this be a lie, please, please don't let me have sacrificed my childhood, and my children's childhood, for something that was a lie. Well I'm sorry love, but you have.
>
> (Fraser, 2013)

Broadcast television programmes have large audiences, but possibly the single most popular message about boarding school, in terms of sales in the millions, was the rock group Supertramp's 1979 hit *The Logical Song*. The lyrics of this song, by Hodgson and Davies, are well worth a listen. They speak of a boy's 'wonderful, magical' life before he gets sent away to boarding school to learn how to be 'sensible, logical, intellectual' – but 'cynical'.

References

A Very English Education (2013) Film. Directed by H. Berryman, UK: BBC.

Arnold, B. and Basset, T. (2005) 'Stiff Upper Lip?', *Openmind*, 131, January/February, pp. 16–17.

Barclay, J. (2011) 'The Trauma of Boarding School', *Self and Society*, 38, 3, pp. 27–34.

Basset, T. (2006) 'Emotional Courage', *Independent Practitioner*, Winter, pp. 10–13.

BMJ (2001) 'The Making of Them: Book Review', *BMJ*, 322, 7289, p. 803.

Browne, S. (2011) 'Editorial', *Therapy Today*, 22, 3, p. 3.

Clark, J./Brick. (2010) *Depresso or: How I Learned to Stop Worrying and Embrace Being Bonkers!*, London: Knockabout.

Duffell, N. (1990) 'The Old School', *Independent*, 1 September.

Duffell, N. (1995) 'Boarding School Survivors', *Self and Society*, 23, 3, July, pp. 20–3.

Duffell, N. (2000) *The Making of Them: The British Attitude to Children and the Boarding School System*, London: Lone Arrow Press.

Duffell, N. (2011) 'Old School Ties', *Therapy Today*, 22, 3, pp. 11–15.

Duffell, N. (2014a) *Wounded Leaders: British Elitism and the Entitlement Illusion*, London: Lone Arrow Press.

Duffell, N. (2014b) 'Wounded Leaders', *Therapy Today*, 25, 6, pp. 14–18.

Fraser, S. (2013) *Boarding Survivors*, 11 November, available from: https://sallyfraser-writes.wordpress.com/tag/boarding-survivors/ (accessed: 2 September 2014).

Gottlieb, M. (2005) 'Working with Gay Boarding School Survivors', *Self and Society*, 33, 3, pp. 16–23.

Lambert, A. (1990) *No Talking after Lights*, London: Hamish Hamilton.

Lambert, R. and Millham S. (1968) *The Hothouse Society: An Exploration of Boarding-School Life through the Boys' and Girls' Own Writings*, London: Weidenfeld and Nicolson.

Leaving Home at 8 (2010) Film. Directed by C. Russell, UK: Channel 4.

Mair, D. (2005) 'The Best Years of Your Life?' *Therapy Today*, 16, 7, pp. 7–9.

Modjeska, D. (1995) *The Orchard*, London: Pan Macmillan.

Monbiot, G. (1998) 'Brutality in the Dorm: A Decorous Form of Parental Neglect', *Guardian*, 26 March.

Monbiot, G. (2012) 'The British Boarding School Remains a Bastion of Cruelty', *Guardian*, 16 January.

Palmer, J. (2006) 'Boarding School: A Place of Privilege or Sanctioned Persecution?', *Self and Society*, 33, 5, pp. 27–36.

Partridge, S. (2007) 'Trauma at the Threshold: An Eight-Year-Old Goes to Boarding School', *Attachment: New Directions in Psychotherapy and Relational Psychoanalysis*, 3, November, pp. 310–12.

Raphael, F. (2003) *A Spoilt Boy: A Memoir of Childhood*, London: Orion Books.

Renton, A. (2014a) 'Abuse in Britain's Boarding Schools: A Personal Story', *Observer Magazine*, 4 May, pp. 28–37.

Renton, A. (2014b) 'The Damage Boarding Schools Do', *Observer Magazine*, 20 July, pp. 28–33.

Rivers, W.H. (1918) 'The Repression of War Experience', *Procedures of the Royal Society of Medicine*, 11 (Sect. Psych), pp. 1–20.

Schaverien, J. (2004) 'Boarding School: The Trauma of the "Privileged" Child', *Journal of Analytical Psychology*, 49, 5, pp. 683–705.

Schaverien, J. (2011a) 'Boarding School Syndrome: Broken Attachments: A Hidden Trauma', *British Journal of Psychiatry*, 27, 2, pp. 138–55.

Schaverien, J. (2011b) 'Lost for Words', *Therapy Today*, 22, 3, pp. 18–21.

Schaverien, J. (2015) *Boarding School Syndrome: The Psychological Trauma of the 'Privileged' Child*, Hove: Routledge.

Smith, A. (1759) *The Theory of Moral Sentiments*, London: A. Millar.

The Making of Them (1994) Film. Directed by C. Luke, UK: BBC.

Thompson, H. (1997) *Peter Cook: A Biography*, London: Hodder and Stoughton.

Worrall-Thompson, A. (2003) *Raw: My Autobiography*, New York: Bantam Books.

Chapter 2

What therapists can do

An overview

I had the strange experience of attending a talk by Professor Schaverien about therapy for ex-boarders. During the questions after her talk, I began to realise that I was the only person present who was asking questions as an ex-boarder myself. Everybody else present was asking questions about what they could do as therapists when helping such clients. Towards the end of the talk the Professor asked us all to raise our hands if we had been boarders. I raised my hand and was a bit surprised when about three quarters of the people present also raised their hands.

(Anonymous Boarding Concern supporter)

Key points of chapter

*   Ex-boarders are increasingly seeking access to therapy and are amongst the most difficult client group.
*   Boarding is a *psychosocial* issue.
*   Until now, therapeutic work with boarding school survivors has been an unknown quantity. This book proposes:

    I. a motivation model *From Survival to Living* for ex-boarders and their therapists;
    II. a broad procedural framework, the *RAC Model (recognition-acceptance-change)*, for therapeutic work with ex-boarders;
    III. a typology of survival personalities;
    IV. a range of theoretical understandings. Of these sources, Attachment Theory, its effect on behaviour and neurology is a good starting place.

The challenge for therapists

The problems associated with boarding have only recently attracted the attention of mental health professionals, but with the gradual publicising of the issues surrounding *Boarding School Syndrome* (Schaverien, 2011), ex-boarders are now increasingly seeking psychological help. Counsellors, psychotherapists, psychologists, GPs and mental health workers need therefore to familiarise themselves with the signs and symptoms of this syndrome, as well as possible healing strategies.

Therapists may be ignorant of the needs and tactics of this client group; others may struggle to skilfully address them. In our experience ex-boarders are amongst the most difficult clients, for the self in distress is frequently masked by a very competent, if brittle, socially rewarded exterior. Hence – in the absence of an accepted methodological approach – the need for this book.

Sometimes it may also be the case that therapists themselves have not yet addressed their own boarding-related issues, whether as ex-boarders themselves, as parents of boarding children or partners of ex-boarders, as the observation quoted above suggests. A prerequisite, therefore, for working with this group is that if they are ex-boarders themselves, therapists should have worked on their own boarding issues.

In this book we set out approaches and techniques that we feel are useful with this client group. Sometimes, therapists may find that they have to 'shift gear' with these clients. For example, some psychodynamically trained practitioners may find a more empathic and personal style is called for. On the other hand, some who have been humanistically trained may have to learn to make interpretations and investigate transference phenomena in a way that is new to them, or jars with the model in which they have trained. Above all, the work has to be framed in the context of a *psychosocial* understanding, which may be new to many therapists who are used to working primarily with individual issues.

In these pages, we will offer a generalised structural framework as an overview for the stages of recovery work with boarding school survivors. To this end we recommend:

I. A broad-brush *contextual* framework, in which to place the work of recovery: A perspective that has proven useful for boarding school survivors to stay motivated is to envisage the therapeutic engagement as a journey *from survival to living*. This path – unlike his or her previous expedition away from home on the road to self-sufficiency and social privilege – is one that the client takes accompanied by the therapist, with all the accompanying dilemmas of dependency.

II. A broad-brush *procedural* framework, in which to place the therapy over time: We use what we call the *RAC Model* (Recognition – Acceptance – Change) to establish the guidelines of how successful therapeutic work might proceed. A first step for a client is to *recognise* that their boarding experience, and their adaption to it, has had a major impact on their life. Following on from this recognition is the *acceptance* of its impact. This needs to be supported by further recognition and understanding of how strategies adopted at a young age have influenced their adult life. *Change* involves the implementation of the recognition and acceptance stages and the substitution of *adult* strategies for living that are not still rooted in the strategies of a young and abandoned child.

III. A broad-brush *typological* framework: This helps both clients and therapists understand the continuum between motivation and resistance, by viewing ex-boarder survival patterns within three classical boarding school survivor personality types (Rebel, Complier and Crushed).

IV. An extensive range of established theoretical understandings and methodological interventions: To support therapists in the difficulties of working with ex-boarders, therapists are encouraged to find helpful ways of working across a wide range of disciplines. Our suggestions form what we call the *Trauma, Abandonment and Privilege Toolkit*.

Our hope is that this approach will be useful to all manner of therapists, regardless of the theoretical background underpinning their own work. We shall come back to points I to III throughout the text, but first we would like to introduce how we see the theoretical issues.

The *Trauma, Abandonment and Privilege Toolkit*

It is now widely accepted that the theory and methodology make much less of an impact in treatment programmes than the relationship between client and therapist. This may be especially true for those who have suffered neglect and abandonment by cold primary caretakers and domineering authority figures. Nevertheless, it is important to articulate a theoretical stance appropriate to a consistent approach to *Boarding School Syndrome* and especially the process of survival.

The therapeutic methods and thinking that we have evolved over 25 years of working with boarding school survivors involve drawing from a variety of disciplines. This is not to argue necessarily in favour of 'integrative' approaches, but rather we have sought to fit theory and methodology *to* the client group, rather than the reverse. In this way, we hope to preserve the integrity of the specialised approach, which allows practitioners trained in many different styles to enter the field. This can also help them become curious in the areas where they might need to acquire extra skills or understanding.

The integrity of such a method centres on three key concepts underlying the work and expressed in the title of this book: *Trauma, Abandonment and Privilege*. Naming Boarding School Syndrome as *trauma* is the starting point for work with ex-boarders; it is absolutely vital since the social *privilege* that this education represents regularly blinds sufferers, therapists, educationalists and legislators alike to its pathological dimensions. This can be further masked by ex-boarders exhibiting high social functioning, being in powerful positions in social institutions, and sometimes exhibiting an unconscious sense of entitlement.

The shocking revelation of the traumatic dimension of boarding was first made explicit in the introduction of the provocative term *Boarding School Survivors* by Nick Duffell (1990) and his associates. Since then there has been discussion amongst the pioneer theorists of the syndrome about how to classify it. At the time of writing, Post Traumatic Stress Disorder (PTSD), a personality disorder, or complex trauma all are contenders. The most promising label, however, seems to be *developmental trauma*, a term adopted by some practitioners within a recently emerging field of study that combines insights of psychotherapy with research data of neuroscience. The developmental problem of boarding is central: first, since traumatic symptoms are usually initially hidden by the need for boarding children to survive the socially accepted abandonment to the institution by parents, which kicks off the trauma. And, second, because of the gradual development of the effects, which then become chronic over time.

We shall return in more detail to this as we proceed. Below we outline those theories and streams of influence that we have been drawing on and adapting, so that practitioners who work with ex-boarders have an understanding of the varied approaches that bear fruit with these clients. We will start, not with trauma, which heads up our title, but with the *abandonment* that produces the broken attachments, which is where it all begins.

1. **Attachment**: Understanding attachment in boarding children and its consequent effect on development.

Boarding involves the rupture of attachments in dependent youngsters, under an externally imposed ethos of self-reliance, not fitting their ongoing developmental needs. Attachment, for us, is seen as an ongoing process throughout and beyond childhood. Transgenerational boarding issues frequently mean that caregivers have not been able to make good attachments in the first place. The work of theorists John Bowlby and Iain Suttie, who stressed the cultural significance of what he called 'the taboo on tenderness', are seminal here (Suttie, 1988, p. 65).

We shall elaborate on Bowlby's *Attachment Theory* and its relevance to boarding later in this chapter, but disrupted attachments do not alone account for the developmental challenges that boarders face. For as children grow, they do not just need parents – they need *parenting*. A developmental context that encompasses the changing life stages is essential when considering how boarders spend most of their latency, puberty and adolescent periods within institutions without parental guidance. Human beings' primary developmental continuum is *sexual* and here we encounter the limits of Object Relations and Attachment Theory, arising in a Britain that was extremely uncomfortable in any sustained thinking about sex. Freud, Reich, Horney and Erikson (who first identified the *psychosocial* approach) are worth revisiting in this context, but much more useful is the recent work of the Dutch developmental psychologist, Willem Poppeliers, *Sexual Grounding Therapy* (Poppeliers and Broesterhuizen, 2007).

2. **Survival**: Understanding how children learn to survive the trauma of the boarding experience through adopting a survival personality and employing dissociation.

The impulse to survive is primary and affects all other human needs and development, including conscious and unconscious formations. When we are young we look to the outside for the necessary protection for our survival; when we find ourselves in environments which are too powerful to control, the protective impulse is turned inwards and becomes control of the self, self-negation and defence. In this way, self-betrayal occurs in order to serve survival and the secondary – and often dominating – problem is shame. A wide range of theorists – from Darwin through Freud and Klein to Maslow and Liedloff (1986) – may be helpful here.

The existential conflicts of power and vulnerability within and between persons are frequently in extreme crystallisation in adult ex-boarders, who have been trained to eschew all forms of vulnerability and emerge as competent 'winners'. The disowning and projection of vulnerability is therefore inevitable. In particular, therapists will need to understand what might be best called the 'architecture of survival', and some key concepts are mentioned below:

i. **Structural defence**
   The need to survive and the absence, or failure, of caring adults necessitates an extreme employment of protective self-negation and use of defence mechanisms. Functionally, the result could be said to be *structural*, as in the form of an outer carapace, like Winnicott's (1971) *False Self* – although this is still a metaphor. It is useful to think that the boarder has to erect a similar structure, which we call the *Strategic Survival Personality*, in reference to the specific nature of the neglect and abandonment within a rule-bound institution and the consequent need to constantly avoid censure and punishment. The prime additional shaming element is the psychosocial dimension of privilege.

ii. **Psychic wisdom**
   Individual psyches are geared towards defence in order to serve survival, and this may be seen as wisely protective. Yet the survival ego is not the whole self. Under such an understanding the defences are only designed to last until the individual may be mature enough to dispense with them. The breakdown of a survival personality can become a 'breakthrough' for the psyche as a whole. The Freudian proposition of 'regression in service of ego', and Winnicott's (1954) 'regression in service of the true self', can be expanded to 'regression in service of recovery and growth'. Jung's

notion of *Individuation* and transpersonal theorists such as Assagioli (1965 and 1975) are helpful here.

iii. **The plural self**

The survival personality expresses itself in various behaviour patterns, which can create virtually distinct identities, even though they do not 'exist' as such. These identities are variously known as *sub-personalities, roles* or *life-scripts*, and can function at various levels of organisation, complexity, and refinement. Humanistic approaches such as Psychodrama, Process Oriented Psychology and Psychosynthesis, from which a five-fold process of *recognition, acceptance, co-ordination, integration* and *synthesis* has influenced our three-fold procedural model, are useful here. John Rowan's (1993) writing provides a good summary.

iv. **Transactional ego states**

Eric Berne's (1964) *Transactional Analysis*, whose model of the psychodynamics of Parent-Adult-Child offers a simplified schema of Freud and Fairbains' understanding of internal conflicts, is helpful in understanding the ex-boarders' toxic *Inner Parent* dynamic. Stone and Winkleman (1989) further elaborated Berne's Ego States model in relationships, into what they call 'Bonding Patterns'. These have in turn been developed by Duffell and Løvendal (2002) in couple work, which is one of the main areas where ex-boarder issues may arise unannounced.

3. **Trauma:** Understanding the profound defensive nature and physiology that adults develop as a result of childhood trauma.

In boarding the soul is not honoured. The Strategic Survival Personality is dedicated to defence and therefore represents an organism under stress, and, in many cases, crystallised in a 'freeze response'. Boarding can be seen as a trauma, which, like PTSD of war veterans, presents itself in a *secondary*, post-event, and well-established form, where the only available attachment object is the *survival personality itself*. The writings of Leonard Shengold (1989) and Donald Kalsched (1996) can give important context and insight into the traumatised personality.

Therapists do well to become versed in both the physiology and process states of trauma, and should develop familiarity with:

i. **Dissociative processes**

Boarding children have little option but to disown those feelings and thoughts not permitted in the institution, and ex-boarders may well not have reintegrated the parts of themselves that they disowned in order to survive. Dissociation can be understood as an entirely natural result to being exposed to trauma; it is probably mediated by the Autonomic Nervous System and is therefore entirely unconscious. Dissociation must be recognised and its levels must be understood. In particular, what psychoanalysis calls 'splitting' has to be distinguished – in terms of degree – from repression; similarly 'projective identification' from 'projection'. The work of many psychoanalysts from all schools, especially Heinz Kohut (1977), beautifully summarised by Josephine Klein, is helpful here (Klein, 1987).

ii. **Transference and counter-transference**
The psyche has porous boundaries, especially where there has been trauma, neglect and disrupted attachments, when its porosity can become pathological. Disowned elements only re-enter consciousness when they are projected onto others, and then reclaimed. In particular, Kleinian and Independent Psychoanalytic understanding of work with projective identification is key. The work of Kohut (1977), Searles (1979) and Casement (1985) will be especially useful here.

iii. **Trauma and neuroscience**
Familiarity with the neurobiology of post-trauma symptomatology and the stress response will be useful for therapists working with ex-boarders. The work of Sue Gerhardt (2004), Felicity de Zuleta (2006) and, in particular, Stephen Porges (2011) will be extremely helpful here. We return to trauma in detail in Chapter 8.

Other sources of knowledge

Some of the other theories and methodological approaches that have a bearing on the work with ex-boarders include:

i. **Systemic**
We live within a network of relations that influence behaviour and belief, encompassing family, ancestors, class and nations. Problems are easily normalised in a particular social setting and this collective field has extreme influence on individuals. While individuals are unique and ultimately unknowable, it is meaningful to speak of collective imagery, transgenerational problems, national identities and character types. Field theory, systemic therapy, particularly the pioneering work of Bateson (1972), and his understanding of double binds, as well as Jungian archetypal therapy, is useful here.

ii. **Cognitive**
Survival personalities and behaviour patterns of ex-boarders both serve and limit psychic health. Being designed *in extremis* by a child they tend to become maladaptive over time, offering in their failure a chance to substitute more realistic behaviour patterns. Sometimes cognitive analysis of the unconscious benefit – or *pay-off* – of negative patterns can help free creative insight, stimulate self-acceptance and change, and structure a path towards more healthy patterns. Neuro Linguistic Programming (NLP) and Game Theory may provide a background for such cognitive

work, but, in our experience, it is not effective where there is dissociation at play.

iii. **Characterology**

One of the most challenging aspects of ex-boarders, especially *Rebel Types* (about whom more later) can be their lack of self-care, their commitment to self-defeating patterns and their ability to self-sabotage. This can be understood as a form of *social masochism*. The complex interventions that masochism requires are often counter-intuitive and are best explained by somatic therapists, such as Stanley Keleman (1994) and especially Stephen M. Johnson (1994) with his well-organised schema of *Character Styles*.

iv. **The power of love**

Finally, therapists to ex-boarders should be comfortable with the reality of love as a generative force and the reality of the pathology engendered in its absence. Iain Suttie wrote meaningfully about 'the flight from love' (Suttie, 1988, p. 245). However, the understanding has to go slightly further than Attachment Theory, especially to work with the specific double binds that affect boarders. This, in the classic form, could be summarised as: 'they say they love me but then they abandon me'. These inevitably corrupt future intimate relationships, often with unconscious misogyny. This can be hidden by active parenting where the unloved inner child is projected onto the real offspring. The problem of love, therefore – in terms of letting it in, believing in lovability and learning to love – becomes important soul work.

Following on from this overview, we will look a little closer at Attachment Theory and its relation to early boarding.

Broken attachments, broken behaviour

Perhaps the most difficult experiences in relation to boarding and the problems for ex-boarders are the loss of family – mother, father, siblings, grandparents – who have been present and part of everyday life for the child, and the loss of home – pets, environment, familiar smells and atmosphere.

This loss can be quite sudden – like young birds being ejected from the nest when they are not yet ready for the outside world. It can be the equivalent of an acute shock: one to which children have no option but to adapt. Henceforth they find themselves thrown back on their own resources for very long periods, but in the continual company of other children who are similarly without loving caretakers. The loss of key attachment figures becomes adapted to and normalised and soon becomes a chronic problem. Its effects stretch seamlessly forward into adult life.

Attachment Theory was principally the work of John Bowlby (1907–90). Bowlby believed that many mental health and behavioural problems could be attributed to experiences in early childhood. After the Second World War, he developed infant observation at the Tavistock Clinic in London within the newly created National Health Service (Bowlby, 1965).

Born into a prosperous family, the young Bowlby rarely saw his mother, who like many others of her class considered that parental attention and affection would lead to the dangerous spoiling of a child. Bowlby was brought up by his nanny, but lost her when he was 4 years old. At the age of 7, he was sent to boarding school. In *Separation: Anxiety and Anger* (Bowlby, 1973), he revealed that he had a terrible time and later said: 'I wouldn't send a dog away to boarding school at age seven' (Schwartz, 1999).

Bowlby's Attachment Theory suggests that children come into the world biologically pre-programmed to form attachments with others, in order to survive. He was influenced by the biologist Konrad Lorenz who, in his study of imprinting, demonstrated that attachment was innate in young animals and therefore had survival value (Lorenz, 1935). In evolutionary terms, babies who stayed close to their mothers would have survived to have children of their own. Bowlby suggested that a child's attachment figure acted as 'a secure base' for exploring the world and that the attachment relationship acts as the prototype for all future relationships (Bowlby, 1965).

If all goes well, a child's attachment relationship with their primary caregiver leads to the development of what he called an *Internal Working Model* (Bowlby, 1973). Three principle benefits of internalising this framework are:

1.   The self can be regarded as valuable.
2.   Other people can be regarded as trustworthy.
3.   The self is regarded as effective when interacting with others.

In effect, this is a cognitive framework comprising mental representations for understanding the world, self and others, which today is better known as *Mentalisation* (Bateman and Fonagy, 2006). Mentalisation is regarded as an important tool for people with a diagnosis of Borderline Personality Disorder. Although the majority of ex-boarders present as functioning, in terms of their outer selves or their *doing* capacity, they may be much less able on the inside in terms of their interior, relational or *being* capacity.

Disruption of the attachment process would, according to Bowlby, prevent the adoption of a good internal working model and have very severe and long-term consequences and result in cognitive, social and emotional difficulties. The separation or loss of the mother, as well as failure to develop an attachment, Bowlby called *Maternal Deprivation* (Bowlby, 1965). This concept has been highly influential in social work, since it is realised that it may be a major causal factor in delinquency, depression, excessive aggression, reduced intelligence and an inability to show affection or concern for others.

A summary of the key points of Attachment Theory:

- Attachment to a primary figure, usually the mother, is essential to good childhood development.
- Human development is a process of creating and maintaining attachments towards the primary attachment figure and other significant people.
- Eventually, using the attachment figures as a *secure base* a child will move on to form attachments outside of their close family.
- Without this secure base, worry and anxiety tend to rule the psyche.
- The bonds between attachment figures and a child start off as very strong and secure but, over time, they loosen to allow the child more self-determination.
- Eventually the child becomes an adult through a process of gradual maturation over a number of years.
- Attachment and mutual empathy, learned as a child, become the cornerstone of adult intimate relationships and family life.

Growing up in an attachment-deficit environment

Attachment-oriented therapists have developed Bowlby's work into a precise typology for identifying attachment issues, and it may well be fruitful in future to extend this work to encompass boarding school survivors. For now, it is sufficient to understand that the boarding school is – by definition – an 'attachment-deficit environment'. This means that:

- Being sent away to boarding school at a young age effectively breaks the strong attachments that have nurtured a child.
- Children find themselves in an institutional world, sometimes run on masculine and patriarchal lines, with little feminine or maternal influence.
- This is an entirely unnatural rupture: no psychological or developmental theory of any kind supports such practice.
- Instead of growing through a process of gradual maturation over a number of years children are forced to grow up too quickly, to put away childish ways and become adults before their time.
- Instead of having a secure base of good attachments, boarding children tend to grow up emotionally and relationally detached.
- Children compensate by developing an internal refuge: the *Strategic Survival Personality*, to which they transfer their attachment and reliance (Duffell, 2000).
- In consequence, ex-boarder adults often seem to show signs of a child inside of them who has been frozen in time and never organically grown up and who tends to dominate some of their behaviours, especially in intimate relationships.

Psychological theorists of all denominations, through Freud to Winnicott to Biddulph, have supported the notion of sound parental bonds to provide children with a good start so that they can progressively and age-appropriately develop autonomy and become adults who can give a similar good start to their own children. No theories of child development support an opposing view. It goes almost without saying that these principles have to be extended to children's education.

> In the West, Piaget, Erik Erikson, John Bowlby, Rudolf Steiner and others have demonstrated that the needs of children vary according to recognisable stages of physical and psychological development. Unfortunately, education in the private sector seems hardly to have been touched by the enormous developments in psychology during this (20th) century. The boarding schools have carried on as ever, barely influenced by psychology, politics, or even much educational theory, because the social and economic position of the system has made them a special case.
>
> (Duffell, 2000, pp. 45–6)

There is a now a mounting body of evidence that the optimum conditions for the physical development of children's brains are provided by close bonds to loving parents (good attachments) plus relational stimulation (Gerhardt, 2004). Under such conditions children actually grow more healthy brain tissue while learning proper regulation of their nervous systems. Under conditions of lack, they fail to grow in this way.

It is becoming increasingly clear that attachment-deficit institutional-based residential education has very serious impediments, because it is based on psychological processes and mechanisms that have more in common with trauma survival than psychic good health. In the case of ex-boarders, their learned high functioning and the imposed ethos of self-sufficiency camouflages underlying anxiety, stress and the impoverishment of relational brain tissue.

Survival mechanisms involve an overuse of the major *defence mechanisms* – chiefly *dissociation* – that are dedicated to adaption to an otherwise uncontrollable environment. Dissociation is an important concept to which we will return in more detail. For now let us say that it is a kind of everyday avoidance technique, ranging from simply thinking of something else (while opening your mouth for the dentist, for example) to levels of repression or denial that can become chronic, habitual and profoundly toxic.

Beginning to think therapeutically about ex-boarders

Here are two sample case examples to get you thinking about therapeutic work with boarding school survivors. Read through the brief description of the client and perhaps make some notes prompted by the questions below. At this stage, it is a good idea simply to let yourself be open and curious.

Case example 1: Patrick

Patrick, a self-employed surveyor who does some teaching at a local university, is 46. He is experiencing a difficult time at work. Having been very successful, he now seems to have lost all desire for his work. A bit of a perfectionist, he feels standards have dropped. His wife has put pressure on him to see a counsellor since he seems to be always hanging around aimlessly at home, irritable and drinking too much.

He agrees to see you for six sessions at first and clearly wants a quick fix. He tells you that his father was a diplomat and that his family often moved home and also lived abroad. He talks about his childhood with his family in a rather dismissive way. He says he was perfectly happy and can't recall any difficult times.

He tells you he was sent to boarding school at the age of 7. At first, he says that he got on fine there and achieved very good exam results and a good place at university. However, when you ask him to describe his time at prep school from the age of 7, he drops his calm and ordered persona and becomes visibly upset. He describes various incidents of feeling homesick and being bullied, but is able to very quickly return to what he calls his 'normal self' and leaves the therapy session in the same ordered and detached mood that he arrived with.

On the fifth session, he says he has had enough of talking about school, which he didn't like; it is so long ago and he doesn't want to dwell on it. He reckons he has found the therapy useful but wonders if he need come to the sixth session. He has voted in the local election before coming to see you and launches off into a rant about politicians: he hates them all with their double standards and endless spin. He says he is a socialist but has no party he can now vote for. 'Politicians are all like Nero – on the fiddle while the planet burns up.'

Questions for reflection

- *What feelings do you imagine you might be left with after sitting with Patrick?*
- *What is your sense about Patrick's situation and how might you try to work with him in the future?*
- *Might there be any thoughts arising in you that you imagine you wouldn't want to mention?*

Case example 2: Susan

Susan, aged 35, comes into therapy because she feels unable to sustain an intimate sexual relationship. She has had boyfriends and some relationships that last for about 18 months, but they always seem to unravel. This has not bothered her so much in the past but now she feels she wants 'to settle down more'.

Susan is bright and intelligent. She works as a psychologist in an NHS Trust and is very passionate about her work. She sees clients herself in her role as a psychologist. She uses Cognitive Behavioural Therapy and many of her clients find it useful. However, she tried it herself and it didn't really help – or rather it worked for a while and then she got a bit stuck. She has seen therapists before and found them helpful up to a point. She makes it clear that she is at least as well qualified as you are – probably more so!

She describes her family as loving and her childhood as uneventful. She did, however, go away to what she describes as a 'progressive' boarding school at the age of 11. She was very homesick at first but soon got over this. She excelled academically at school. She acknowledges the significance of her boarding experience but is very reluctant to talk about it. She has left all that behind and is not in touch with any school friends. She doesn't really have any women friends, as she is generally mistrustful of women. She reckons she gets on better with men, especially with her slightly older brother. Some of her ex-boyfriends are still friends with her.

Her parents live a few miles away. She describes them as 'peace-loving and easy-going'. They always say to her 'Whatever you want to do with your life it's OK with us.' Her mother says 'Why do you need to go to a therapist? You can talk to me about anything.'

When she comes to therapy, she always has a long list of what she wants to discuss and areas she wants to work on. She talks a lot about her work and the difficulties of working in the NHS. She talks about other people in her life, seeming to avoid talking about herself. Susan presents as a very capable and coping adult, but you have the sense of a very vulnerable child lurking beneath this bold exterior.

Questions for reflection

• *What feelings do you imagine you might be left with after sitting with Susan?*

- *What is your sense about Susan's situation and how might you try to work with her in the future?*
- *Might there be any thoughts arising in you that you imagine you wouldn't want to mention?*

Exercise 1: boarding experience

Ask your client to brainstorm and list their experiences of boarding which can also be divided into both good and bad experiences. Although the likelihood is that bad experiences will predominate, it is also important to look for the good within an overall bad situation.

Examples of what might come up in this exercise:

- loss
- sadness
- hope
- fear
- survival
- friends
- secrets
- coping
- bullying
- motherless
- denial
- confusion
- abuse
- freezing
- helplessness
- suppressing tears
- missing daddy
- disconnecting

Exercise 2: lost and gained

Ask your client to consider and perhaps write down what they feel they both gained and lost from their boarding experience. This is a more specific exercise that should elicit both gains and losses.

Examples of what might come up in this exercise:

Gains: space, friends, independence, got away from difficult family
Losses: mother, home, family, safety, feeling secure, pets, cuddles, bedroom, love

References

Assagioli, R. (1965) *Psychosynthesis: A Manual of Principles and Techniques*, New York: Viking.

Assagioli, R. (1975) *The Act of Will*, New York: Penguin.

Bateman, A. and Fonagy, P. (2006) *Mentalization-based Treatment for Borderline Personality Disorder: A Practical Guide*, Oxford: Oxford University Press.

Bateson, G. (1972) *Steps to an Ecology of Mind: Collected Essays in Anthropology, Psychiatry, Evolution and Epistemology*, Chicago, IL: University of Chicago Press.

Berne, E. (1964) *Games People Play*, New York: Grove Press.

Bowlby, J. (1965) *Childcare and the Growth of Love, Second Edition*, London: Pelican.

Bowlby, J. (1973) *Attachment and Loss. Vol. 2: Separation, Anxiety and Anger*, London: Hogarth Press.

Casement, P. (1985) *On Learning from the Patient*, Hove: Routledge.

de Zuleta, F. (2006) *From Pain to Violence: The Traumatic Roots of Destructiveness*, Chichester: John Wiley.

Duffell, N. (1990) 'The Old School', *Independent*, 1 September.

Duffell, N. (2000) *The Making of Them: The British Attitude to Children and the Boarding School System*, London: Lone Arrow Press.

Duffell, N. and Løvendal, H. (2002) *Sex, Love, and the Dangers of Intimacy: A Guide to Passionate Relationships when the 'Honeymoon' Is Over*, London: Thorsons.

Gerhardt, S. (2004) *Why Love Matters: How Affection Shapes a Baby's Brain*, Hove: Brunner Routledge.

Johnson, S.M. (1994) *Character Styles*, New York: W.W. Norton.

Kalsched, D. (1996) *The Inner World of Trauma: Archetypal Defences of the Personal Spirit*, Hove: Routledge.

Keleman, S. (1994) *Love, A Somatic View*, Berkeley, CA: Centre Press.

Klein, J. (1987) *Our Need for Others and Its Roots in Infancy*, London: Tavistock Publications.

Kohut, H. (1977) *The Restoration of the Self*, New York: International Universities Press.

Liedloff, J. (1986) *The Continuum Concept*, London: Arkana.

Lorenz, K. (1935) 'Der Kumpan in der Umwelt des Vogels: der Artgenosse als auslösendes Moment sozialer Verhaltensweisen', *Journal für Ornithologie*, 83, pp. 137–215, 289–413.

Poppeliers, W. and Broesterhuizen, M. (2007) *Sexual Grounding Therapy*, Breda, NL: Protocol Media Productions. See also www.sexualgrounding.com.

Porges, S.W. (2011) *The Polyvagal Theory: Neurophysiological Foundations of Emotions, Attachment, Communication, and Self-Regulation*, New York: W.W. Norton.

Rowan, J. (1993) *Discover Your Subpersonalities: Our Inner World and the People in It*, Hove: Routledge.

Schaverien, J. (2011) 'Boarding School Syndrome: Broken Attachments – A Hidden Trauma', *British Journal of Psychiatry*, 27, 2, pp. 138–55.

Schwartz J. (1999) *Cassandra's Daughter: A History of Psychoanalysis*, London: Viking/ Allen Lane.

Searles, H. (1979) *Countertransference and Related Subjects: Selected Papers*, New York: International Universities Press.

Shengold, L. (1989) *Soul Murder: The Effects of Childhood Abuse and Deprivation*, New York: Fawcett Columbine.

Stone, H. and Winkelman, S. (1989) *Embracing Each Other*, San Rafael, CA: New World Library.

Suttie, I. (1988) (first published 1935) *The Origins of Love and Hate*, London: Free Association Books.

Winnicott, D.W. (1954) 'Metapsychological and Clinical Aspects of Regression within the Psycho-Analytical Set-up' in *Through Paediatrics to Psychoanalysis, Collected Papers* (1992), London: Karnac.

Winnicott, D.W. (1971) *Playing and Reality*, London: Tavistock.

Chapter 3

Managing separation and loss

I hope you're not missing me because I'm certainly not missing you
(Hickson, 1995, p. 150)

Key points of chapter

- Young children who board have to cope with their initial feelings of sadness and loss by denying them; this often means that, as adults, they are not in touch with their emotions.
- In the mismatch between knowing their parents love them and being miserable in the institution where they have left them, children find themselves in a bind.
- Disowned feelings of vulnerability can end up in the ex-boarder's partner or therapist.

The emotional threshold

The first issue confronting new boarders is how to deal with the separation and loss they experience.

The natural way to do this would be to feel and express the accompanying emotions: anger, grief, loneliness and bewilderment, perhaps even a sense of betrayal.

At boarding school, however, the authorities do not encourage such expression; it is believed to upset and tire the child. Nor do they want to worry their customers, the parents. The theory is that in the first weeks, while the child is in what is called 'the settling-in period', contact with home is inadvisable because it would upset all parties. Homesickness is seen as something that children will naturally get over; the aim is to encourage children to be self-reliant and used to what is called 'community life'.

Amongst their peers, children may also discover an explicit or implicit prohibition on sharing feelings. While apparent weakness may be frowned upon, other children do not want to see evidence of the feelings that they themselves are desperately trying to hide.

Therapists should not be surprised that ex-boarders have a serious problem with feelings: not being in contact with them, or perhaps despising
them in others, or being unable to authentically share them in relationships.
Sometimes they think they have too many feelings; sometimes they imagine
that they are sitting on an emotional volcano and fear that if they once start
to express them there may be no way of ever stopping.

In a way, boarding children never fully come home from school. Going to
boarding school for the first time is like crossing a threshold. When someone
crosses a symbolic but real threshold the person who walks over never comes
back the same. It is like an initiation, but one that the child has not chosen
and is still too young and unprepared for. This is what it looks like to a counsellor working in a boarding school:

> I have observed the pain in the child and indeed the parent, when that
> moment finally comes that each say farewell in a hallway, by the car or
> in a dormitory. Some don't touch, embrace or find words to say fare-
> well, but turn away and 'don't look back'; others occasionally collapse. In
> some ways, it has echoes of when a child is placed in care and the struggle
> for child and parent to separate in such tragic circumstances.
>
> (Anonymous school counsellor)

The threshold can be thought of as a discrete moment as one Boarding School
Survivors workshop participant relates:

> At the prep school threshold a terrible violence, disguised by privilege,
> is done to children and parents – ordained by a powerful and unques-
> tionable Establishment. This is where the upper lip of the (mostly) upper
> classes quickly learns to lose its expressive ability, where it sets into stiff-
> ness, where the face always knows 'how to act' but can seldom show what
> it really feels.
>
> (Partridge, 2007)

Binding the boarder

Boarders are sent away from their homes in the knowledge that their parents
have chosen this form of education and are paying large sums of money for
it. They do not want to disappoint their parents so they need to adopt and
maintain a brave face. This is why journalists investigating the 'to board or
not to board' dilemma never spot unhappy children when they visit boarding
schools. School counsellors can tell a very different story:

> When I worked as a school counsellor, I attempted to find many creative
> ways of holding/containing the contradiction of children separating from
> those they love versus what they gain from the total boarding experience.
> Attempting to hold the classic position of 'neutrality' as a therapist was

exceedingly difficult. The resolution for the child's pain and behaviour would be that the child returns to the familiar world of 'home'.

The rhythm of separating from what has been your normal identity – leaving your own bed, toys, curtains, bedroom chaos, clothes – leaving that normality of regular rhythms and chaos of family life – the affirming sensory experience of smells, touch, sounds, tastes and adapting to such different sensory experiences of a boarding school can be exciting but also totally traumatic. A child's identity must adapt or not survive. The separating can make a necessary hardening of the heart with the loneliness of trying to understand this new world, whilst inside the heart is aching.

Leaving behind the everyday affirming physical touch of your loved ones, that helps make you feel safe and whole, must be very unsettling. This is especially important in allowing the mind to wind down and feel able to rest and allow the body and mind to enter restorative sleep. It is often at this time that the child gets in touch with all that they are missing and a deep experience of loss sets in. It is very regular for therapists to be dealing with children who are having insufficient sleep because either they or others in the dorm are having very restless nights and traumatic dreams.

(Anonymous school counsellor)

Boarding children are well aware that it is a social privilege to attend one of these schools. They know it to be especially important to their parents, and now they have already been sent away, they fear an even worse fate if they were to cause unhappiness by not appreciating parental generosity or sacrifice. So, internally, they find themselves in a no-win situation called a *double bind*. First identified by anthropologist and social scientist Gregory Bateson, double binds over time develop into a compulsive self-negating behaviour complex (Bateson, 1972). Fraser Harrison describes the boarder's double bind as:

A python with many coils ... my parents were the last people to whom I would have complained. They had, after all, sent me away from home, which was bad enough; what might they do to me if I made a fuss? It could only be worse. And anyway I wanted to please them, not to irritate them. I was frightened of losing their love by telling them how much I needed it.

(Harrison, 1990, p. 67)

Such thoughts may never get actually spoken or put together by the child in this way; nevertheless, we have heard enough stories from ex-boarder adults about how they coped with being sent away to believe it to be fairly universal. In general terms, the boarder's double bind may be expressed something like this:

I know Mummy and Daddy love me. They have told me so. I know it's important to them to send me away to school and that it costs a lot of money and that I should be grateful.

But I hate it. If they love me, why did they send me away?

Either they don't love me or there's something very wrong with me for feeling like this. If they don't really love me it must be because I am bad. If they do, and I feel like this, it must be because I am bad.

(Duffell, 2000, p. 140)

One of the benefits awaiting ex-boarders from pursuing recovery in therapy is the loosening of such double binding. Simon Partridge suggests that the young boarder's bind is so strong as to require a new word, and proposes instead 'triple lock':

First, as usually a member of a family where an avoidant attachment style predominates: where physical contact is sparse or non-existent, in which emotions are discouraged or inexpressible, where intra-familial relationships are already 'detached' or 'professionalised' through nannies or au pairs. Second, by entry to a pedagogy which removes the child from what elements of secure attachment that might exist – e.g. pets, siblings, nannies/au pairs and familiar surroundings, yet at the same becomes a surrogate caregiver of sorts demanding its own avoidant attachment (hence the often extraordinary 'allegiance' to School or Club), and which then compromises any simple return to 'home'; and third, this 'avoidant attachment' is legitimised by, and the norm of, the wider culture of the ruling elite which places power, influence and instrumental control (rationalised as 'public duty' – the 'Stiff Upper Lip' well demonstrated this) at the core of its raison d'être, leaving little or no room for emotional warmth and security.

(Partridge, 2013)

Partridge reasons that this triple lock is 'impossible to escape without informed and empathic therapeutic assistance'. The chief reasons for this is, once again, the lack of recognition and the profound effect of the normalisation in society, which can be seen as a collusion of denial.

In a closely related field, the work of Elaine Arnold with families of African Caribbean origin offers an interesting comparison. Arnold has worked with children who were left behind in the Caribbean and only joined their mothers in the UK many years after they had settled. One child, now a mother herself, recalls:

I did not have an understanding of it all; it just made no sense to me. No one questioned: did you feel rejected? Did you want your mum? But they reminded you that you should not be an ungrateful child, your Mum was doing her best, and you should accept. They did not know better, I suppose, it wasn't made much of, so I suppose I did not give the feelings much thought.

(Arnold, 2012, p. 103)

Lost for words

It has been said that human beings can endure almost anything as long as they are able to tell their story afterwards. Many ex-boarders recount that their parents did not seem curious about what it was like at boarding school. All parents want to know that their child is safe and happy, but boarders' parents also want to be reassured that they have made a good investment. No parent wants their child to be unhappy, but few seem able to bear and mirror the distress that separation and loss brings. In consequence, it tends to go underground. Eventually, as the child becomes an adult, this survival mechanism is more than likely to become pathological.

In the first weeks, the school authorities discourage contact with home. As time goes on, the events and particular nuances of school life become so complicated and involved that a person who has not been through it will seem never to understand. Being witnessed in their distress at being sent away is not straightforward for boarding children. Parents who have not boarded may well find it difficult to imagine the world that their child is now in. Ex-boarder parents who have been in denial about the problems, perhaps with such phrases as 'It never did me any harm', or 'It's character building', only make the child's isolation worse. Expressions like 'You'll soon be back at home' don't help. Rather they encourage a cycle where a child finds it very hard to be mindful and live in the present: longing to be at home while they are at school and counting the days until they go back during the holidays.

Eventually, because they cannot find an ear to hear their story from their own perspective, boarding children give up on ever being listened to:

- They don't want to tell their parents that they are unhappy for fear of disappointing them.
- They can hardly speak to the school authorities, who don't want to know about unhappy children because it is bad for business.
- They dare not share their vulnerability in the peer group because there would be too much shaming and bullying.

Boarders can therefore end up being 'lost for words', as Joy Schaverien says (Schaverien, 2011). Ex-boarders, therefore, are likely to enter therapy having already learned to mistrust or disconnect from their own feelings. We may think of them like soldiers returning from a war: survivors, but in shock, struck dumb, because no one wanted to hear their stories.

During the First World War, only one psychiatrist seemed to have any understanding of what was really going on inside the shell-shocked soldiers and how they might be healed. William Halse Rivers was a student of Freud's brand new talking therapy, which offered a conception of the workings of the unconscious mind. In particular, Freud suggested that what was not permitted by society was expressed as physical symptoms by so-called 'hysterical' patients. Rivers maintained that the soldiers' neuroses did not result solely from the war experiences themselves but were 'due to the attempt to banish distressing memories from the mind' (Rivers, 1920). In other words, the soldiers' attempts to dissociate from what they had experienced – for the sake of their own sanity – had produced a *secondary* problem. This is exactly the case for boarding school survivors.

Instead of trying to forget what they had been through, Rivers encouraged his patients to recall their memories and to share them with an empathic listener. This early methodological step laid the foundations of treatment for all trauma counselling, as well as for what later became known as *post-traumatic stress disorder*, which today's military have begun to take seriously. Rivers' story is movingly retold in Pat Barker's *The Regeneration Trilogy* (1992), in which she highlights the terrible double bind that he found himself in. If his patients recovered they would inevitably have to go back to the front; in order to survive again they would have to practise more of the repression that Rivers had taught them to reverse.

In her remarkable survey of madness, feminist historian Elaine Showalter also turned to the story of Rivers and the shell-shocked soldiers, explaining how they had something in common with many women psychiatric patients of the time: their most common neurotic symptom was that they became, quite literally, dumbstruck. Hundreds of soldiers lost the ability to speak, as Showalter describes: 'When all signs of physical fear were judged as weakness … viewed as unmanly, men were silenced and immobilized and forced like women to express their conflicts through the body' (Showalter, 1987, p. 171).

Today, in hindsight, we can easily understand that what the men had experienced in the trenches was beyond words – literally unspeakable. Nor was anyone interested in what they had to say, for they had been betrayed and sacrificed in an affair in which they had absolutely no voice, one that had been conducted at the highest hierarchical level by Field Marshall Haig and his German counterparts, whose rationale had almost completely been obscured. In this sense, their inability to speak was the greatest expression of truth that was possible. But Showalter mentions one other salient point. She tells us that the '*dumbness*' generally only affected the enlisted men and not the officers, suggesting that: 'For the public-school boys, the university aesthetes and athletes, victory seemed assured to those who played the game' (Showalter, 1987, p. 169).

These men were already trained to withhold their personal responses. Rivers noted that the officers expressed their sickness differently because they had experienced the 'benefit' of public school education. In what is possibly the first ever serious psychological commentary on the problems of boarding, Rivers saw that these officers had mentally organised their experiences differently from the regular soldiers. He understood that they were *already* practised in the art of dissociation, learned at school: 'The public schoolboy enters the army with a long course of training behind him, which enables him successfully to repress, not only the expression of fear, but also the *emotion* itself' (Rivers, 1918). Dissociation, however, carried with it secondary problems which might be masked by their ability to present themselves in the way they had been trained to. Rivers realised that this level of defence was distinct and felt the need to write a paper on the differences. In fact, without the dubious skill of dissociation, the war could not have continued, so futile were so many of the assaults that were ordered. The war's continuation relied on a belief in 'playing the game' whatever the cost.

C. S. Lewis famously describes his experiences at English boarding schools as worse than anything he endured in the frontline trenches of the First World War. Referring to his war experience, Lewis says:

> It was, of course, detestable. But the words 'of course' drew the sting. That is where it differed from [the boarding school] Wyvern. One did not expect to like it. Nobody said you ought to like it. Nobody pretended to like it. Everyone you met took it for granted that the whole thing was an odious necessity, a ghastly interruption of rational life. And that made all the difference. Straight tribulation is easier to bear than tribulation which advertises itself as pleasure. The one breeds camaraderie and even (when intense) a kind of love between the fellow sufferers; the other mutual distrust, cynicism, concealed and fretting resentment.
>
> (Lewis, 2012, p. 218)

The militaristic conception of boarding schools means that the normalisation of repression for the boarder and the ex-boarder's continued habit of dissociation from emotions becomes a seamless and barely-questioned legacy. Re-learning the habit to speak about loss, feelings, trauma, shame and about double binds will inevitably need to form a major and challenging part of therapeutic recovery work with boarding school survivors.

Filling the place created by loss

Nature abhors a vacuum: children cannot only lose and separate – they have to put something in the place of this loss. Children have no choice about whether they are sent away and what happens to them. They have to cope with it. The only choice they have is in *how to* cope with it – in *what* they put in its place. Sometimes we ask ex-boarder clients to make a drawing of what they have lost and then what they put in its place. Over the many years of doing this exercise, both with men and women, we have noticed that the first picture is usually more rounded and brightly coloured than the second, which is frequently filled with square shapes and dark colours. For the boarder's loss is real, even if it can only be retrospectively symbolised.

Boarders have to create a new personality, a self, to cope with, to compensate for the loss, and with which to adapt and survive the unknown environment of the boarding school. In the next chapter we will look into this *Strategic Survival Personality* in much greater depth; we shall see that the strong attachment to the parents that boarding children have to sever is transferred to the survival personality itself. This makes therapy with ex-boarders particularly challenging as it may feel to the client that the therapist wants to take away the one constant that has been present through his or her life: their very own survival personality. For now, we will concentrate on the child's initial adaptation to the loss and the inability to talk about what has been experienced.

Alastair Hickson, a sociologist researching some of the problems associated with boarding, was passed a letter home from a new boy, kept by his mother. 'I hope you're not missing me because I'm certainly not missing you', he lied, poignantly demonstrating how complete the disowning process can become (Hickson, 1995, p. 150). This is how it starts, painfully pulling on a happy mask; but gradually, repression, denial and splitting become a habit. He learns to successfully repress, as Rivers hypothesised, 'not only the expression of fear, but also the *emotion* itself'.

But this is not the end of it: a further feature crucial to this state of affairs fills the place created by loss. This is the availability of another person, in this case the boy's mother, who is likely to be identified with the amputated sad feelings. This is why the peer pressure to maintain the illusion of no feelings is so vital, since the group will be on the lookout for someone amongst them to carry the disowned homesickness and feelings of vulnerability, loss, childishness or incompetence. The dissociation from feelings is much more readily accomplishable when they can be located within someone else. In this way the boarding child can say to him or herself 'I am not the one who feels sad – it is him (or her)'.

The ex-boarder's therapist has to be alert to the continuing presence of these kinds of phenomena. Frequently, the disowned feeling states turn up in a partner. By having a vulnerable-seeming partner, a dissociating ex-boarder can continue to fill the place created by the loss and can maintain the identity of 'not being the one who is vulnerable'. Whilst the refusal to be the unhappy one is quite understandable at the beginning of a child's boarding career, over time such psychic strategies become very harmful, as the partner will frequently take on feelings of unhappiness and loneliness which do not belong there. Over time, they begin to feel very real and the partner's identification with them can become complete. Below is an example of a partner who has struggled with this:

> I am about to reach 15 years of marriage to a very corporate highflier, ex-public school, man and am not sure if I can take any more of it. I found your site after listening to something on Radio 4 about boarding school survivors and I realised that that is exactly what I have been dealing with all these years. I have a husband who has no concept of or apparent need for relationships of any kind other than those which can bring short-term business benefit. He has no ability for intimacy and no perceptible sex drive. Despite the destruction and unhappiness this causes, he also has never willingly sought help for it: *it is my problem rather than his*. I want so much to resolve some of this and not ruin the lives of my children by blighting them with a divorce.
>
> (Anonymous contact through the Boarding School Survivors website)

This is why boarding school survivor therapists *must* have an understanding of transference phenomena. Sometimes a sign that the work is progressing is that the therapist begins to feel suffused by disowned feelings of vulnerability and loss, of childishness or incompetence. It is important that the therapist is able – often by means of supervision – to take on a third perspective and find a way to comment that they seem to have become part of the process of filling the place created by loss, beginning to identify with the amputated feelings of despair, helplessness or rage. Only when the other end of the split-off material has been identified can the client begin to experience how in adaptation he or she has trained him or herself to compensate for the loss.

Sometimes an ex-boarder client will experience physical symptoms that may be a way of pointing to an emotional trauma for which he or she is still 'lost for words'. When specific memories are not recalled but a certain anxiety associated with the experience is present, for example a travel phobia, or unaccountable feelings at a particular time of the week or of the year, it is a sign that the client has experienced trauma. These can become part of strange mood swings or depressive incidents, or superficial emotional states such as irritation, which cover deeper feelings. More difficult to deal with is that these kinds of feelings or moods, if they do not find words of expression, can erupt into behaviour involving other people which then take considerable detective skill to allocate to a correct source.

Here is one example from the British political scene, where ex-boarders occupy many positions of power and which may have a 'back-to-school' atmosphere that ex-boarders often struggle with. In the autumn of 2012 the then Minister for Overseas Development, Andrew Mitchell MP, got involved in a scandal, the so-called 'Plebgate' affair. He was alleged to have got very upset with policemen guarding Downing Street and insulted them. Specifically he was said to have called one of the policemen a 'pleb'. This unusual word is a common slang word at public school that denotes either a child from the local town who was not sufficiently privileged to be boarding or a child who has just recently arrived, such as a 'new boy'. In other words, it is another way of compensating for the loss by singling out someone who is in an apparently inferior position.

The whole affair reveals just how divided a society the British culture of elite schooling maintains, but whatever happened, within the enormous media coverage and legal proceedings, no one has yet explained why the minister was so particularly frustrated at that time; in fact, he had just been promoted. Those of us who are used to working therapeutically with ex-boarders may have been struck by the time of year in this extraordinary affair: it was mid-September, back-to-school time for the public schools. Ex-boarders regularly report sensing an unaccountable misery at that time of year; their bodies tend to remember the rhythms of their year-long institutionalisation and its seasonal breaks. They may register unaccountable dreads and longings, even if their minds have split off their feelings about it. Some, when they feel safe enough, will say they feel very stressed then. If pushed they may acknowledge that behind the anger or irritation there may be a well of unexpressed sadness.

Did Rugby-educated Mitchell have those kinds of unallowable feelings percolating through him while he was running late along Downing Street with his pushbike? Certainly many family members of ex-boarders may recognise that in mid-September, or on Sunday afternoons, there may be plenty of unacknowledged irritation or anger floating around or dripping out and spoiling things.

The purpose of conducting exercises with clients at this point is to reverse the 'lost for words' problem, to help the client integrate boarding experiences and reflect on how these have impacted on behaviour. Frequently it will emerge that behaviour that was quite appropriate at the time is still continuing despite the fact the context has utterly changed. This is the principle problem that the boarding school survivor will have to tackle, and doing this alone is virtually impossible. To start with, the ex-boarder will have to return to the earliest days to recognise that he or she was powerless to influence what happened

In some cases, the client may have words and memories but they may not yet have been able to serve integration of the experience. Here an exercise may give a structure, a narrative into which events and emotions can live together and be witnessed by an outside authority. If it was never mirrored or witnessed by a parent then the therapist can usefully take that role and reflect back to the client that he or she had no choice in the experience but to adapt him or herself to it, and that nowadays it is this adaptation which remains problematic in living in an age-appropriate and healthy way.

Sometimes there may be no accessible memories, and this may well be because the events were so painful that the client has dissociated from them very strongly. A frozen memory bank is not the same as an empty memory bank, so therapists can suggest to the client that it is not that memories do not exist, but that there most likely are memories but that they seem to be frozen for now. When the client starts to feel safer in the therapeutic environment, it is quite possible that memories may begin to return, as the memories thaw out, as it were.

Exercises in returning to memories, such as the one suggested below, are not to be underestimated in their power and may have to be done in stages or repeated over several sessions. It is important that the client is able to proceed at a comfortable pace so that the benefits of the exercise can be integrated.

Exercise 3

The first day at school: a guided visualisation.

Have a pen and paper handy. Relax and breathe deeply; close your eyes.

At home

Remember your home, as it was before you first went away to boarding school. See yourself at home on the day before your first day at boarding school. Remember your room ... your bed ... the view from the window. Fill out the memory ... your toys, your pets. Maybe you had brothers and sisters, perhaps your friends were there. Now recall the morning of the day you were to go off. When did you wake up? Who woke you? Remember your things all packed to go, trunk, tuck box, suitcase.

The journey

Remember your journey to school, how you travelled – by car, by train, by plane ...? Do you remember any sounds or smells? Who was with you? What is the atmosphere like? What is being said and what are you thinking? Can you remember any feelings you had?

Arriving

As you get nearer you can see the school. Is it the first time? Perhaps there are school gates, a driveway. What are the sounds, what can you see? Take in the buildings, the grounds, the other people. What are you thinking? How do you feel?

Goodbye

Now it is time to say goodbye to those who brought you here. How do you say goodbye? Who are you saying goodbye to? Are they around when you want to say goodbye? What do they say? What are you thinking? What do you feel?

Separating

Now perhaps you enter a building, or go up some steps. Stop and freeze at this point, on the school steps, at the moment of separation. What is it like? What is happening inside of you? Do you feel welcome?

The threshold

Be aware that there is a threshold between your familiar life and the new one you have been left in. Try to stay at this threshold – even if you can't remember it.

Now step out of being the child you were; try to step back and look at him or her – even if you can't remember.

This is the moment that your life was to change for ever ... this is where your separated life begins. How does it feel to see him? How do you feel towards him? How does it feel as you step into this separate life? What are you thinking. What do you feel?

School

And now go back to being that child again. You are inside your school; it is your first night away from home. Maybe you lived in a dormitory ... perhaps you have a room. Look around ... see and feel your bed. What are the smells, the sounds? Even if you can't remember, acknowledge your feelings at this point. Even if they are conflicting emotions, just allow what is there.

Now, very slowly, let all these memories and reflections begin to fade away, and take a moment to allow your experience to settle within you.

Gradually become aware of the present moment. Let go of being that child and gently open your eyes. Become aware of where you are and who you are now. Take some time.

Here the exercise may be paused to be continued or repeated at another time. Your client can make notes about the experience and discuss what thoughts, memories and feelings arose during the process.

Now ask your client to reflect with you on these questions:

- What were you expecting on your first day at boarding school?
- What did you imagine you were coming to?
- What picture did you have?
- How had you been prepared?
- What did you find? What was it like?
- What were you leaving?
- What did you need at that time?
- Were any of your needs met?
- Was there anything you enjoyed about that day?

References

Arnold, E. (2012) *Working with Families of African Caribbean Origin: Understanding Issues around Immigration and Attachment*, London: Jessica Kingsley.

Barker, P. (1992) *The Regeneration Trilogy*, London: Penguin.

Bateson, G. (1972) *Steps to an Ecology of Mind: Collected Essays in Anthropology, Psychiatry, Evolution and Epistemology*, Chicago, IL: University of Chicago Press.

Duffell, N. (2000) *The Making of Them: The British Attitude to Children and the Boarding School System*, London: Lone Arrow Press.

Harrison, F. (1990) *Trivial Disputes*, London: Flamingo.

Hickson, A. (1995) *The Poisoned Bowl: Sex Repression and the Public School System*, London: Constable.

Lewis, C.S. (2012) *Surprised by Joy*, London: Collins.

Partridge, S. (2007) 'Trauma at the Threshold: An Eight-Year-Old Goes to Boarding School', *Attachment: New Directions in Psychotherapy and Relational Psychoanalysis*, 3, November, pp. 310–12.

Partridge, S. (2013) 'Boarding School Syndrome: Disguised Attachment-Deficit and Dissociation Reinforced by Institutional Neglect and Abuse', *Attachment: New Directions in Psychotherapy and Relational Psychoanalysis*, 7, 2, pp. 202–13.

Rivers, W.H.R. (1918) 'The Repression of War Experience', *Proceedings of the Royal Society of Medicine*, 11: 1–20. PMCID: PMC2066211 *Lancet*, 2 February.

Rivers, W.H.R. (1920) *Instinct and the Unconscious: A Contribution to a Biological Theory of the Psycho-Neuroses*, Cambridge: Cambridge University Press.

Schaverien, J. (2011) 'Lost for Words', *Therapy Today*, 22, 3, pp. 18–21.

Showalter, E. (1987) *The Female Malady: Women, Madness and English Culture 1830–1980*. London: Virago.

Chapter 4

Survival

My headmaster's report early in my stay at prep school said: 'My one complaint concerns foolish behaviour – nothing serious, merely pestilent – and much of his tiresomeness concerns Matron's department. In a third term he must put away these childish ways.' I was eight at the time.

I didn't enjoy boarding school but I learned to *survive*. The patterns of behaviour I learned have stayed with me all through my life. In some ways they have served me well, but in others they have fundamentally limited me.

(Arnold and Basset, 2005)

Key points of chapter

- Boarding children cope with their feelings of loss and abandonment by adopting a *strategic survival personality* in order to keep themselves safe.
- There are broadly three main types of strategic survival personality – Compliers or Conformists, Rebels, and Casualties or the Crushed.
- Therapists have to appropriately challenge the strategic survival personality, which may have served the child well at school, but now prevents the adult from leading a meaningful life or enjoying loving and reciprocal personal relationships.

The hyper-vigilant child

Boarding school places demands on children to grow up very quickly and become premature adults. The glossy brochures that advertise the schools promote 'self-reliance' and 'the value of community'. Dependence and childishness are therefore seen as obstacles to be overcome. Children have to somehow survive in what is essentially an alien environment, conceived by adults who are not their caretakers. Despite this, children are very resilient and will work out ways to survive, often rather quickly.

Losing the security and comfort of their homes, boarders now have to live in an institution, without parents, siblings, toys and pets, constantly surrounded by their peers, who are scared and missing their families but not allowed to show their feelings. The institutions are beset with rules, which are easily infringed, but said to be for the good of the children.

As we know from the novel *Lord of the Flies*, by William Golding (1954), whose father was a schoolmaster in the town of Marlborough, children growing up without families can be very cruel to each other. Boarders have to be on high alert to protect themselves. They will be on the lookout for any signs of vulnerability to scapegoat and bully in others. The need for hyper-vigilance is ever present, since boarding schools are 24/7 institutions. Unlike most children, if their school day was difficult, boarders cannot relax in the comfort of being with their family at home, or retreat to their own bedrooms at the end of the day.

In the absence of grown-up loving protectors and a place to be truly safe, boarding children must hide their internal anxiety and develop self-protection in order to have a chance of surviving. The resulting hyper-vigilant anxiety state is a survival pattern, but soon becomes taken as normal and often maintained long after leaving school, unrecognised as anything unusual. Excessive anxiety as a base pattern becomes a seamlessly unconscious way of facing the world, but frequently hidden behind a veneer of confident self-reliance as the education demands.

Please note: Therapists who have not boarded may be more likely to spot such unreasonable attitudes and inappropriate emotional states than those who have – because they have not been so normalised.

Equally alarming is the plethora of rules and customs in boarding schools. The ease with which the boarder can break them is retained in the memory of most ex-boarders. Being brought up in such an overcharged atmosphere of multiple rules and the consequent hunting down of transgressors is fertile ground for boarders to develop an inauthentic way of life dedicated to trying to stay out of trouble: *strategic* survival. Again, this situation reinforces that the world is a dangerous place. This is arguably a reasonable training for soldiers, but for children in the modern world it is hopelessly inappropriate. Healthcare professionals now understand that unconscious chronic fear brings about very serious long-term problems, and new scientific evidence emerging in recent years shows how excess arousal brings about further ongoing neurological problems over time.

The work of neuroscientist Stephen Porges, Professor of Psychiatry at the University of North Carolina and author of *The Polyvagal Theory*, demonstrates that people who regularly greet the world with hyper-vigilance and hyper-arousal (such as trauma sufferers) begin to lose their vagal nerve connections to the many muscles that the Vagus supplies in the upper face (Porges, 2011). This means that they lose their ability to read other people's facial signals, which is the prime means that higher mammals have of checking out safety or danger in social settings. They may then resort to a default position that the world is fundamentally unsafe, driving a cycle of more anxiety, all of which can be hidden by the survival personality's basic 'happy mask' of confident functioning. Approaches that may be friendly, loving or intimate may be ultimately subject to the same kind of suspicion, as the ex-boarder remains in an unsafe, isolated universe. Therapists need to be alert to any clue to this hidden anxiety, because once the ex-boarder identifies with it the work of recognition can begin.

Survival

All children are pre-programmed to rely on their parents for protection, support and guidance, but boarding children have to discover on their own how to survive. Here is a brief overview of how it is done.

- Children, sent away from their attachment figures to board, experience a loss of love and find themselves surrounded by other separated children in an unknown institution.
- In order to cope in this new, alien world, where emotion must be repressed and crying is frowned upon, children have to work out how to survive.
- Children adopt survival strategies, which are very helpful in coping with the trauma of separation and living in an alien world.
- These survival strategies are *strategic* because they are constructed to keep the child out of trouble.
- These often take the form of a seemingly real personality with special traits.
- They may be very creative and serviceable ways of getting through school.
- But they usually become less than helpful when the child becomes an adult and needs to live, learn and love in the wider world outside.
- Survival strategies are based on the prediction of the world as a hostile place and keep away loving approaches just as they are designed to keep away hostile ones.

The kind of survival personality constructed depends on the child's individual proclivity, how well attached they were before being sent away, as well as the kind of child that was acceptable to their family of origin. Because this protective self is so closely identified with the sense of who they are, most ex-boarders do not recognise that they have built a strategic survival personality. To acknowledge it as being a protective structure would seem like a failure, because it admits the vulnerability that the construction guards against.

However, many well-known figures in the world of arts or entertainment have described how their need to survive at boarding school became finally a way of life that even provided a successful living. Comedian Peter Cook, for example, used humour to survive his time at Radley: 'I could make fun of other people and therefore make the person who was about to bully me laugh instead' (Thompson, 1997, p. 18).

It may be no coincidence that so many successful but anarchic British comedians are boarding school survivors, including John Cleese, Harry Enfield, Hugh Laurie, Tim Brooke-Taylor, Stephen Fry, Ian Hislop and Craig Brown. Asked in an interview about what first drew him to comedy, Eric Idle replied: 'probably spending 12 years at boarding school – comedy became a survival gene' (Idle, 2012).

Many successful British actors discovered that surviving boarding school required an acting ability, which they later put to good use. 'If I stood on the stage ... I might just fool them if I keep moving my lips', explained the actor Damian Lewis, famous for playing Brodie, the spy or hero (you never really know) in the TV series *Homeland*, to the BBC's Kirsty Young on the radio programme *Desert Island Discs*. Lewis had already got his interviewer's interest with his ambivalent comments about his time at boarding school. 'Who were you at boarding school?' asked Young. Lewis was very clear:

> Going away at eight is a sphincter-tightening exercise. An eight-year-old is asked to deal with a new situation that I think can be overwhelming. Some swim some sink. It definitely informs who you become later.
>
> (Lewis, 2014)

The strategic survival personality

Boarders' survival personality frequently gets built around one of the twin obsessions at school: keeping their heads down and breaking the rules without getting caught. One day, when he was seeing an ex-boarder for therapy in his practice in the 1990s, Nick Duffell came to realise that boarding produces a specific style of protective self, whose essence is best described as *strategic*:

> A high-flying corporate lawyer in his late forties had sought psycho-therapy to explore how he developed sudden unexplained fits of panic when making presentations. At a certain point he described himself as 'strategic', and explained why. He revealed how, despite his outward success, all his life he had been trying to stay out of trouble. It had ruined his personal relationships, because he tended to mistake any approach to

him – even an intimate one – as a potential threat. He had always led what he described as a 'double life'.

(Duffell, 2014, p. 72)

This man was describing the essence of the *Strategic Survival Personality*.

Boarders do not have any choice but to be dedicated to their own survival, so their character becomes, above all things, strategic. Sometimes this means being self-effacing, at other times Machiavellian. The name of the game is trying to stay one step ahead, staying out of trouble, anticipating danger, promoting the outer self they are selling – a personality that is 'Born to Run'.

Over the years, many things have confirmed the strategic hypothesis. For example, boarding school survivors as clients in psychotherapy frequently recount dreams with similar elements, in which they are on the run from something or someone, or about to get caught and be unmasked, or are up for trial and facing the death penalty. The novels of the famous spy author John le Carré endlessly feature the dilemmas of ex-public school men caught between being (like Brodie) against and within the establishment, living lives full of duplicity, subject to repeated acts of betrayal.

Here is Damian Lewis again, describing the conditions that create this strategic compulsion to avoid failure:

> Eton really is a high-octane privileged entitled environment ... it's a massively competitive environment, there's no question, and I think probably somewhere like that just feeds this idea that you better not be the one that's caught out, because if you're the one that's caught out you'll be turned on, so it feeds this readiness to be quick-witted, nimble, agile of mind at all times, which of course is its own defence mechanism and is there by the time you leave, very much as part of you as a young 17 or 18 year old.

(Lewis, 2014)

This strategic necessity clearly can become the basis of a very skilful self and the learned duplicity may be very helpful for spies or diplomats. It makes a lot of sense when we realise that the great era of the boarding public schools was the mid- to late nineteenth century when Britain needed to raise loyal dependable administrators to run her Imperial project. But when added to the double bind about being either wrong or unloved, *plus* the need to live without any emotions, *plus* the inner shame of having a privilege, it is not difficult to see how evasive secrecy or 'strategic-ness' becomes a way of life at school. But, it becomes a dangerous two-edged sword as Lewis so clearly explains: 'by the time you leave' the strategic habit becomes 'very much a part of you'. It is hard to shed in later life because ex-boarders are hardly aware they are doing it – to them it is normal. They have no other experience to compare it with.

The strategic habit has a very dark side, as Le Carré shows in his novels, and therapists must be alert to this. In a strategic way of life anything or anyone may get sacrificed through a variety of face-saving behaviours, including betrayal or bullying, or simply being dropped. The latter is very prevalent in intimate relationship situations and causes enormous hurt, even if unintentionally done. As an ex-boarder himself, Duffell remembers his wife painfully pointing out to him that he seemed to find it enormously challenging to support the notion of a 'We'.

The habit learned long ago of being thrown back on one's solo resources as a child, not expecting to live in a greater or shared unit, becomes closely identified with who the ex-boarder becomes. It is extremely difficult both for the one who is dropped to name and for the ex-boarder to recognise, let alone lose the habit, simply because the self that has been formed is not used to being in situations of loving mutuality. He has had to look after 'Number One' as long as he can remember.

Dependence, dissociation and denial

While also having to manage on their own from a young age, boarding children have to cope with multiple realities. They still have to be able to function in the home world that they have left behind but return to at intervals during their boarding career, while also being part of the school where they spend most of their childhood. Moving backwards and forwards between these locations at the beginning and end of terms, and sometimes these days also at half term, boarding children find themselves literally geographically divided. At the most basic level, boarding children have to split their identity into a home child and a boarding child and keep both sides of their identity going. It is no wonder that they have to master the art of what is known in psychology as *dissociation* or *splitting*.

The strategic survival personality that boarders develop and ex-boarders maintain is therefore like a Janus, the two-headed god of the Romans. It relies on showing one face to the world – usually confident, coping and upbeat – while keeping another part of the self – the sad, vulnerable, childish part – hidden, including hidden to themselves. This part is the dependent, scared, unconfident side that does not believe itself to be loveable. What is more, the construction of the falsely competent side is encouraged by the values of boarding schools, which want to promote successful independent products of their establishments in order to appeal to their customers, the parents. But nobody is fully independent in an inter-dependent world, especially little children, who have a right to be dependent.

So boarders have to learn how to dissociate, just as they are learning how to repress their feelings. They have to practise denial, to put on a brave face and delete all the things that make them unhappy – not just the *expression* of emotion, as Rivers noted, but the *emotion itself*. Once learned and taken for normal, this is a habit that is very hard to unlearn in later life. John Le Carré's fictional characters, which were based on the author's extensive experience in the hallowed institutions of the British Secret Service, show how this cultivated duplicity can resemble giving favours with one hand, while the other hand is plotting to do precisely the opposite (Le Carré, 1995, p. 44). This learned duplicity is arguably useful training for a soldier or a spy, but it invariably tends to ruin normal life, such as being in an intimate relationship or a family.

Clearly, boarders have not been encouraged to be authentic. They are then severely hampered later on in life, especially in adult relations and family situations that rely on authenticity and an ability to express emotions and empathise with the feelings of others. Worse, they may not know themselves to what extent they have managed to successfully keep apart the conflicting sides of themselves, to what extent their right and left hands have entirely separate agendas, as Le Carré proposes.

Here is where the actions and attitudes of the boarding school survivor's therapist can have considerable effect. When these problems emerge in therapy, the therapist will need to keep the client to task, and in this will have his or her work cut out.

The strategic survival personality in the consulting room

Initially, what is likely to emerge in therapy is the lonely, vulnerable side of the client, for which most therapists will have a strong attraction. Temporarily, the client may well enjoy being seen in this light, since he or she will have invested a lifetime in disowning these aspects. However, if the therapist is not seeing the client's partner or family members in couples or family therapy, then the other side of their personality, the one who has not learned empathy, who has discounted that human beings have needs, who has assumed the false boarding values of independence and the horror of vulnerability, who may be a bit of a bully, may well remain in hiding.

Therapists who are overly prone to seeing these more attractive and vulnerable sides, taking pride in the emergence of these aspects, may be reluctant to pursue the darker aspects of their client's personality. Or they may be fooled. In this way, therapy ends up colluding with the client's tendency to split rather than reveal. Further collusion can occur if therapists have their own reasons, such as having also boarded or having sent their own children away to board, or being impressed by the social status of their client.

Whilst the initial phase of being vulnerable may suit both therapist and client, as the work develops the client is more than likely to rediscover the distaste for this side of his or her character. Alternatively, the sense of being the powerless or dependent person may begin to reassert itself and the client then begins to feel increasingly uncomfortable. At this point, in both subtle and not so subtle ways, the client may begin to question the process and cast doubt on the skill of the practitioner. The therapist may believe it, may start to feel like an incompetent, stupid child, may wonder what on earth he or she is doing. In short, the split-off vulnerability and childishness may begin to land fair and square within the person of the therapist. Here it is vitally important that the therapist interrogates the counter-transference, as recommended by Patrick Casement (Casement, 1985).

The client holds a trump card – of deciding to terminate the therapy – and, if the therapist does their job, he or she may well be tempted to play it. The therapist must always remember that successful therapy will involve very ambivalent feelings on the part of the client. For it consists in helping to deconstruct the client's strategic survival personality, tracing the aspects of the personality that have been denied, disowned and split off. It means challenging the ways by which the client has survived so far. This will produce an unconscious counter-reaction. Retaliation usually occurs first in the threat to quit therapy, which is itself an ambivalent, self-negating action, of the kind which, unfortunately, the boarding school survivor is all too used to from childhood.

The Jungian analyst Joy Schaverien first began to learn about the complex psychodynamics of boarding school survivors when she realised that there were certain male clients who tended to exit therapy. This happened whenever they were becoming more vulnerable, because of what was emerging, or more dependent because of the need to fit their lives around the analytical breaks. She explored this issue in a 1997 paper entitled *Men who Leave too Soon*. Schaverien (2004) followed this up with *Boarding School: The Trauma of the 'Privileged' Child*, in which some of the obstacles a therapist can face when working with the dissociating survival personalities of ex-boarders were described. Here is an extract from one of her clinical vignettes:

> Mr A, in his late forties, was the son of a banker who had travelled abroad. His mother had often travelled with the father leaving their son in the care of a nanny from an early age. Mr A had been sent to a boarding school at the age of 7 and in the school holidays his parents were often absent and made arrangements for him and his younger sister to be cared for by a succession of nannies. Now he came to see me reluctantly, on the recommendation of his doctor, who thought that there could be a psychological component to some of the physical symptoms that he was suffering … As he began to talk about his early life, the link with his physical symptoms became apparent, first to me, and then gradually he began to see the connections.

So far so good, as this represents the honeymoon period when client and therapist seem to be cooperating. Schaverien continues:

> Initially, as he recounted his childhood experiences, he was quite dismissive of their import. However when he talked about his prep school, it became evident that this had affected him profoundly. The feelings

associated with it were emotionally present and, as he recounted various incidents related to this time, he became tearful and momentarily the vulnerable child, that he had once been, was present in the room. Each time this happened he would quickly recover and the coping persona would emerge and take charge.

This developing rhythm seems to have become too much for him and, after he had attended for a few months, he began to consider increasing from one to two sessions a week, but eventually decided to stop the therapy and come no more. Here is how Schaverien frames his dilemma:

> This was at the point when the self was breaking through its encapsulation and there was an intermittent, dependent atmosphere generated in the analytic relationship. I understood this to be generated by the dawning consciousness of the neediness of the vulnerable child-self.
>
> (Schaverien, 2004)

Strategic survival personality typology

Over many years of working with ex-boarders, we are able to define an approximate typology of strategic survival personalities, which relate to the different ways of approaching school life that we mentioned earlier, either keeping one's head down or breaking the rules but staying out of trouble, or not managing either. The three main types are (Figure 4.1):

1.   Compliers or Conformists
2.   Rebels
3.   Casualties or the Crushed

Figure 4.1 Survival personality types

Compliers or Conformists

These survivors are usually in denial of the problems of boarding and have identified with the values of the school – better to be on the winning side! Their motto can be: 'It never did me any harm.' Compliers tend to thrive in institutions after school. This is the class which is naturally most represented in the public world of business and politics.

Compliers tend not to seek therapy; but sometimes life intervenes. All goes well until they seem no longer to be on the winning side, for example, when something happens such as the loss of their job or an ultimatum from their spouse or partner. When their own child is born or reaches boarding age they may discover a chink in their armour. Then they may suddenly connect to some of the unrecognised needs of their inner child from whom they have distanced themselves.

At such crisis points, at the mercy of a sudden, unpredicted problem that threatens to break down their functioning level, they may appear desperate to change themselves. All the feelings of failure that they have been trying to keep at bay come flooding into their minds. They are in disarray when their carefully hidden negative self-concept is unmasked. In breakdown they may become completely paralysed. Their ability to repress, deny or generally dissociate suddenly evades them. This may be permanent or temporary, according to how they deal with it.

Here the therapist will do well to remind the client of the inherent opportunity in the breakdown. It feels like a disaster, but from the vantage point of getting out of the grip of the survival personality it can be reframed as a huge opportunity. The loss of ability to split or to function is a sign that their unconscious mind wants them to do more than just survive – it wants them to embrace living!

At the same time, the therapist should let the client know that they understand the ambivalence generated by this lack of functioning. They will probably find it too much to persevere, for the Complier's tendency is to leave therapy and abandon the change process as soon as the problem is 'fixed' and they feel able to function again. The Complier has invested heavily in a self that is dedicated to functioning.

Rebels

These survivors have recognised the problem of boarding and care about what happened to them as a child. However, they may develop a tendency to excessively blame boarding school, parents and all authorities in general for all the problems in their life.

Rebels have not been able to practise complete dissociation: they know they've suffered at school. They may be keen on personal development and therapy, but they often try to befriend their therapist, which makes therapy all the more difficult. The most common tendency is to reject their own potential along with the whole of the established order. In this way they 'throw the baby out with the bathwater'. Rebels often struggle with basic self-care. They can be very poor in looking after their own health and wellbeing, as if waiting for someone to take care of them.

Rebels are often more comfortable with displaying anger than grief and may get caught in an anti-authority stance towards the whole of society. The fallout is that in consequence they find it difficult to engage their own inner authority. Because it is in group life that they have suffered, they tend to be loners, avoiding joining groups at all costs – particularly that mother of all groups: the Establishment. They are often to be found in solitary professions where skill and hard work are necessary, such as carpentry or writing, and where the casual observer would not realise that they had 'benefited' from an elite private education.

A rebel must have a cause, so they often get involved in political or spiritual issues. If they do join a group, it is likely to be a left-wing or new-age movement, where anti-authoritarianism is required, and which often tend to be riven with internal conflicts. The Rebel's anger preserves the value of the outrage about what happened to them, which is life-promoting. However, the source may still be not properly recognised as Rebels rarely want to know that their own survival style has now become the problem. It is here that therapists will find their greatest challenge.

Some Rebel survivors are so busy seeing all the problems that they may ignore just how difficult to live with they can be. Rebels can be superior, over-friendly or seductive, with a delightful child inside. They tend to have a pronounced split between the inside and the outside, which is very confusing for their partners. They can be charming in terms of their friendliness, their preoccupation with freedom and their liberality.

Most challenging is that Rebels often adopt a masochistic stance to the world and are shy of real intimacy. Their rebellious survival defence has a healthy side, but because it is constructed along rigidly self-negating lines, it endlessly snatches defeat from the jaws of victory. Masochistic styles are well known to be challenging for any therapist (see Chapter 10) and the Rebel's strategic survival personality will put up serious resistance to any attempts at deconstruction.

Casualties or the Crushed

These people may have been neglected, abused or subject to double binds even before they went to school. Being already so damaged, they were unable to create a competent survival personality and suffered bullying and scapegoating at school from staff and children alike. Alternatively, they were abused at boarding school – often sexually – and were unable to make a cry for help. Or their cry for help was glossed over or ignored.

Their situation is often accompanied by drug and alcohol problems, poverty or social isolation; even some ex-boarders from quite 'privileged' backgrounds can fall into this group. Included in the Crushed are those who may have come from good enough homes but whose attractiveness had subjected them to unwanted attentions in the sexual hot-house atmosphere during their puberty.

As we know, the outward face of the strategic survival personality tends to exhibit high, if brittle, functioning. A Casualty might have been able to put on a brave face just enough to'avoid annihilation. But those crushed by boarding will be exhibiting some signs of distress, even if takes an effort to realise that they are not just misfits. In these cases, bullying leave its mark ineradicably. Being bullied can lead to a life dominated by much sadness and depression. For example, an anonymous ex-boarder contacted the Boarding School Survivor website with this message:

> I am a 42-year-old male who suffers with acute depression. I was bullied relentlessly at boarding school and have only just been able to disclose to my support worker that I feel my condition is entirely down to my childhood experiences at the hand of bullies. I need to speak about this to someone impartial about how this has affected my life. I do not want to feel suicidal constantly!

In addition to the three main types of survival personality described above, Boarding School Survivor women's workshops facilitator Nicola Miller has proposed three persona profiles:

- Henrietta – successful and confident in the work setting but unsuccessful and unconfident in the field of love and personal relationships.
- Eliza – a flamboyant and colourful 'lady' who feels worthless and unfulfilled despite everything in her life appearing so 'rosy'.
- Calamity Jane – tough, can cope, and a good friend to others, but always escaping another complicated personal relationship – often a therapist, who can understand everybody else's feelings, but not her own.

(Miller, 2009)

From survival to living

We have said that the habits of strategic survival and dissociation are really hard to unlearn. However, the stress of practising the amount of denial and dissociation that is needed puts a strain on a survivor. Often the ex-boarder is seen to have a rather brittle outer shell. Sometimes, this outer carapace can fail altogether and result in a crisis situation, as it did for the high-flying lawyer referred to earlier. In his case, the signs of failing to survive only occurred when he had to address an audience and then he found his words had dried up. When he began to talk in therapy about what his childhood was like – especially his time at boarding school – and how it had affected him, his symptoms began to disappear. He had begun the journey *from Survival to Living*.

The first task for clients is to recognise and then really get to know their strategic survival personality, to map out their patterns of survival and to understand the context for deconstructing these patterns. This involves considerable self-observation, guided by a perhaps unfamiliar attitude of self-compassion.

Children must survive. Survival patterns protect and hold them, give them an identity and some structure, in lieu of parental protection and guidance. We could say that the strategic survival personality is the one *in loco parentis* rather than the school. But there is a cost to this survival. In exchange for the undeniable privilege of the small classes, competitive atmosphere, the social perks of the old school tie and the right accent, boarders have had to sacrifice something of their *inner* selves. Because the survival personality operates by denial, by self-reinvention and by self-negation the price is actually a level of self-betrayal.

The journey back is fraught and the therapist must be alert but it is not without hope. What can seem like a desperate situation can become an opportunity to embrace life-giving change.

Sometimes breakdowns can be new beginnings.

Exercise 4: learning to survive

Questions for reflection:

- Think about how you learned to survive in your early days as a boarder.
- Did you have any specific strategies that you adopted?
- Did you play a particular role in your peer group?
- How similar or different was it from the role you had at home?

References

Arnold, B. and Basset, T. (2005) 'Stiff Upper Lip?' *Openmind*, 131, pp. 16–17.
Casement, P. (1985) *On Learning from the Patient*, Hove: Routledge.
Duffell, N. (2014) *Wounded Leaders: British Elitism and the Entitlement Illusion, a Psychohistory*, London: Lone Arrow Press.
Golding, W. (1954) *Lord of the Flies*, London: Faber and Faber.
Idle, E. (2012) Interview sourced at http://www.imdb.com/name/nm0111756/news?year=2012.
Le Carré, J. (1995) *Our Game*, London: Hodder and Stoughton.
Lewis, D. (2014) on 'Desert Island Discs', *BBC Radio 4*, broadcast 30 November.

Miller, N. (2009) 'Some Issues that Arise for Women Attending Boarding School Survivor Workshops'. Paper given to Boarding Concern Conference, 14 November, accessible at www.boardingconcern.org.uk.

Porges, S.W. (2011) *The Polyvagal Theory: Neurophysiological Foundations of Emotions, Attachment, Communication, and Self-Regulation*, New York: W.W. Norton.

Schaverien, J. (1997) 'Men who Leave too Soon: Further Reflections on the Erotic Transference and Countertransference', *British Journal of Psychotherapy* 14, 1, 3–16.

Schaverien, J. (2004) 'Boarding School: The Trauma of the 'Privileged' Child', *Journal of Analytical Psychology*, 49, 683–705.

Thompson, H. (1997) *Peter Cook: A Biography*, London: Hodder and Stoughton.

Chapter 5

Signs, symptoms and relationships

Well, obviously a fear of abandonment. A tendency to shut down emotionally, and freeze out, in the face of something sad, or frightening or infuriating. There's the 'timetabling' – you're resented (as a partner) if you just want to relax and put your feet up, like a normal person. There's always got to be a plan or a task.

(Sally Fraser, describing the symptoms of a boarding
school survivor, Renton, 2014)

Key points of chapter

- Among the signs and symptoms that therapists need to be aware of when working with ex-boarders are an extreme inability to feel and express emotion and a compulsion to be in task mode. These factors make intimate relationships a potentially very tricky area.
- As they grapple with the problems of maintaining a loving and intimate relationship with an emotionally absent boarding school survivor, it is often the intimate partner who seeks advice.
- Some ex-boarders access therapy after a major crisis in their lives, while many do not see their boarding experience as centrally problematical.

Signs and symptoms

In our experience, the effects of boarding require the following key steps towards recovery:

1. Recognising the signs and causes of the problem.
2. Understanding the functioning of the strategic survival personality.
3. Putting an end to strategic living and recovering emotions.
4. Stepping away from *survival* into *living*.

This recovery process represents a major undertaking for both client and therapist. So in this chapter, to illustrate the complex process of recognition that *Boarding School Syndrome* and the *Strategic Survival Personality* necessitates, we will use some of the many thousands of letters and emails that the authors and Boarding School Survivors have received over the years. This recognition is a precursor to the succeeding stages of acceptance and change.

Ex-boarders will often have a very competent exterior but it is built on survival strategies adopted many years ago to cope with feelings of loss at being abandoned very young to an institution. Faced with the inevitable losses that belong to adult life, the competent exterior of an ex-boarder reveals itself as brittle; it will sometimes begin to fracture. Perhaps the most common facet or symptom of an ex-boarder can be described as 'emotional absence'. Cognitively, they may be razor sharp; but emotionally, they can be rank beginners. Inevitably, an inability to deal with anything emotional makes the business of intimate relationships a veritable minefield for ex-boarders. Here is an example:

> At the age of 11, I suddenly suffered from terrible homesickness which lasted about a year. I then recovered (on reflection I just shut down this emotional part of me) and continued to board and do well at school until I left at 18. I am now 26 and have found life since school very difficult on an emotional level. I have great difficulty building relationships and have developed a very independent but lonely existence. I have never suffered any bullying and generally considered myself likeable, but something within me prevents me from getting close to people and is stopping me from fulfilling my potential. I can't help but think that this is connected with those tough days when I was very young and was so desperate to be at home. I would like more than anything else to have the help of a therapist to tackle these issues and move forward.
>
> (An anonymous unsolicited email enquiry)

Other signs or symptoms are:

- a fear of being left or abandoned
- a sense of shame and not feeling worthy
- submersion in work and a compulsion to succeed
- an inability to relax
- 'timetabling': always busy
- substance misuse
- anger and irritability
- relationship breakdown.

Picking up on Sally Fraser, quoted at the beginning of this chapter, signs include an obsessive preoccupation with work, with achievement; a fear of failure or a horror of laziness may emerge, either in the presenting issue or unravelled as the therapy proceeds. This is a classic sign which could alert the therapist to the possible presence of the syndrome. Why should this be so linked with boarding, readers may ask, when our whole modern culture seems to favour a tendency to overwork?

Keeping busy

The reforms of the public school system, spearheaded by Dr Arnold of Rugby in the mid-nineteenth century, turned a *laisserz-faire* educational system into one in which the boarders were constantly regimented, kept occupied, put to work or into obligatory activities such as chapel, games or cadet training. In this way all spare time was eliminated: everything was on the timetable. This process was a way of controlling the unruly children; the secondary tactic was to distract them from their emotional reality and to prevent sexual liaisons amongst pupils. This tradition remains a durable facet of boarding life in Britain, continuing in an unbroken line, supported by such modern ideas as the results culture, and it has a profound effect on the adults these children become.

Here is an example of how it is taught to boarding children in modern Britain. Colin Luke's remarkable television documentary *The Making of Them* (1994) discreetly followed and filmed a group of 8- and 9-year-old boarders in their first six weeks at two different prep schools. One sequence in the film features a young woman teacher addressing her class in a way that seems very modern and rather sympathetic. She begins:

> It's quite natural for you to miss mummy and daddy; we all miss our family when we are away from them and if we have a few tears that's nothing to worry about, it's very normal – I have a few tears every now and then too, so you being much younger are quite allowed to have a few.
>
> (Luke, 1994)

But now she begins to deliver the *coup de grace* by recommending the boys to betray themselves in the time-honoured way: reject feelings and adopt 'time-tabling'. The teacher continues:

> Don't worry, that [missing family] gets better too. You'll find that every day that you are here, as things become more familiar, and you get busier and busier, and you are doing more and more, you begin not to forget about mummy and daddy – well you never forget them of course – but it gets easier and easier being away from them. Alright?

What choice do they have when it is put with such apparent empathy? Is it any wonder that 40 years later ex-boarders find it nigh impossible to give up these ingrained habits? Is it surprising that the fantasy of what might happen if the ex-boarder stopped doing and started feeling is a vague but calamitous one? Unless the therapist – and eventually the client – can recognise and accept it in this way any attempts to change behaviours will certainly be fruitless.

In the same year that Luke's film was shown, sociologist and writer Alisdare Hickson (1995) conducted a large survey of ex-boarders asking them to speak anonymously about their sexual experiences at public school and the effect of these experiences on their sexual orientation. His unusual methodology was to write a letter to every male name that appeared in *Who's Who*.

Hickson draws many interesting conclusions from his courageous feat of anecdotal history gathering. His idea is that the constant business and obsession with rules was a deliberate policy of the disciplinarian movement to reform the public schools that kicked off in the puritanical 1860s. The chief motive was to counteract the boys' tendency towards 'beastliness'. The less the boys met each other in free time the less they would be tempted to have sex with each other, which left only the vice of 'self-abuse' to be policed. In consequence, every second of the day was regimented with volumes of pointless tasks, codes, rules and regulations invented to limit the boarders' freedom – always something on the timetable.

The tyranny of the timetable, the propensity to overwork, to always be in 'doing' mode is one that affects countless adult ex-boarders and can turn up as a presented problem or a symptom of the ex-boarder. Here is one senior manager looking back in Luke's film:

> I think I came out really believing that work makes free, and that stuck with me for many, many years, to the point that it cost me the ability to parent my children, it cost me my marriage, it cost me, in fact, the *quality* of my career. On the one hand, you're prepped in this way to be part of the Establishment, to be successful, to be self-reliant and aggressive and all those things, but in fact, somewhere inside you, when it comes down to dealing with *real* relationships, with the *real* things in life, you are very, very *weak* and ill-prepared, and the tendency is to run away into work mode. I can remember making a virtue of leaving home at 5 o'clock on a Sunday afternoon to catch the plane to go somewhere: I'm going back to the front, I'm going back to my troops, I'm doing my duty.

In 1977 Jonathan Gathorne-Hardy wrote a history of the public schools in which he remarked on some of the effects he thought peculiar to ex-boarders, chiefly their tendency to be excessively conscientious (Gathorne-Hardy, 1979, p. 219). Recalling John Betjeman's long poem about public school life (which he hated), *Summoned by Bells*, Gathorne-Hardy suggests the result of this constant orchestration and exhortation 'to do' to be: 'so obvious that scarcely a single social study mentions it – the English upper classes were absurdly over conscientious' (p. 242). Very much of his day, Gathorne-Hardy does not seem quite certain whether this tendency is a vice or a virtue; he is quite sure of its ubiquity and its usefulness, however, and links it with boarding's original purpose for training colonial administrators and officers: 'This is why so many of them could be sent 7,000 miles away and trusted to govern or administer or fill in ledgers' (p. 243).

We call it 'timetabling' and it is one of the universal curses of ex-boarders, though of course it can be useful at work, but when it rules domestic life, it is a calamity that therapists will need to spot, name and do their best to help and tame. It affects all ex-boarders. George Orwell's memoir of his prep school, *Such, Such Were the Joys* reveals him well prepped for 'doublespeak' and totalitarianism before the age of 12. On the recent Penguin edition the back cover reads: 'I think the characteristic faults of the English upper and middle classes may be partly due to the practice, general until recently, of sending children away from home as young as nine, eight or even seven' (Orwell, 2014). Whether Orwell knew in what ways he himself had been affected by boarding is doubtful; he seems not to have been very good at self-care and he certainly smoked himself into an early grave. Below we quote his own words showing how even this renowned literary figure was tormented by his workaholic timetabling, learned, we can safely imagine, during his ten years of boarding. This poignant passage was taken from a notebook found by his bed at his death:

> It is now 16 years since my first book was published, and about 21 years since I started publishing articles in the magazines. Throughout that time there has literally not been one day in which I did not feel I was idling, that I was behind with the current job, and that my total output was miserably small. Even at the periods I was working ten hours a day on a book, or turning out four or five articles a week, I have never been able to get away from this neurotic feeling that I was wasting time.
>
> (Gathorne-Hardy, 1979, pp. 242–3)

Ex-boarder clients and therapy

Some ex-boarders will seek the help of a therapist or counsellor to address their boarding issues; others will avoid seeking therapeutic help at all costs. Some will be pressured into it by their partners. However, there is also a further group of ex-boarders: those that enter therapy for a number of reasons, but specifically not to look at boarding issues. Whether this is in individual therapy or couple therapy the task for the therapist is the same – to make a mental picture of the signs and symptoms presented and to find a way of feeding back a hypothesis that there is a boarding issue at play, without putting the client off or exciting their resistance at the beginning of the vital recognition stage. The issue for therapists is how to raise the subject and, once it is put on the agenda, how to keep it there to enable their client to begin to explore an area of their lives that may be initially relatively inaccessible.

For example, an ex-boarder client may come to therapy after the loss of a parent with a view to getting help with their grieving process. In obtaining details of their life history, they may state that they went to boarding school from an early age; but this information may be delivered without any real emotion, flatly as a bare fact. As therapy progresses, the therapist may begin to notice more emotional absence in the client. Nevertheless, the client says that therapy is helpful, even when to the therapist there is no obvious sign of this. Whenever boarding school comes up, the client speaks in a rather flat way, reporting things like 'there were a lot of us there'.

This is not an easy situation for a therapist, but we have found that recommending the book *The Making of Them* (Duffell, 2000) or film (Luke, 1994) can lead to small or large breakthroughs. Often clients will see their own experience mirrored back to them through the experience of reading or watching. This then can lead to a more likely chance for deeper exploration in therapy.

Client scenario

A therapist contacted us in 2014 to say that he had recommended a client, who had been a boarder but was reluctant to explore this experience in therapy, to watch the film *The Making of Them*. The client returned the week after and said to the therapist, 'I watched that film and I loved the bit when the boy is talking about boarding school and being all sensible and adult but then he goes on to say about eating the nose on his birthday cake.' At this point the client had a big grin on his face and the therapist noticed a big shift in his energy. The disowned inner child had begun to return. The recognition process could begin.

Sometimes, boarding issues are concealed behind a web of other problems, frequently conflicting situations at work, where the presence of authority figures, or the need to be one, unconsciously reminds the client of the bad authority figures experienced at boarding school or those who were ready to send them away from home too soon. Alternatively, difficult wider family situations can reveal the client's inexperience in being in a family, and this is a symptom that can easily be missed. All these hidden issues require some real analytical work on behalf of therapists to identify them. Here is one such scenario.

Case study: Jacqueline and Mark

Jacqueline was in her late thirties when she started seeing a therapist. The topic of their discussions invariably centred round Jacqueline's relationship problems. For the past year she had been seeing a man, Mark, in his early fifties, a widower with two teenage sons. These boys were in constant trouble – at school, with girlfriends and with the law. Their conduct at home seemed close to anarchic. Mark would fret and rage and tell all his troubles to Jacqueline, who told her therapist how she thought the boys needed both love and boundaries, commodities that seemed to be in short supply at Mark's house. Jacqueline's life seemed to be disappearing down the black hole of Mark's chaotic family. Her therapist encouraged her to try to persuade Mark to seek his own therapeutic support, which he eventually – and reluctantly – did.

Mark's therapist also noticed the drowning nature of the saga of these boys and their constant worrying activities. He noted Mark's struggle to be a parent and found out that Mark's father had been absent and preoccupied with work, leaving the parenting to his wife – as Mark himself had done, until his wife's fatal accident. His therapist imagined that Mark's reluctance to be a parent, his difficulties in loving the boys and exerting realistic discipline stemmed from his unconscious anger at his father's absence. The therapist also tried to reframe Mark's current issues as part of the grieving process of losing his wife two years earlier. But Mark continued to talk about the awfulness of his sons and how unfair things were. Not much changed.

Eventually, Mark revealed that he had been a boarder from the age of 13 and that although he hadn't wanted to go it had 'been alright, generally speaking'. Gradually Mark and his therapist together began to realise that he had no experience of being parented as a teenager – when he came home he was 'spoiled' by his mother, which had made his relationship with his father even more distant. The trips home had increasingly seemed like visits, since where he really lived was at school. Mark was recommended to read up on the psychological effects of boarding, which made him cry for the first time in many years. One year later Mark asked his therapist if he thought a group workshop on boarding would help him become a better father. Mark had begun the difficult work of recognition, acceptance and change.

Sometimes the issue of boarding is avoided because the therapist is unaware of the profound impact that boarding can have. Alternatively, some therapists may be reluctant to explore these issues with their clients. Another enquiry to Boarding School Survivors highlights this difficulty:

> I am writing to thank Mr. Duffell for this book as my husband read it (as a public school boarder from age 7) and it has helped him hugely. He was already in counselling, but hadn't really tackled/recognised just how much his boarding school experience has scarred him. So thank you, it is good to see him working through his survival mechanisms and recognising his little adult and trying to love him … finally.
>
> (Anonymous enquiry, 2012)

A partner's story

In Chapter 3 we introduced the difficult issues that partners of ex-boarders often face. Indeed many partners contact organisations such as Boarding School Survivors and Boarding Concern. The most usual enquiry is from a woman seeking help for a male partner or spouse, for example:

> I've just found your Boarding School Survivors website and read the sample chapter of *The Making of Them*. My husband and I need this book! He's now 70 and still scarred from being sent away to sink or swim in a public school at age 14. He's basically a good man, but he's still that teenager defending himself from a hostile environment, still wanting mother (or a series of mother substitutes) to atone for abandoning him, and acting out forever because there is no atonement. He dreams nearly every night of packing his trunk in a dormitory, not knowing where he's going to next or where he belongs, just as your chapter describes.
>
> We've been married 27 years, and I've been imprisoned in that school with him all that time. We're on the point of divorce because I can't stand any more his want home/hate home, need love/don't need you, bully-or-be bullied attitudes. I don't want to leave him, but I'm worn out by that poor boy, forever with his fists up braced for a fight, so busy dealing with his neediness that he can't care for others.
>
> (Anonymous enquiry, 2010)

Here we see a marriage of 27 years in crisis. As the wife puts out an appeal for help, it is to be hoped that her husband is able to respond to her call to change. To do so he will have to acknowledge that boarding without his family to love and touch him, in an institutional hothouse that valued self-reliance and achievement over love and relationships, has cost him a heavy price. He will need to recognise that while he has been busy surviving, as if he were still at boarding school, his partner has been explicitly paying that price. He will be very unlikely to be able to do this without some good professional help.

If he does end up in therapy, one of the first jobs of the therapist will be to help him with his recognition work. In most cases, this usually needs a good creative partnership. The process of recognition may not be possible at the therapist's usual rate of patience, when a marriage is in such crisis and the client has been so split off from memories and emotion. Consequently, the therapist may have to intervene in a didactic way more than he or she is used to.

Of course there are many ways to proceed and many different styles, but this is how we would recommend approaching such a case.

- The first step will be to *normalise* his relationship failure, letting him know that his woefully inadequate training for relationships makes the normal difficulties of intimacy almost insurmountable.
- After that, the therapist will have to help him see that loving attachments and good relationships were forfeited in his privileged abandonment; a deal was done for social success and a life of the mind, and it was done at a cost.
- Next, the therapist will have the difficult task of helping him recognise that the one who has been trying to love him is not the same as the one who abandoned him when he was a child.
- The therapist may now reframe his relationship trouble: it actually means that he has a chance to put things in the right order now, as he was unable to in childhood. Now he can prioritise love, attachments, relationships, intimacy.
- But in order to move from survival into living he will have to do the long hard work of rebuilding trust in his relationship.

Sometimes, as we have already referred to in Chapter 3, a partner may end up experiencing the feelings that the ex-boarder has not let themselves feel. A partner can be a bit mystified about why they may feel shame, despair and loneliness. The psychodynamically trained therapist will recognise these feelings as a transference of the shame, despair and loneliness that the partner has disowned. If an ex-boarder has been denying and dissociating from their feelings for a very long time, this can lead to *projective identification*, whereby their partner begins to feel and experience all the emotions that the ex-boarder cannot feel. These emotions feel very real, and the partner begins to consider them as their own.

In *Wounded Leaders*, Duffell calls this problem 'Dump Truck Ethics' and proposes that the incidence of this problem in marriages/partnerships in the UK is in: 'epidemic but as yet unrecognised proportions, so that many partners regularly think they are going crazy for unknown reasons' (Duffell, 2014, p. 87). Clearly the challenge here for therapists is to be able to spot these processes and to deliver what they have recognised in ways that do not make the ex-boarder feel more stressed, shamed or criticised than they already do. Even highly trained therapists will have to draw on all their skills to do this.

In the initial stages of making such a revelation the partner who is in receipt of the projective identifications will feel relieved because someone has finally named the harmful game that they have been involved in. This relief may well be accompanied by increased shame, panic and denial on behalf of the ex-boarder and sometimes by the aggressive accusation that the therapist is supposed to make things fair and not take sides.

Obviously no real progress can be made until the ex-boarder recognises that they have a problem and makes the commitment to do the work of withdrawing the projections, feeling the shame, despair and loneliness, and making amends for the harm committed. One of the great difficulties for the therapist in guiding this task is that the client may well be recognising for the first time that they are victims of their privileged abandonment in childhood.

At the same time they will have to face the fact that in their intimate relationships they have become persecutors. This can cause very complex internal conflicts, with the therapist risking being seen as the favoured rescuer to the partner rather than the client. A journey round the famous Drama Triangle (victim/rescuer/persecutor) is to be expected, which will keep the therapist on his or her toes! As in all such cases, not taking things personally and allowing these transitional processes to occur will help. Only a joint journey into the heart of the matter, into the original situation which caused the innocence to be abused, can do the trick. For as the psychoanalyst James Grotstein said: 'When innocence has been deprived of its entitlement, it becomes a diabolical spirit' (Grotstein, 1984, p. 203).

Steps towards recovery

There is an order to recovery. Effects cannot be reversed before the signs and causes of the problem have been acknowledged and the strategic survival personality recognised; only then can the client begin to step out of 'survival' towards 'living. This is a long process and in subsequent chapters we will look at the areas of acceptance and change. Recognition is the important first step.

We will end this part of the book with some testaments from people who have recognised their boarding issues and have begun their journey from survival into living. First, an example of two ex-boarders helping one another in dealing with their issues:

> I'm now 62, and have been blessed by marrying a wife who herself was a boarder for a number of years, so has been incredibly patient in encouraging me out of my 'survival patterns'. I just hope our own children (5 in all – 4 now themselves married) haven't suffered too much from the backlash, although we never seriously even considered sending them away to school, despite offers of help with fees from well-meaning relatives. I think both of us were aware from an early age of the fact that we had both suffered from boarding, though, as you say in your book, actually

dealing with the problems takes the best part of a lifetime, and is still an on-going process!

(Comment on Boarding School Survivors website, 2013)

Next, psychotherapist Nicola Miller describes what female ex-boarders gained from attending Boarding School Survivors workshops:

> They survived their school days somehow, and they come away from the workshops more consciously aware of their survival as a testament to life. The fact of surviving two weekends with twelve BSS women gives many hope and the knowledge that, in a safe-enough environment, bonding and attachment are possible. Sharing and learning from each other, we see parts of ourselves we never knew existed, mirrored all around the room. This experience also breeds courage, courage to accept what was needed in the past was lost, courage to accept we do not have the power to change our history, and the imperative – we must surrender the constant struggle to recreate what we needed then. So we grieve our female nature, we acknowledge with respect the characters we have become, and we start to really listen for the loving and creative girl who has all the beauty and potential of a woman.
>
> (Miller, 2009)

So far in this book we have tried to explain the trauma that a child experiences when their attachment to their family and all the many facets of life at home is deliberately ruptured by early boarding, often at the age of 7 or 8. It is not a trauma that occurs through a chance or fateful unwanted accident or disaster; nor does it come about through a violent or abusive intrusion into a child's life. It is a planned and deliberate trauma, part of a deliberate process of social engineering which goes largely unchallenged and masquerades as a privilege and a benefit.

An example of how the boarding experience can profoundly affect a person's life is offered here by Anni Townend, a boarding school survivor and now a leadership consultant, who contacted us in 2014. In her eloquent piece, she summarises some of the themes of this book so far and also shows how with a lot of work and effort ex-boarders can make sense of their experiences. She speaks of the privilege of boarding and how it was the unhappiest time of her life, although she does acknowledge some benefit from the educational experience. Townend writes of the trauma of crossing the threshold and being handed over and signed for like a package:

> I do feel privileged now to live the life I have here in the UK with my family, however in the past I have felt ashamed of being at boarding school. I didn't know how to talk about it. I felt different and even now when I say that I went to boarding school I feel there is an assumption

of privilege. This assumption both holds a myth and a truth with which I have never really come to terms.

I have many memories of 'my time' at boarding school and knew then, as now, that they were not the happiest days of my life. Indeed I would characterise them as the unhappiest days of my life. The educational experience benefited me intellectually in that I was given much to think about. Spiritually I was given the space to reflect in silence and to decide for myself what mattered to me. It is the only thing really that I am grateful for from that time.

The dreadful handover on that first day at school found me walking down a long corridor with great distrust, as each step took me closer to the inevitable saying Goodbye. I was 10 years old. A formidable woman met us, and a rather smaller and timid woman stood by her side. I did not take to them or them to me. As I stepped over the threshold I knew deep inside me that this was not going to be a good experience. I was right. It was something to be got through, to be endured. The feeling was one of going inside from the light into the dark, of leaving all I knew and that was familiar. As I stepped into the dark everything closed in on me and I left most of myself, if not all, outside. It has taken years of therapy and support from family and friends for me to find myself again.

I was handed over and signed for like the delivery of a package. My mother was not prepared for how awful this handover would be. Should it be done fast, slow, should there be hugs, how to say Goodbye and leave a small child in this big place? My father in his inimitable way was impatient to get going thus hastening on the painful parting. At some point my parents left and I was on my own. I felt abandoned. And therein lies the thing, I was on my own, and remained really on my own for the next 5 years. I left aged 15. During that time I managed. I survived. We have never really recovered from this as a family. It is a conversation that my mother and I return to with difficulty from time to time. Even writing about it is not easy.

So why am I sharing this? I have for some time wanted to write about these years at boarding school and their impact. My story is not of sexual abuse. It is a story of emotional abuse and neglect, of deep unhappiness and of physical neglect. It has had a huge impact on my life as an adult and on my relationships. I have had to learn to look after myself in ways that are affirming and nurturing, rather than neglecting and undoing. I am grateful to my friends, to my partner and daughters who have helped me to do this and to writers like Jeanette Winterson who have shown me that writing is a way of making sense of stuff and of getting on with it, with true northern grace and grit. Sharing my story is another way of coming out from the dark and of stepping towards the light.

Exercises in returning to memories, such as the one suggested below, are not to be underestimated in their power. They may have to be done in stages or repeated over several sessions. It is important that the client is able to proceed at a comfortable pace so that the benefits of the exercise can be integrated.

Exercise 5: replacing what was lost

Lead your client through this guided visualisation, which includes drawing:

- Close your eyes and relax.
- Try to remember your home before you left, who you were then.
- Remember your home, your bedroom, your siblings, toys and pets. Think of all the people and things you had to separate from when you went away to school.
- Now try to sum up all that you had to separate from and lose and allow one image for this to appear in your mind's eye.
- Trust what comes to you. Don't censor this image – it comes from your unconscious mind, which means you well.
- Now open your eyes and quickly draw and colour this image – don't worry about making a beautiful drawing, it is simply a representation for you to do further inner work with.
- When you have finished your drawing, again close your eyes and relax.
- This time, remember your boarding school, if there were more than one, you may like to choose the one you first went to or the one that has most energy for you at this moment.
- See yourself in this school, wander round in all the different places, dormitories, classrooms, common rooms, playing fields and so on.
- How did you behave toward different people? What were you like in these different situations?
- And when you went home for the holidays, how did the person you were becoming behave at home in the family, with home friends and so on?
- Now, with all that you had lost, you had to put something in its place. Allow an image for this to appear in your mind's eye. Trust what comes to you.
- Now open your eyes and quickly draw and colour this second image. Again, don't worry about making a beautiful drawing, it is simply a representation for you to do further inner work with.

Now ask your client to reflect with you on these questions:

- Looking at your two drawings – how do you feel when you see them?
- In what way are they related?
- Can you appreciate your unconscious mind for producing these images?

References

Duffell, N. (2000) *The Making of Them: The British Attitude to Children and the Boarding School System*, London: Lone Arrow Press.

Duffell, N. (2014) *Wounded Leaders: British Elitism and the Entitlement Illusion, a Psychohistory*, London: Lone Arrow Press.

Gathorne-Hardy, J. (1979) *The Public School Phenomenon*, Harmondsworth: Penguin.

Grotstein, J. (1984) 'Forgery of the Soul', in Nelson, C. and Eigen, M. (eds), *Evil, Self and Culture*, New York: Human Sciences Press.

Hickson, A. (1995) *The Poisoned Bowl: Sex Repression and the Public School System*, London: Constable. The *Independent*'s comment is at http://www.independent. co.uk/arts-entertainment/books/boys-will-be-boys-1617532.html.

The Making of Them (1994) Film directed by C. Luke, UK: BBC.

Miller, N. (2009) 'Some Issues that Arise for Women Attending Boarding School Survivors workshops'. Paper given to Boarding Concern Conference, 14 November, retrieved from www.boardingconcern.org.uk.

Orwell, G. (2014) (first published 1953) *Such, Such Were the Joys*, London: Penguin Classics.

Renton, A. (2014) 'The Damage Boarding Schools Do', *Observer Magazine*, 20 July, pp. 28–35.

Part II

Acceptance

Chapter 6

Remembering

The boys do not take on board what I say about being more open emotionally and in communicating. Talking and creating emotional awareness is like talking to the cat. How do I proceed as a woman to get the young men to open up? There has to be an open sesame somewhere that somehow I am missing, a door to emotions that do not exclude me and make me feel I am constantly trying to relate. Very unrewarding … I would like to be more efficient as a tutor.

(A non-British private tutor working with older boarders in email enquiry to Boarding School Survivors, 2015)

Key points of chapter

- Remembering is a key stepping stone on the path to recovery.
- Often one of the first goals for ex-boarders is to get back in touch with their emotions, in particular the sadness from their original abandonment.
- Therapists can positively promote *emotional courage*: learning to override the stiff-upper-lip training and facing the return of feeling, letting sadness and tears back into one's life, and sometimes anger.
- Therapists can encourage a level of awareness to recognise the impulse to survive by discounting feelings or becoming strategic.
- Ex-boarder clients can unpack their personal childhood history and restore an image of themselves at school.

Re-membering

Some people say that the boarder never comes home again.

How do therapists proceed in helping their ex-boarder clients to 'come home'? The job has to start with helping them remember what has been lost and learning to be comfortable with feelings again. It is not straightforward: there can be a similar dilemma to that of the well-meaning tutor quoted above who wants to love her pupils back to life when she wonders how, as a woman, she can get the young men to open up.

Even experienced therapists can be puzzled by just how far away from feeling and memories some of their clients can be. Sometimes therapists are distracted by strange thoughts and feelings that arise in the field between them and their clients; sometimes by their own desire to reach out across the divide. Here is a short vignette from an ex-boarder group experience to describe one way such therapeutic dilemmas can arise.

Vignette: Roger

'The thing is, I just can't remember anything about those first days at school.'

It was Roger who spoke, a man in his early fifties sitting in a room along with 13 others in a circle of chairs. They were on the second day of a group workshop, convened for the express purpose of working therapeutically on how boarding had affected them. Roger was elegantly dressed in up-to-date fashion, if in rather a youthful style. His long legs, encased in tight-fitting trousers, ended in light brown leather brogues and stretched out confidently into the room.

'Perhaps', said one of the two facilitators, a man about the same age as Roger, noticing the expensive outfit and momentarily pausing as he silently reproached himself for not having worn his own new designer jeans. 'Perhaps there's a good reason', he continued somewhat hesitantly, 'why you don't remember anything. Perhaps it is too painful for you to recall. Most likely you were traumatised, and your feelings are sort of on ice.'

The intervention seemed on the mark, but Roger looked like he wasn't going to unthaw in much of a hurry. Nor did he look particularly troubled by his lack of memory or feeling. It appeared as if it had become part of how he presented himself to the world.

What *was* he doing here if he didn't want anything to change, and how can we get behind his solid wall of defence, both facilitators had wondered at their coffee break debrief.

'It's like, *here* … it's OK to be me', continued Roger, seemingly oblivious of the therapist's comment, looking at no one in particular. 'We are all the same here … we're all victims of the system', he said with a certain note of triumph.

OK. That's it, he is here to belong, to be part of something, to have his identity confirmed, not to differentiate at all. Everyone is apparently the same, even if actually they are not, was how the facilitator's thoughts now ran. It was a room full of men in different states of awareness, different stages of readiness to engage with the psychological problem, which, in the present, had become their own selves, still driven by the need to survive.

His colleague seemed to have similar musings, and the two facilitators both relaxed, recognising that all Roger was going to manage this weekend was to belong in a group of men and feel safe. There was no point forcing him: he just needed to be included. They were not going to try to push the river upstream and get distracted in their efforts towards those who were in a different place.

There are some ex-boarders who are very sure that boarding was a major problem in their lives, but less interested in how they are behaving *now*, as adult survivors, which is the real problem in their lives now that needs tackling. Often these people fall into the survival personality category we described earlier as Rebels. Sometimes they are equally, if not more resistant to therapeutic endeavour as Compliers. The therapist's key to understanding this is to recognise that they can be equally cut off from feelings and memory, as if something has been amputated from them and just does not exist anymore. Sometimes they may seem to belong to more than one of the personality types at the same time, like Roger, who appears part 'Rebel' part 'Crushed'.

It is not that they are *repressing* memories or emotion but that they have *dissociated* completely from them, and have reinvented themselves thereafter. Consequently, the therapist who attempts to be helpful by insisting that they remember what is lost will be resisted. It will seem to the client as if the therapist wants to seek out and destroy their survival mechanism. Despite their apparent willingness to enter therapy, this will inevitably put them on 'red alert'. In such cases therapists *must* learn to pace themselves. In a group situation, therapists must assess whether the participant is able to fully benefit from a group therapeutic approach.

Psychodynamically speaking, it is a question of needing to make an assessment of 'ego strength', which may easily be disguised by the client's self-presentation. Roger's smartly dressed, confident body posture and Rebel stance belies his very fragile sense of self. Where the dissociation is very severe it may be that a group participant will need a dedicated one-to-one approach. In such a case, the group setting will be unlikely to do much, except perhaps to offer the participant a place to belong, where they can feel accepted – loved even. Focusing too hard on the resistance towards remembering or feeling or to even 'staying in the present', as a Gestalt therapist may want to, is unlikely to work. If this is pursued in a group setting it can endanger the dynamism of the group, forcing it to be dominated by, as it were, its lowest common denominator.

Working with such an ex-boarder in individual therapy, therapists must recognise just what an amputation has been suffered. At the initial stage, recovering lost memories and feelings may not be the immediate best approach. As in the example above, the need may simply be to belong and be loved. And for this to happen, they must be affirmed, as they are. The therapist's respectful, patient and skilful approach might be to say: 'Yes, there are very good reasons why you shut these feelings and memories away'. For such a client an interpretation will be necessary, so humanistic therapists may have to learn a new style. Interpretations can be much more compassionate than their reputation suggests, since very often the good interpretation begins with an affirmative 'Yes', which is always good to hear. And, as in the example above, an initial interpretation is not the last word. It is an affirming recognition, and it may be followed up by something like:

> Perhaps one day they'll come back, or perhaps you've banished those demons for ever. Maybe we'll discover this together one day.

Primarily, this is all about respecting the client's trauma and creating safety. Secondly, but by no means less importantly, it is about understanding and allowing the wisdom of the psyche. Mostly, wise Psyche allows all of us to deal with what we can deal with – *when* we are able to deal with it. Sometimes this takes much longer than one might expect. Patient, consistent therapeutic support will go deep down into the recesses of the psyche and help the client remember.

Now, when we say 'remember', we take that word very seriously and employ it in several different senses. The most important are:

- Remembering in the conventional sense, recalling what *actually occurred* so ex-boarders are not driven by an imperative to maintain self-protection in relation to an unconscious trauma.
- *Re-membering* in the sense of developing awareness or mindfulness (*re-* meaning 'expressing intensive force' plus Latin *memor* meaning 'mindful').
- *Re-membering* in the sense of becoming a *member* once more of the group of humans trying to live rather than survive; group workshops can be extraordinarily useful in this sense.
- *Re-membering* in the sense of restoring what has been amputated – the emotional limb, as it were. (Origin Middle English, from Latin *membrum* meaning 'limb'.)
- *Remembering* in the sense of maintaining an ongoing, lifetime self-awareness and self-regulation discipline; not slipping back into old habits of survival at any cost, such as abandoning their partner to save face to avoid vulnerability.

Learning to feel again

The therapeutic job involves guiding the client to accept that what happened was in the past and that a different strategy is needed to move from survival to living as an adult. Starting to recognise issues connected to boarding and remembering what it was really like may eventually lead to acceptance: coming to terms with the trauma of the broken attachments, acknowledging that adopting a survival strategy was necessary for the child to survive.

In the previous chapter we saw how ex-boarders struggle with emotions, since survival at school meant learning not to be emotional. An emotional homesick child will bring up similar feelings in other children and such a child becomes a threat to the group identity and is liable to be scapegoated and bullied. Boarding children therefore learn, from an early age, to bite their lip, bury their feelings and not cry, but ex-boarders have to learn how to feel again.

In this process the mutual support of themed group therapy can be helpful and may be an important first step in this direction. Here participants gain an increased understanding of how past experience of boarding affects their current lives, and especially intimate relationships with others.

The will to recover that emerges within a group can give enormous leverage for the healing process. Below we eavesdrop on the email correspondence of a group of men – all strangers to one another – sharing their immediate feelings, just after a weekend workshop exploring their boarding school experience. It is the first time any of them have spoken about those days in public; some were sent away at the age of 6. The men consented to our sharing this in the hope that others would find their own courage:

'In the same boat': aftermath of a Boarding School Survivors workshop

John: Hello my new friends. Wow – what a weekend – I have spent most of today walking up and down – inside and outside. Things going round in my head – feelings churning up in my stomach. Too distracted to do any work/anything at all.

Edward: Thank you John for kicking the ball into the air … it hasn't touched the ground yet. What an extraordinary weekend it was for me. Amongst many other things I felt privileged to be seated amongst men who had the courage to make that step into the unknown.

Mike: Hi, my feelings are similar … Leaving you all on Sunday felt OK – a bit like the end of a business course where you make very temporary friendships meaning to keep in touch but never following it up – but yesterday I found myself with an unexpected longing to be back with you all – not a case of duty or I really ought to – but a feeling of separation – that had made me realise what an impact this weekend had on me.

Brenda (my wife) met me from the train – it was strange because I had built up a lot of tension about that moment – I guess because I knew she would quiz me on what went on – on the plus side I did something totally out of character for me – when she asked how the weekend went, I said it was 'fantastic'. My normal response to these types of questions is usually at best 'it was quite nice really'. Like I said on Sunday, I feel like a veil is being lifted. I hope it continues.

Brenda and I talked for a while about the weekend, but I found myself quickly becoming detached and analytical. She eventually burst into tears and said that she felt that I was putting her through the same emotions that I had felt going to school. At this point my emotional barriers blocked this out and I felt nothing – no sympathy – no sorrow. I'm not ready to deal with her needs – maybe in time this will change. Yet when we were all together talking about our experiences, I felt a real sense of empathy and understanding. Looking forward to hearing from you all.

James: Hi, team! As I think we all felt – what an amazing weekend. I thought I had got a good understanding of what was going on from reading the book *The Making of Them*, but from hearing all your stories I got a whole load more insights. It seems I have still got a lot to learn.

When I got home my wife, who, like most women we brush up against, is desperate for signs of some belated emotional development, then gave me a thorough grilling! So I have not really put the whole experience 'in order' in my mind yet. At least I did not retreat into my usual sullen silence when emotionally challenged!

So now busy spotting the well-worn behavioural patterns that prevent me from having to emotionally engage – like not responding to these messages until I got home, even though John sent it to my work address as well (with my wife prompting from the wings – aren't you going to answer, then?!). My 'inner parent' needs to challenge the lazy 'little boy' to get out in the emotional world, instead of shutting up in his own room saying petulantly, 'Why should I?' All goes back to the need to be cherished, which in one of my most common and perverse behaviour patterns means going for isolation to avoid possible rejection. Still much to sort out, then!

William: Well, yes. What an amazing weekend. What a magical space we all created together. As though we opened up a new doorway somehow. An alternative reality where it was both Manly and Noble to feel emotions. Where it was Heroic to show them, and where rewards are measured, not in engraved silver or caps or different blazers, but in Actual Real Life Emotions. Wonderful.

Hang on though – three days later, grey drizzle, too much work – perhaps it was just a dream, something just out of reach – or maybe not … It really does feel like a turning point. Physically I have found myself stretching a lot. Emotionally there is much sadness and, oh boy, such anger!

What a blessed relief it is to shine a bit of light into that long forgotten cupboard. There, half mad from 30 years of isolation, hides a little boy who simply wishes that his parents loved him enough not to send him away. Loved him enough, so that he didn't have to hide. Come on out now lad. The danger is passed. Ugly duckling like, you have to become a man. Look in the mirror. Doesn't the cupboard feel a bit small? Step Right Up! It's a bit like the ultimate Adventure Theme Park. Welcome to the Wobbly World of Emotions! All rides free, once the one-off entrance fee is paid.

Jonathan: Hello all! What can I add? I feel privileged to have spent the weekend in your company and heard all your experiences. Above all, as (in one strange but very real sense) the group's oldest survivor, I'm full of awe and admiration for those of you who had to start so much younger than I did.

The weekend's bringing into stark relief two parts of me that I'd love to tackle: fear of standing out from the crowd, and fear of showing my emotions. I was struck by how many common themes came up over the weekend, and how many similar experiences I heard. I feel I could have written James' words, about going into isolation to avoid possible rejection, about myself.

A final thought. We may call ourselves cold or unemotional, but in our discussions over the weekend and afterwards, I see from everyone an abundance of vivid language, poetry and emotion. So I wonder: how can we harness this? Good luck to you all.

What we witness in the above above is the euphoric, surprising and unfamiliar effect of finally having permission to experience emotions, encouraged by the facilitators and their joint commitment over a four day project based on remembering events and sharing feelings. It is the result of the facilitating therapists' work in building a safe-enough container for their clients' inner work to begin and to be inspired and sparked off by each other. The communality is a crucial part of the mix: not that they are all the same, but their suffering and experience has enough similarity to motivate each individual to come fully into the present and to confront the dysfunctionality of their current lives.

Amongst the many themes in this account we have picked out:

- The power of sharing stories and experiences developing an atmosphere of shared empathy.
- A sense of something shifting in both the minds and the bodies of workshop participants.
- The emergence of sadness and anger long buried and put to one side.
- A realisation that fleeing from emotion, for example through work, is a strategy to avoid rejection in intimate relationships.
- The challenge of sharing new feelings with partners.
- An acknowledgement that there is much work to do and that the road to recovery is long.

Emotional courage

The courage that is needed to break the mould and welcome emotions back after the trauma of early boarding has been described by Thurstine Basset:

> Facing up to this damage and speaking out about it takes courage. Not the courage of 'grin and bear it'. Not the courage of the 'stiff upper lip'. Not the courage of 'boys don't cry'. These characteristics are often seen as strengths but in fact they are weaknesses masquerading as strength. The courage I am talking about here is the 'emotional courage' to recognise and face up to pain and hurt, to acknowledge it and through experiencing it to grow through it into a more complete person. In this context, crying is a sign of strength not weakness.
>
> I have always liked the concept of emotional intelligence as it acknowledges intelligence that is not just cognitive. Emotional courage seems to me to be a means for the expression of emotional intelligence.
>
> (Basset, 2006)

Courage with feelings is a quality that ongoing therapeutic work can encourage. It involves 'making friends with emotion', as John Wellwood suggests:

> Emotions are often problematic because they are our most common experience of being taken over by forces seemingly beyond our control. Usually we regard them as a threat, imagining that if we really let ourselves feel our anger or depression, they would totally overwhelm us.
>
> (Wellwood, 2000, p. 181)

Wellwood speaks of accepting emotions, going towards them and facing them directly and fearlessly, and by so doing, using their energy as a renewing and awakening life force.

One way that Basset experienced this was at a poetry workshop for people who had survived the mental health system, with whom he was working. The task was to write a personal poem about the mental health system, but he decided to write instead about his experience of the boarding school system. It was a key point where he realised he too had a story to tell:

> A boy of 8 goes off to school
> sadly he doesn't know the rules
> but happily he works out a way
> to survive the system day by day
>
> A lad of 18 he leaves one day
> sadly it's now too late to play
> by chance he finds a useful role
> to fight the system and make it whole
>
> A man of 55 finds out
> what his choice in life's about
> he fought the asylums until they closed
> he helped survivors along the road
>
> This other thing he learned to do
> to help out others and be true
> the only trouble with this plan
> he never learned to help his man
>
> Twenty years of survivor stories
> before I learned to tell my own
> let flow my tears like a running river
> how I wish I'd stayed at home.
>
> (Basset, 2006)

Unpacking personal history

When working with ex-boarder clients who have recognised the psychological harm that has been done to them through the trauma and the breaking of attachments, it is important to reinforce the truth that their reaction and adoption of a strategic survival personality was an entirely normal thing for them to do when placed in a very *abnormal* situation. The patterns of behaviour that they learned from this time are a manifestation of the system that they were sent into – the fault, if there is one, lies with the institution and not with the individual.

In therapy, the client will hopefully begin to feel safe enough to commence the important work of unpacking personal history, in order to reconnect with the child they were before boarding and to express some of the sadness that the historical child repressed. But the client's partner may not have the same patience, as our group chat also reveals. Why should they? The partner may have already failed as an 'unofficial' therapist, and the journey back for the ex-boarder requires much patience, as one client recounts: 'It is easy to love the nine year old, but it's hard to love the survivor with his inability to touch or be touched' (Duffell, 2000, p. 30).

Alongside any significant traumas, such as holidays not spent at home, bullying, or sexual assaults, the most important single moments to remember in this unpacking are transitions. Significant moments of transition pepper the boarder's life: from home to school, school to home; but also from abandoned child to survivor. The client may remember the choice to self-invent or to *choose* survival at such moments. The sense of having at least *some* choice in who was created at such moments can return a missing sense of agency. If the client is able to remember some of the critical moments, the loss of more global memories may not be so important. Such points are:

- the moment of first being left by parents at boarding school
- the first day at boarding school or prep school
- the moment of first choosing to survive or to self-reinvent
- the return home on the first holiday
- the first day at the secondary boarding, or public, school
- the moment of choosing to survive or to self-reinvent at the secondary school.

With a foundation of such remembering, the adult client may now have recognised the route they took towards a survival pattern. For this reason, whilst remembering the abandonment or bullying may unlock feelings, remembering the moment of choosing how to survive is the best way towards unlocking the grip of the strategic survival personality. Recognising their own agency paves the way for being able to re-choose a more appropriate kind of living in the present.

One such remembered example is the comedian Tim Brooke-Taylor, who is said to have remembered how at boarding school he suddenly realised that making people laugh was a sure route to safety. He recognised that he had a gift for it, that he had committed to keep doing it at school; and of course he eventually made a successful career out of it (Duffell 2000, p. 23).

Perhaps the most brilliant description of how a survival personality is constructed, that we have come across so far, comes from spy-novelist John Le Carré, who boarded during the Second World War. In his semi-autobiographical *A Perfect Spy* (Le Carré, 1986), most likely written as part of his own self-motivated remembering process 40 years later, Le Carré charts a boy's compensation for lack of love in a world where the thing *seen* to be done outweighs the thing actually done. In an extraordinary Faustian passage, the novel shows a young boarder, Magnus Pym, exchanging his innocence for a watertight strategic survival personality. The would-be ex-boarder therapist can learn much about how boarders survive from it.

Determined to avoid being any more a victim, Magnus' survival personality is rooted in duplicity and motivated by his contempt for the bad authorities he experienced. In this instance it is not a sudden moment that kicks the process off, as in the case of Brooke-Taylor, but it is consciously developed, perhaps over a term at his prep school. There is a pivotal moment of enlightenment when young Magnus Pym suddenly gets it that he has to reinvent himself. For this, he draws on all the resources his life has offered so far. First, from observing his con-man father (in the author's life as in the novel) he learns how important duplicity is. He must defy the authorities and get away with it:

> Pym had lied to policemen before and knew that you had to look honest. He learned the great lesson of Rick's [his father] example, namely the importance of a respectable appearance. He learned that the only safety was in seeming legitimacy. He developed his determination to be a secret mover of life's events.
>
> It was Pym, for instance, who let down Mr. Grimble's [the headmaster] tyres and poured three six-pound bags of cooking salt into the swimming pool. But it was Pym who led the hunt for the culprit too, throwing up many tantalising clues and casting doubt on many solid reputations.

> (Le Carré, 1986, pp. 128–33)

Magnus Pym's education has only just begun. With the loss of his mother he became 'entrenched as a self-reliant person, confirmed in the knowledge that women were fickle and liable to sudden disappearances' (p. 133). From observing his arch enemy at school, Sefton Boyd, who came from an aristocratic family, he learned how to pose as an authority.

> You kept your hands lightly linked behind your back, shoved your head forward and fixed your eyes on some vaguely pleasing object on the horizon. You walked high, smiling slightly as if listening to other voices, which is how the flower of us wear authority.
>
> (p. 128)

But his greatest moment is when he perfects the art of duplicitous sincerity and is able to humiliate the posh bully. The ecstatic heights of this transformation are as dizzy as Dr Jekyll becoming Mr Hyde, as secret as Clark Kent becoming Superman. It happens in the forbidden and luxurious staff lavatory, a place of majesty, as Le Carré explains: 'Pym loved luxury as only those can, who have love taken from them' (p. 131). In this magical chamber Magnus decides that he will never more live life as a victim. He will survive and do it in style.

He stared at his face, making it harder, then softer, then harder. He ran the taps and washed his cheeks till they shone. His sudden isolation, added to the grandeur of his achievement, made him unique in his own eyes. His mind whirled with the vertigo of greatness. He was God. He was Hitler. Henceforth, nothing on earth need happen without his intervention.

(p. 131)

Next, propelled by an interior voice, which he imagines as 'divine', he ostentatiously carves the initials of his pompous rival into the wood panelling. Then he waits for the crime to be discovered, having convinced himself that *he did not do it*, erasing memory according to the impulse to survive. Finally, the carving is spotted and the usual corporal punishment of the era is meted out to Sefton Boyd.

'It had a hyphen', Sefton Boyd told him next day. 'Whoever did it gave us a hyphen when we haven't got one. If I ever find the sod I'll kill him.'

'So will I', Pym promised loyally, and meant every word. Like Rick, he was learning to live on several planes at once. The art of it was to forget everything except the ground you stood on and the face you spoke from at that moment.

(p. 132)

This moment of choosing survival is a re-creation of reality. It often coincides with the moment of finally disowning feelings altogether, for emotions lead to truth and will give the survivor away. Such self-inventions can therefore be quite dark, albeit in the service of survival. We remember the poignant statement from the psychoanalyst Grotstein quoted in the last chapter 'When innocence has been deprived of its entitlement, it becomes a diabolical spirit' (Grotstein, 1984). The therapist must help the client hold this difficult dilemma. This is an especially crucial and difficult task which needs the development of what psychosynthesis calls *Bi-focal Vision* – seeing the event both as necessary and as a profound self-betrayal; both a step in service of the ego and a potentially near-fatal wound to the soul.

To recognise their own wounding, self-betrayal and survival, ex-boarder clients must learn to empathise with the child who had to self-reinvent, while accepting that behaviour patterns learned then have not been helpful to the adult. Often therapists have to show the way here, so that clients can learn this new skill, unlikely to have been picked up at the side of earlier attachment figures.

The start of such a process, while attending a group workshop, was richly described by Simon Partridge. In front of the other participants, Partridge relives the experience of crossing the threshold on the very first day he was left by his parents at boarding school:

'OK', says Nick, 'sit right down on the floor and hug that cushion'. Then in a move, which completely throws me, he invites me to turn my murderous hatred into a plea of what I would have liked my Ma to have said at this moment of dreadful parting. That seems an impossible one; I have to flip to the other side of hatred. Somehow I'm rescued by the mutual sadness I'd seen in the faces of the mothers and sons in the film [*The Making of Them*], and by the empathy which I feel is streaming towards me from my fellow sufferers. To my amazement the words my mother couldn't utter come tumbling, imploringly out of my mouth, accompanied by sobbing:

I'm so sorry I have to leave you here – but it's something our sort of people just have to do – it happened to me – I'm hugging you so tightly because I love you so much – I'm crying too because I'll miss you so – I found it too difficult to get your name tags all sewn on in time – I'll come and see you as quickly as I can – if anything nasty happens I want you to let me know as soon as possible and I'll come and rescue you.

For good measure Nick asks me to repeat my 'mother's plea' with added feeling, as if I haven't quite got it all out.

Dazed I get up off the floor and, worried about the emotion let loose on my fellows, say, I'll be all right. And I think I will. I seemed to have reversed the 'switching moment' at which boarding school survivors are able to turn off all emotion – a ploy that Nick and Darrel (the workshop facilitators) have picked up time and time again in the course of the workshop. I see how the deadly 'skill' has to be mastered, on pain of annihilation, at the moment when the vulnerable little boy has to transform himself in an instant into that precocious man, able to survive in an institution stripped of parental love, domestic warmth and familiarity, and when mother's heart must turn to stone.

(Partridge, 2007)

Exercise 6: letter/phoning home

Introduction

Many will have had the experience of learning to suppress their real feelings when contacting their parents in the early days and terms of their boarding experience. Letting parents know how you *really* feel is frowned upon by schools. One supporter of Boarding Concern recalled that she wrote a letter home to her mother saying how unhappy she was and how she wanted to be taken away from the school. The next thing she experienced was being summoned to see the headmistress a couple of days later, who gave her a stern telling-off for upsetting her mother – the school's customer, it has to be remembered. This little girl never wrote such a letter again; she just had to live with her unhappiness and her loss of her mother was confirmed.

In the past, children's letters were regularly censored. During the First World War the job of censoring letters home from the trenches fell to the junior officers, who were only just out of boarding school. Such censorship is much less likely in more recent times, but even so, letters, phone calls and emails getting through to parents showing unhappiness at school may rebound on the child. The child rapidly learns the art of self-censoring. Mostly, letters only tell parents banal events, as in this example from Fraser Harrison:

> Dear Mummy and Daddy,
> How are you? I am well. I played football yesterday. I nearly scored a goal. I sit next to Bailey 11. Please send me a cake.
>
> (Harrison, 1990, p. 69)

Exercise

This exercise can be very powerful so it must be followed up on.

First ask your client if they remember the letters that they used to write home from boarding school. Allow them to reminisce about this. Do they remember what they used to say?

Ask if they were permitted to phone home, and if so, to try to remember the kind of conversations they had. Ask your client to:

- Remember what they said and did not say.
- How their parents responded to their letters and phone calls home.

Next, suggest that your client writes a letter from the child they were at the beginning of their boarding experience and tell their parents what they would have *really* wanted them to read. Ask them to write as if they were still a child, but with the perspective that they have now, as an adult.

When they have finished, or at a subsequent session, or group seminar if this is being done as 'homework', ask them to read this letter back to you.

Both therapist and client are to reflect on this, and to consider the process the exercise has evoked.

The client may well like to keep this letter. Alternatively, the therapist can suggest they 'send' it to the parent in a ceremonial way. Now ask them to take this letter and put it in an envelope addressed simply to Mum and Dad, or whatever they called their parents, next putting the letter into a real or pretend post box, knowing that they have now spoken up for the child that they were.

References

Basset, T. (2006) 'Emotional Courage', *Independent Practitioner*, Winter, pp. 10–13.
Duffell, N. (2000) *The Making of Them: The British Attitude to Children and the Boarding School System*, London: Lone Arrow Press.

Grotstein, J. (1984) *Forgery of the Soul*, in Nelson, C. and Eigen, M. (eds), *Evil, Self and Culture*, New York: Human Sciences Press.

Harrison, F. (1990) *Trivial Disputes*, London: Flamingo.

Le Carré, J. (1986) *A Perfect Spy*, London: Hodder and Stoughton.

Partridge, S. (2007) 'Trauma at the Threshold: An Eight-Year-Old Goes to Boarding School', *Attachment: New Directions in Psychotherapy and Relational Psychoanalysis*, 1, 3, November, 310–12.

Wellwood, J. (2000) *Towards a Psychology of Awakening*, Boston, MA, and London: Shambhala.

Chapter 7

Adapting

In making the case for the importance of infancy, it is easy to lose sight of the subtleties of human development over the life span. Babyhood is an intense, concentrated moment of development that can have a disproportionate impact on our lives, but it is not the whole story by any means. Important pathways continue to be established through childhood, especially up to the age of 7. Then in early adolescence there is another intense moment of brain reorganisation, until the brain is fully fledged at 15 years old. But, even after that, change and development continue because life is a process of continual adaptation. It just tends to happen at a much slower rate. Early patterns become habits which enable us to respond quickly without laboriously figuring out everything afresh each time we meet a particular experience. We tend to preserve the way that we respond unless there is a powerful challenge to established systems.

(Gerhardt 2004, p. 195)

Key points of chapter

- The boarder's adaptation becomes the problem.
- The adapted inner child is always hiding and survival focused.
- There is conflict between the inner child and inner parent, whose message is to 'grow up, don't be needy and don't show your emotions'.
- Understanding dissociation and its three levels as a natural response to trauma and how to work with dissociated clients.
- Making room for vulnerability, differentiated from weakness.

Accepting the adaptation imperative

Psychotherapist and author Sue Gerhardt reminds us that human beings are able to adapt throughout their lives. However, as she points out, adaptation happens faster early in life and then at a slower rate as the child approaches adulthood. She confirms that adaptive patterns may be very difficult to unlearn once fully embedded in the psychophysical structures that comprise our basis for behaviour. As we shall explore more fully later, the rigidity of adult patterns of behaviour and response that were laid down in childhood are taken to the extreme when there has been trauma.

Now the ex-boarder adult has suffered a strange trauma. Let us assume that most children who board at a young age belong to a loving, warm family. There will inevitably be some children who find boarding a respite from a difficult or abusive family life; but surely the majority will not. So most children are nurtured and loved within a family for the first seven or eight years of their lives, only to have the loving attachment deliberately broken when they go to boarding school. Boarding is one of the most unusual kinds of trauma in that it is imposed deliberately and carries with it the benefits of social privilege. It entails a requirement to emerge as a competent person destined for societal success. Until very recently it has also been an unrecognised trauma, and there are many interests at stake to keep it hidden.

When considering optimum ways of raising children in a society, all serious thinkers today emphasise the value of good attachments; common sense suggests that the removal of children from families goes against the grain. Supported by modern psychological and neuroscientific evidence, it is becoming clear that societies eventually prosper or fail by how securely attached and empathic their citizens are – especially those in power. Gerhardt's *The Selfish Society* (Gerhardt, 2010) and Duffell's *Wounded Leaders* (Duffell, 2014) employ such reasoning on a societal scale.

Meanwhile, boarding continues in full swing in Britain: the children of the elite and aspirant classes still have to adapt to institutional life at a time when they might expect to have their innocence cherished. Our case is that boarding children have no option but to adapt to their situation of privileged abandonment by adopting a strategic survival personality. We saw how adult ex-boarders, while they are still in the inner grip of needing to survive, end up at the mercy of their own now maladaptive behavioural patterns, and what harm these do in their current families. In *Attachment and Loss*, John Bowlby was pretty clear about the process:

> The more the social environment in which a human child is reared deviates from the environment of evolutionary adaptedness (which is probably father, mother, and siblings in a social environment comprising grandparents and a limited number of other families) the greater will be the risk of his developing maladaptive social behaviour.
>
> (Bowlby, 1969, pp. 208–9)

Earlier, we saw how ex-boarders are inevitably prone to resist the identification of these behaviours as stemming from boarding and, if they enter therapy, especially resist the therapeutic deconstruction of this adaptive structure. But once ex-boarders have recognised that the issue at stake is not whether they were damaged, but that they had no option but to survive, they are ready to begin to move on to the next stage of the journey, which we call the Acceptance Stage.

This means that the ex-boarder client embarks on the acceptance that the self-adaptation process, with all the self-negation, self-denial and self-betrayal that it involves, was a perfectly reasonable strategy under the circumstances in which they found themselves. Their powerlessness in the environment in which they found themselves, where the only limited power they had was over their own bodies and minds, made it inevitable. They only had any choice in the sense of *who* they would become.

A framework for acceptance

Once the ex-boarder has understood and accepted this situation, thera-pists can help frame it in a way that makes cognitive sense while embody-ing self-compassion. At this point, a cognitive focus can provide scaffolding for the further work of recovery. It may also help the rationally trained ex-boarder to keep faith in the therapeutic process when some of the normal explanations such as 'it's the relationship between us that will do the healing' are likely to fall on deaf ears.

Below we outline a three-stage model that speaks to the ongoing process of survival. This way of working originated in the 1980s in therapy with sexual abuse survivors, who often seemed to be in a kind of stunned trance. It was based on affirming reality principles. Something very invasive happened to them; it ought never to have happened; it was not their fault. Many ex-boarder clients will have suffered abuse on top of traumatic neglect, for whatever statu-tory provisions are in place, boarding in a 24/7 institution means that children can never be fully protected from physical and sexual abuse. These things are difficult to talk about, because the world does not really want to hear them, so it is not so surprising that a framework for sexual abuse work is applicable to boarding school survivors.

First we consider the process of survival.

Three elements of survival

1.   Trauma: something traumatic happened to them, which ought never to have happened, and it was not their fault.
2.   Survival: they did well to find ways to survive; survival is not guaranteed.
3.   The cost of that survival: the way that they survived saved their life, but over time will have become counter-productive in being able to live fully and naturally. It will remain so as long as the behavioural mecha-nisms of survival are not fully identified and rejected.

In accepting the first point, boarding school survivors identify as victims of something that was outside the sphere of their own control. Victim identification is controversial: it bewilders and overexcites the Complier type. But the key is in the second point, that this identification is only *temporary*. Actually, they survived and the identification with Survivor is key, even if it is a provocative concept. Again, this is a subtlety that escapes politicians and legislators, who often still refer to survivor groups as 'victim' groups. The survivor has taken control by adapting the self in circumstances when outside help was not forthcoming and the environment was too difficult to control.

Professor Stephen Porges at the University of Illinois is a specialist in the effect of trauma on the nervous system, and in the next chapter we will explore his important work. Porges has an optimistic overview of the value of understanding points 2 and 3, which fits very well with our own approach. In somatic terms, getting to know the body's autonomic response to trauma, people begin to understand:

> that they're not victims – they are part of the control system that enables them to adapt and survive. Their body has not done something bad – actually it has saved their lives. It has enabled them to really suffer without fighting back, and that is very adaptive.
>
> (Porges, 2014, p. 6)

When we come to point 3, survivors have to recognise that this cannot be done without cost. It has involved self-betrayal *in service of survival*. The journey of healing now involves acknowledging the price that they paid, making amends to whomsoever they may have harmed, and finding ways of living that are beyond the limited formula of being a survivor. In short, the second identification of survivor has to be put to one side.

This brings us next to consider the three levels of identification: the one who was traumatised, the victim; the survivor; and the one who came up with the way to survive, the *designer of survival patterns*.

Three levels of identification

1. Victim: they know what happened to them and how bad it was; they are clear that they were not responsible.
2. Survivor: they know that they had no choice but to survive as best they could.
3. Designer of survival patterns: they know precisely *how* they survived, what kind of behaviour patterns they adopted, and how that involved betraying themselves in order to save themselves. They are clear that they themselves are responsible for *how* they survived.

Each of these need to be recognised, identified with and, most importantly, accepted, before real change is possible.

The inner child and inner parent

The recovery from survival to living involves a 'regression in service of ego', as Freud said. The buried child who suffered privileged abandonment has to become real, and the child's needs have now to be heard.

One way of doing this is to follow the inevitable conflict between the ex-boarder's 'inner child' and 'inner parent' parts. The ex-boarder's inner child is always in conflict with an inner parent, whose message is to 'grow up, don't be needy and don't show your emotions'. Fraser Harrison gives an insightful account of how the inner parent is created at boarding school and how the inner parent's main role is to suppress the inner child:

> For most of us, who had been raised in families where every little worry was drawn out and soothed, this was the beginning of that process by which our feelings were first numbed and then disconnected, giving us the distinctive quality of the boarding-school 'man'. At all events, I am sure something vital was killed off inside me during this period which I have never been able to revive.
>
> (Harrison, 1990, p. 68)

The boarding school child experiences external abandonment, tyranny and oppression; but when this child becomes an adult, the tyranny and oppression are on the inside, becoming part and parcel of daily existence:

> To begin with, you had no friends whom you could trust, but in any case you quickly learnt that no one was more despised than a 'blubber', a boy who broke the prevailing code of stoicism. It would have been deeply shaming to admit that you wanted your mother and would have made you very vulnerable. In fact, there was next to no bullying in the school, but that perhaps only showed how effective the code was. Our stoicism required no promotion by the staff; it was one of those unwritten and virtually unspoken mores which nevertheless is fully understood by each member of the community.
>
> (Harrison, 1990, p. 68)

Such a pseudo-adult inner critic frequently drives boarding school survivors. And living life from the inner parent position is supported by the pervasive public school ethos of self-reliance at an age when reliance on others is to be expected, and gets reinforced by social mores. Yet at times – especially of emotional distress – the inner child rises up to challenge and occasionally overcome the inner parent, and the carefully built edifice collapses. These are the times when the Complier survival personality type may seek therapy.

Inside the ex-boarder lives a child who has not really grown up. This child's development was thwarted by the shock of being placed in an alien institution where the only way to survive was to rapidly appear adult. The end product of such a process is often an immature adult – immature because a needy child whose developmental needs were not met is constantly present under the facade of pseudo-adulthood and sometimes acting out.

Healing the conflict between inner child and parent has to be the key to moving on. Recognising this dynamic and accepting its cost is a significant step in the right direction for an ex-boarder. Someone who has adopted a compliant survival strategy will hopefully see how they can often side with their inner parent, whereas a rebel survivor may question their anti-parent identity and their need to be always fighting for a cause.

Dialogue between the hidden inner child and the ex-boarder's adult self makes up the backbone of this work. Popular psychology provides numerous pointers to ways of doing it, and it is effective in group settings as well as individual work. However, in trying to reinstate the value of this repressed part, there can be a tendency to deify the inner child. This can be misleading, for the inner child of the ex-boarder is always hiding, fighting to survive and often using 'guerrilla' tactics. Inner children can be false and deceitful if they learned to lie and be inauthentic in order to survive. When asked 'are you homesick?' or 'are you missing mum and dad?' young boarders learn inauthenticity early, hiding their real feelings. Writing about her own recovery from anorexia, Sheila MacLeod notes how falsehood and honesty intermingle, as the anorexic's account of feeding the body is replete with lies and deceit (MacLeod, 1981). The 'stubborn' honesty is that her carers want to feed the wrong and superficial self: the real, buried self is starving: 'This starvation of the real self is at the heart of the repressed inner child in the boarding school survivor as in the anorexic' (Duffell, 2000, p. 208).

An understanding of Object Relations theory may help both the therapist and client see how children can remain loyal to 'bad' objects such as the critical inner parent: a case of 'better the devil that you know'. The work of Fairbairn and others can be helpful here (Gomez, 1997). Small things such as carrying round a picture of themselves as a young child in the purse or wallet can aid the work, helping ex-boarders remember and providing a means by which the newly emerging adult can foster self-compassion for the wounded part of themselves.

If the work goes well, eventually the inner parent desists from automatic derogatory messages and transforms into an inner teacher or guide; the inner child rediscovers and releases creativity, energy, trust and lust for life. Here is an extract from an ex-boarder's email to the Boarding School Survivors' website; the writer has understood about the survival personality he adopted and accepted that a new way of being is possible:

I just rebelled against everything my boarding schools stood for. I was a rebel – but not one without a cause! – I fought every cause I could find. Over the years I grew tired of this constant battling, and with the help of both a good therapist and a loving wife, I began to give up the constant battle. My wife recently returned from a meditation retreat and amongst the various pieces of paper she brought with her, I found this quote: 'We are not really fighting with the people with whom we think we are fighting. The arguments go on inside our own heads. We are really arguing with ourselves.' I said to myself 'that's me' and I now have the quote in a prominent position on the wall in my office.

Dissociation

The important work with the inner child depends on this part being accessible in consciousness. It will not always be the case in ex-boarders, because boarding children have had to learn to cut off their childishness, their spontaneity and all aspects of vulnerability in double-quick time. Many, if not most, boarders will have disowned their vulnerability and feelings at a level much stronger than *repression* and will have practised *dissociation*, commonly called *splitting* by UK therapists. Here is Stephen Grosz's elegant description:

> Splitting is an unconscious strategy that aims to keep us ignorant of feelings in ourselves that we're unable to tolerate. Typically, we want to see ourselves as good, and put those aspects of ourselves we find shameful into another person or group.
>
> (Grosz, 2013, p. 69)

Neither inner child work nor themed group therapy will be effective until this archetype has returned sufficiently to consciousness, once the client feels sufficiently accepted and safe to renounce the defensive organisation of splitting. Dan Siegel, Clinical Professor of Psychiatry at the UCLA School of Medicine, gives us dissociation's physical picture:

> Dissociation is defined very simply as dis-association – and that means associated things are now literally not linked anymore. In the model of [brain] integration, this is a great match: dissociation means that which used to be linked is no longer linked and that translates to that which used to be integrated is no longer integrated. Looking at some of the studies of the brain in dissociation, we can see that the brain literally becomes fragmented – it is no longer linking its differentiated parts.
>
> (Siegel, 2014, p. 16)

New research shows that a poor attachment history, especially what is known as *disorganised attachment*, where the caregiver is a figure that evokes

fear rather than protection, creates drastically organised mental representations. These are visible in the brain as a form of disorganisation; integration
and connection is forgone for the sake of acute self-protection in the inability
to rely on the environment. Siegel again:

> As an attachment researcher, I will just say that when we study a form of
> attachment called disorganized attachment, longitudinal studies done by
> Alan Sroufe of the University of Minnesota have demonstrated that at
> least one source of dissociation is disorganized attachment.
>
> (Siegel, 2014, p. 16)

Being sent away to an institution by parents could create such disorganised
attachments, as Siegel describes. The boarding child's employment of dissociation is an entirely congruent response to an entirely unnatural and traumatic situation. But what the brain pictures are not able to show us is that
dissociation is regularly followed by *projection*, which, in its extreme form can
affect another person's psyche, leaving the practitioner, as Alan Schore says,
'dissociatively cleaned' (Schore, 2003). At boarding school it works like this:

> As rule-bound institution and the psychology of the strategic boarder
> collide, the preoccupation with rules and the imperative to not be
> wrong create a further and mind-numbingly perfect but poisonous
> twist inside the boarder's mind. Here's how it works: it's as plain as
> milk that not everyone can make it. Someone has to be 'The Pathetic
> One'; someone has to be 'The Stupid Child' who gets it wrong; some-
> one has to be 'The One Who Gets Into Trouble'. The boarder knows
> this in his bones. 'It had better not be me!' runs the inevitable internal
> logic. Hence the boarder, who learns to live a solitary life in a 24/7 'total
> institution' with zero privacy, cannot be alone but *needs* others around
> him, psychodynamically, to embody the roles and emotional states he
> wants to avoid.
>
> (Duffell, 2014, p. 77)

Lids or splits?

One of the on-the-job tests for splitting is when 'normal' interventions like
dialoguing with the inner child, Gestalt work, or circular questioning with
couples do not work. As long as the impasse is not due to the therapist's lack
of skill, it will be because the client can't *use* such interventions. Frequent
interruptions, inauthenticity, non-sequiturs, the inability to fantasise and so
on are signs that the client's inner world is too *fragmented* to use empathy,
imagination or projection *creatively*. Perhaps helped by their supervisor, therapists must then employ ego-strength diagnosis and realign their interventions, which should be reparative and parental.

Diagnosing is actually much more compassionate than it at first sounds to some humanistically trained workers. It can embody a reverence for the psyche's creativity and resilience, since even in the seemingly most bizarre survival mechanisms it suggests that we are at some level always giving it our best shot. In the 1960s, for example, R. D. Laing proposed that the divided self was a healthy response to an unhealthy situation, even if it may be entirely inappropriate (Laing, 1960).

A useful ego-state diagnostic model, building on Heinz Kohut via Josephine Klein's remarkable survey of psychoanalytic literature (Klein, 1987), was outlined by Duffell in 1992, and employed in *The Making of Them* (Duffell, 2000), and we recommend it here.

In psychic terms, humans mature by progressively releasing material from our unconscious, by renouncing unconscious promises, by releasing what we have disowned and repressed, by taking back projections. In this process the psyche has its own wisdom and timing. One of the ways it works is by *keeping a lid on things* until the time and conditions are right to lift it and become more of a whole person. Repressed parts that don't fit the self-image are kept 'under the lid' to avoid pain or cognitive dissonance. But they are relatively available: therapy can establish dialogues between these parts. They have fairly coherent cohesive self-structures, which require recognition and integrating techniques; they are like the Danish islands, which are separate but are joined by bridges. This state is what Kohut calls *horizontal* splitting (Kohut 1977).

Sometimes, when early stages of dyadic relating, merger or mirroring were not adequate, poor attachment and trauma have forced a dissociative defensive attitude to life, leaving the individuals with serious difficulties in relating to self and others as *subjects*. Now the self-map is distinctly different: disowned parts of the self are much more distant – like islands in the South Pacific with access and connections to each other that are only distant memories. There is no connection: you are either in one or the other. These states of isolation and fragmentation are called (after Kohut) *vertical* splitting.

Interestingly, the new brain pictures that Siegel (2014) refers to confirm the description. Vertical splitters have parts of the self severely divided and effectively employ dissociation; denial and projective identification export split-off parts into others, or even into parts of the self. Self and others are experienced as good or bad objects, not as whole human beings. In these cases, relationship issues reflect individual issues projected out and become self-fulfilling prophecies.

Of course, the level of fragmentation varies on a continuum: at the extreme end of this continuum is the person with Dissociative Identity Disorder. So that therapy has traction, therapists should learn to recognise whether they are talking to parts of a person that are under the lid or vertically isolated. Some therapists, trained outside the traditional fields of psychodynamic theory or psychoanalysis, particularly those trained in humanistic or transpersonal therapies, may fear getting drawn into labelling or have difficulty recognising the difference.

But unless they are able to recognise and accept the distinctions, adapting their models accordingly to include working with clients whose psyches are organised in a defensive mode by means of splitting, they will find the work ineffective and very taxing. Once therapists get this, it will become familiar. At first the picture is confused because the horizontally split client employs the first two levels of dissociation shown in the box that follows, whereas vertical splitting involves all three.

Three levels of dissociation

1. Disowning and repression: 'I am not the one who is needy, homesick, vulnerable, crying, upset, etc.'
2. Projection: 'It's you who's the needy, homesick, vulnerable, despairing one, etc.'
3. Projective identification: partners/spouses/therapists take on and viscerally experience the disowned and projected feelings of the ex-boarder.

Working with dissociation

There is a wealth of information about working with the dissociated client to rely on within the psychoanalytic literature. From the perspective of neuroscience, dissociation in the brain is the opposite of integration, but, with the right diagnosis or formulation, it is amenable to cure: 'Dissociation, while it is one of the most disabling conditions, is one of the most treatable – it is completely curable, and that has been shown' (Siegel, 2014, p. 17). This, we now know, is due to *neuroplasticity* – the ability of the brain to rebuild its own connections under the right conditions. For this to happen, therapeutic empathy is a prerequisite. Work may involve the use of non-conventional therapeutic tools, which we will discuss in the next chapter.

Meanwhile, the psychotherapeutic style with vertical splits needs to be motherly and containing. In 'mother mode', to use the Winicottian notion of the matrix as the maturational space, the therapist soothes the individual, as a mother does to a child through staying calm, slow and reassuring. The therapist models the mother being attuned to the infant and being able to empathise. The mother detoxifies the child's experience by naming it and regulates the child through regulating herself and surviving projective identifications. Their clients may not take responsibility, but therapists should communicate 'All is well in the world. This too is manageable,' even when things are hard or confusing.

Therapists should not expect a vertically split client to have a realistic overview of self, because when parts of the self are like disconnected islands, self-awareness can only ever be partial. Interventions that are questions often get nowhere with a vertically split client, whereas interpretations that start with a 'Yes' are very holding, and allow the client's dissociated world to become alive in the room. But therapists need also to be vigilant: thoughts and feelings that are not made room for in the session can arrive on the door-step and challenge both the frame and the existence of the therapy. Below are some examples of such therapeutic endeavour.

Case example: Andy

Andy, a self-employed carpenter, comes into therapy wanting to discuss whether he should end his marriage. He acknowledges not enjoying his time boarding but he cannot see how this would have affected him as an adult, except by putting him off working in an institution. Andy finds every-thing in his relationship frustrating, and when he tackles his wife they only row, and she withdraws sexually.

'Yes, you don't seem to be able to find a way to be happy', says his thera-pist, who has already formed the hypothesis that he survived by dissocia-tion, rejecting both the authoritarian and vulnerable parts of himself. She adjusts her interventions accordingly:

'Yes, you find that being in an intimate relationship is the hardest thing you have ever done.'

Andy nods, but fails to take responsibility for any of his own behaviour. In therapy, he endlessly complains about his wife: how she doesn't want to get a proper job, how all she does is look at her Facebook page and text her friends. She has started training as a counsellor. 'But she never completes anything', he says with easy contempt.

'Yes, she does seem a bit like a stupid child', his therapist responds, 'she seems to be the incompetent one'.

Andy looks up.

'Yes, she does seem to be the lazy one in your relationship', she continues.

The therapist wants to follow this with a question: 'What happened to the lazy one in you, Andy?' And it is a very good question, and it might come next if the client were only repressing, but it may have to come a bit down the line, in this case.

When working with splits therapists need to develop patience, looking with curiosity for the other end of the split.

Managing adaptation

If the therapeutic work of containment and integration goes well, clients may be able to manage parts of their internal world with less rigid dissoci-ation. When the split-off parts start to come into dialogue, the interventions associated with repression can be used. These include working with the inner child, obtaining an overview from an aware ego, rather than from one who is trying to organise mitigating against the stress of cognitive dissonance, to ward off having to identify with the aspects of the self that have had to be forcefully repudiated.

When the time for a didactic overview is right, the crucial learning for the client is to understand and regulate what happens in intimate relationships. When partners disown their vulnerable side, one or both will aggressively force the other into the vulnerable role, so that they themselves do not have to occupy it. This is a very common relationship dynamic, so common as to be almost a relationship *stage*, known as *Bonding Patterns*. This has been described elsewhere (Duffell and Løvendal-Duffell, 2012, pp. 99–106) and we will return to it later on. But when a partner is practising dissociation as a defensive attitude for survival then the projection of the vulnerable one – the stupid, incompetent, messy child – is done with utmost force. Now, through projective identification, their partner seamlessly identifies with the feelings and roles of this child.

The therapeutic work is first to spot this and note it. Then, when sufficient ego strength or self-awareness has been built, it is to tease apart the projections and offer a welcoming place for the clients' disowned vulnerable parts to return. This is not beginner's work. Sometimes the conditions are too scary, as Grosz points out:

> In denying and projecting a part of ourselves into another, we come to regard these negative aspects as outside of our control. At its extreme, splitting renders the world an unsettling, even dangerous place.
>
> (Grosz, 2013, p. 69)

Below is a case where the client's ability to function and present herself as aware initially distracts the therapist, who then has to become increasingly reflective, learning how to shift gear in order to make the therapy safe again.

Case example: Beatrice

Beatrice is a high achiever in her early thirties, self-referred because she is aware that boarding caused problems. She describes herself as feeling no joy, struggling to sustain intimacy in long-term relationships and plagued by an indefinable sense of longing for something lost. The relationship with her parents is at an all-time low.

The first six sessions go well until she starts to describe how, on a holiday to Italy, she was swept up by a man and hastily married him. Her therapist notices how she describes this without any affect. When invited to talk about the feelings involved she becomes unexpectedly angry – right at the end of the session.

During the following week the therapist cannot get her off his mind. He gradually realises that, despite initial appearances, Beatrice has not yet felt safe in the therapy. They began in a cooperative way, with her being a nice girl, which is how she survived her boarding, but also how she keeps control of the sessions. The day before the next appointment he receives a text message saying that she has decided to end the therapy.

The therapist now thinks he may have underestimated how traumatic it was being sent away and not feeling loved by her parents. She has not begun to talk about her boarding school life yet because it was there that she learned to split off her emotional self; it must be too soon and too scary to bring these feelings back.

He decides to write back to her. In collaboration with his supervisor, he practises what kind of letter might put the client into a 'creative double bind', so that she might permit her curiosity to get the better of her fear and return to the work. In the letter he normalises the difficult feelings that are now arising. He communicates that there is a part of him that wants to let her go and have her freedom away from such difficulties, but he notes that there is also another part of him that knows she will only be able to be fully free when she has got to the bottom of them in safe company. He adds that he will be in his room at the appointed hour, thinking about her.

The therapist wonders if she will turn up and, if not, how he can repair the gap and keep his client in the painful but needed therapy.

As Joy Schaverien writes, ex-boarders often leave too soon (Schaverien, 1997). Writing letters to entice them back can be very useful, both in their success rate and in getting therapists to think about how to 'work in parts'. When therapists learn to work in parts, they discover how to match the split. In this way the client's reality is mirrored and the therapist uses splitting creatively as a model and a tool.

A framework for clinical work with splits

1. Establish sanctuary through holding and mirroring. Dependence and primary ambivalence will be issues. Therapists should work towards a sense of Winnicottian 'indwelling', being with them rather than doing. Guntrip suggests therapists must not be hard-edged objects and must carry the client like water carries the swimmer (Klein, 1987).

2. Understand and contain acting out; hold and detoxify disturbing feelings with interpretations. Therapists should be in touch with their own bodies and regulate their clients through this awareness.

3. Bring about connectedness and thereby integration, if possible, of split-off, disowned and projected parts. Therapists should work with the metaphor of parts to use their own ability to split in a creative rather than defensive way.
4. Build ego strength; help establish a more authentic personality that can tolerate some vulnerability.
5. Establish empathic response – right-brain work (Schore, 2003) – before they are ready for symbolising. Facilitate becoming 'independent centres of initiative and perception' (Kohut, 1977).
6. Test reality before commencing self-awareness and repression work.

Making room for vulnerability

The true recognition of our own self-betrayal is a source of deep human dignity. Once ex-boarders begin to have some understanding of these processes, they are more likely to be able to have intimate relationships that are fulfilling, equal and life affirming. But in order to do this, they need to begin to leave behind the parts of them that need to always be right and in control and begin to embrace their vulnerability. It cannot be done while dissociation is maintained as the prime way of organising their psyche and therefore running their life.

Boarding children have to rapidly cut off their vulnerability in order to survive. So adult ex-boarders take some convincing that vulnerability is worth restoring, let alone attempting the work of retracting their projections and making amends for their projective identifications. But making room for their disowned vulnerability is the key towards a transformative shift – moving from survival into life. Unfortunately, the valuing of vulnerability is not something we see much mirrored in everyday culture, let alone in our leaders, especially if they are boarding school survivors. Here is an example of the fear of vulnerability in public office.

Readers may remember Tony Blair's time as prime minister, though they may have forgotten that he had heart problems, requiring admission to hospital in both 2003 and 2004. On both occasions he and his media team made light of his problems. He was 'not vulnerable' – indeed he was back at work with business as usual, gearing up to be elected for a third term of office, in no time. Fair enough, you might say, as we wouldn't want to think of our prime minister as weak and not up to the job. But contrast this with Kjell Magne Bondevik, who, when prime minister of Norway, was transparent with his electorate about his depression and his need for some recovery time. Here is how he contextualised his absence:

> I wanted to contribute to more openness around mental health problems because the stigma is a big part of the problem. You know that the first

step to recover is to talk to somebody about your situation so you can share your burden and not bear it alone.

(Bondevik, 2008)

In fact, both Bondevik and Blair were re-elected after their respective periods of ill health. So both their strategies worked, although we would want to congratulate Bondevik for his honesty and the Norwegian electorate for their open-mindedness.

In our modern ultra-competitive Western society, vulnerability can seem to be yet another weakness that must be hidden away or treated in a pathological way. Today's online life of tweets, texts, gaming and social media, with social interaction on screen rather than face to face, does not help. Cut off from the emotional patterns of day-to-day life, the exercise of the subtleties of somatic relational communication, people actually become more isolated, despite the appearance of endless connectivity.

The most common trap about vulnerability is equating it to weakness. Brene Brown, Professor of Social Work at the University of Houston, argues that this is a widely accepted and dangerous myth:

> As children we found ways to protect ourselves from vulnerability, from being hurt, diminished, and disappointed. We put on an armor; we used our thoughts, emotions, and behaviors as weapons; and we learned how to make ourselves scarce, even to disappear. Now as adults we realize that to live with courage, purpose, and connection – to be the person whom we long to be – we must again be vulnerable. We must take off the armor, put down the weapons, show up, and let ourselves be seen.
>
> (Brown, 2012, p. 112)

Brown's words should strike a chord for ex-boarders. They illustrate that vulnerability is an important part of being human. It is increasingly important for ordinary citizens to be able to own and indeed work with their vulnerabilities as part of 'life's rich tapestry', but also because vulnerability is the key to relational authenticity, and strangely enough, to personal empowerment.

It may be useful to consider the Japanese concept of *Kintsukori*, which means to 'repair with gold'. It designates a special style of repairing broken pottery with gold lacquer, in which the repaired piece is considered more beautiful and valuable than the original. As humans, we can perhaps begin to see that, alongside the knocks and hardships of life, it is our imperfections that make us who we are; they deepen both our inner and outer beauty. The practice of *Kintsukori* may be a helpful guide for both client and therapist in the little-known art of making room for vulnerability.

Exercise 7: inside and outside

For this exercise, it is best to draw three concentric circles.

The inner most circle is for how the client felt inside at boarding school.
The next circle is for what was lost or missing at boarding school.
The outer most circle is for any external threats felt by the client at boarding school.
Ask your client to come up with words for all three circles.

Example of what might come up in this exercise:

- Inner circle – how the client felt inside at boarding school: discomfort, awe, anger, challenged, told off, rivalry, self-doubt, self-soothing, shy, understanding, panic, anxious, frustrated, identified with others, invisible.
- Next circle – what was lost or missing at boarding school: love, space, privacy, reassurance, encouragement, safety, physical comfort, cuddles, guidance, fun, being held, containment, acceptance.
- Outer circle – any external threats felt by the client at boarding school: cruelty, punishment, rules, deportment, bells, surveillance, abuse, teasing, bullying, uniform, uniformity, gangs, culture, timetables, divide-and-rule.

This exercise is useful to help a client to differentiate between their inner world, how they felt when at school, and what belonged to the outer world of the home they had left behind and the school environment where they spent most of their time.

References

Bondevik, K.M. (2008) Interview with Jeremy Paxman, *BBC Newsnight* blog, 22 January, http://www.bbc.co.uk/blogs/legacy/newsnight/2008/01/bravery_in_the_face_of_mental_illness_1.html.

Bowlby, J. (1969) *Attachment and Loss, Volume 1*, London: Pelican.

Brown, B. (2012) *Daring Greatly: How the Courage to Be Vulnerable Transforms the Way We Live, Love, Parent and Lead*, New York: Gotham Books.

Duffell, N. (2000) *The Making of Them: The British Attitude to Children and the Boarding School System*, London: Lone Arrow Press.

Duffell, N. (2014) *Wounded Leaders: British Elitism and the Entitlement Illusion*, London: Lone Arrow Press.

Duffell, N. and Løvendal-Duffell, H. (2012) *Sex, Love and the Dangers of Intimacy*, 10th anniversary edition, London: Lone Arrow Press.

Gerhardt, S. (2004) *Why Love Matters: How Affection Shapes a Baby's Brain*, Hove: Routledge.

Gerhardt, S. (2010) *The Selfish Society: How We All Forgot to Love One Another and Made Money*, London: Simon and Schuster.

Gomez, L. (1997) *An Introduction to Object Relations*, London: Free Association Books.

Grosz, S. (2013) *The Examined Life*, London: Chatto and Windus.

Harrison, F. (1990) *Trivial Disputes*, London: Flamingo.

Kohut, H. (1977) *The Restoration of the Self*, Madison, CT: International Universities Press.

Klein, J. (1987) *Our Need for Others and Its Roots in Infancy*, London: Tavistock.

Laing, R. (1960) *The Divided Self*, London: Penguin.

MacLeod, S. (1981) *The Art of Starvation*, London: Virago.

Porges, S. (2014) Transcript of *Beyond the Brain: Using Polyvagal Theory to Help Patients 'Reset' the Nervous System after Trauma*, webinar session broadcast 17 October, interviewed by Ruth Buczynski, National Institute for the Clinical Application of Behavioral Medicine.

Schaverien, J. (1997) 'Men who Leave too Soon: Further Reflections on the Erotic Transference and Countertransference', *British Journal of Psychotherapy*, 14, 1, pp. 3–17.

Schore, A. (2003) *Affect Regulation and Repair of the Self*, New York: W.W. Norton.

Siegel, D. (2014) Transcript of *The Neurobiology of Trauma Treatment: How Brain Science Can Lead to More Targeted Interventions for Patients Healing from Trauma*, webinar session broadcast 14 November with Daniel Siegel, interviewed by Ruth Buczynski, National Institute for the Clinical Application of Behavioral Medicine.

Chapter 8

Trauma

'[The trauma sufferer] becomes overwhelmed by emotional disruptions in a way that makes it hard to respond to the reasonable needs and expectations of others, which naturally will make intimate partnership extremely difficult'

(Bancroft and Patrissi, 2011, p. 61).

Key points of chapter

- 'Developmental trauma' may be the most useful designation of trauma applying to ex-boarders.
- Today's therapists can benefit from understanding the effect of trauma on the brain.
- Trauma workers currently believe holistic and broad approaches to be the most helpful.
- This is a rapidly developing arena of work and it is important to keep abreast of developments.

What is trauma?

Perhaps the most difficult thing for the public to accept is that boarding, hidden in privilege, can count as trauma. Even some Rebel Type boarding school survivors, who are angry about boarding as a system that goes against the self-evident needs of children, may struggle to accept this idea. Sometimes, their peripheral anger covers grief – the pain of many years of hiding and dealing with the effects of trauma. The question of what precisely we mean by trauma is fundamental to our analysis.

The word 'trauma' is used in several ways. For example, an A&E doctor might talk about the trauma that happens to the body, while a social worker or psychiatrist might think of an acute event like being in an accident or being sexually assaulted that overwhelms the victim's ability to cope. It can refer to a severe physical injury or medical treatment, as well as the emotional shock following a stressful event or a physical injury, or a deeply disturbing experience or invasion that leads to long-term psychological problems. Witnessing a loved one being harmed, especially when powerless to prevent it, can be a trauma. A trauma can be a one-off event or a chronic occurrence. In some cases, a traumatic situation can be seemingly non-dramatic, but though it may appear banal, its repetitive and inescapable nature is imprisoning.

Trauma can have a 'double whammy' effect, due to its effect on the brain and the central nervous system:

> Modern research has shown that the impact of trauma includes physical changes inside the brain and to brain chemistry. These changes can cause a lasting increase in the person's sensitivity to certain kinds of stress while simultaneously taking away the person's ability to handle that increase.
>
> (Bancroft and Patrissi 2011, p. 61)

Difficulty in maintaining normal coping systems goes under the broad name of Post Traumatic Stress Disorder (PTSD). Under certain circumstances, there is also a third effect: that of normalising the lack of functioning induced by the trauma. Martin Pollecoff, who runs a therapy service for British ex-servicemen called The Long Boat Home, names this problem:

> If it is not spotted before you leave the forces then on average it takes 13 years for ex-service personnel to be diagnosed with PTSD. By that time we are no longer dealing with a trauma. What you get then is a personality that has accommodated itself to the wound.
>
> (Pollecoff, 2009)

Although Pollecoff's observation refers to ex-servicemen who have had to risk their lives under dangerous circumstances and witness body mutilation and death we believe it applies to ex-boarders who, through privileged abandonment in elite institutions, suffer profound wounds to their souls. One of the added difficulties in Boarding School Syndrome getting recognition is the lack of research. Given the centrality of private boarding education to the British Establishment, readers can imagine how difficult obtaining funding for such research would be. Yet, any trauma that tends to begin at the age of 8 and to surface symptomatically 20 or 30 years later, because of a personality that 'has accommodated itself to the wound', would be very difficult to research. But the clinical evidence from ex-boarders' therapists and the traumatic side effects reported by their partners is significant.

Developmental trauma

How should we then best describe the specific kind of trauma that boarding children experience? American authors Bancroft and Patrissi, whose focus is the role of trauma, personality disorder and abusive behaviour in intimate relationships, describe psychological trauma in a way that fits for boarding: 'At the heart of trauma is a sense of complete helplessness combined with feeling abandoned by those who could or should have protected him or her' (Bancroft and Patrissi, 2011, p. 60). Psychoanalyst and couple therapist Frances Grier suggests that a boarding child has to face 'unremitting trauma' and therefore qualifies for Masood Khan's category of 'cumulative trauma' (Khan, 1963, pp. 288–306). According to Grier, Khan noted that a trauma could be comprised of: 'slow-moving, but highly repetitive non-dramatic bad experiences, which eventually overwhelms them and renders them impotent … which slowly but surely traumatises the child' (Grier, personal email correspondence). Boarding creates a deep shock from which there is no relief, writes Grier:

> Almost universally, these children expected relief: their parents loved them, there must be a mistake. If they cried out in anguish, surely the parents or other trusted adults – often loved servants in the case of children brought up in the countries which used to be part of the British Empire – would come to the rescue as they've always had in the past.
>
> (Grier, 2013, p. 149)

Clearly the *context* in which the trauma happened is key, as Dan Siegel, one of the leading neuroscience-based psychiatrists, argues:

> We really need to ask specific questions: what was the context in which the trauma happened, at what time did it happen – what was the developmental framework – and what was this person like before the event? Trauma will affect the specifics of the brain depending on all of those factors.
>
> (Siegel, 2014, p. 5)

From the perspective of neuroscience, the earlier the trauma the more impactful – including physical changes inside the brain and brain chemistry, as well as the consequent effect on sensitivity to stress – it is likely to be, because it occurs at times of intense brain growth. In the sixties, before we had the technology to investigate properly, Bowlby reasoned: 'That there are sensitive periods in human development seems more than likely' (Bowlby 1969, p. 208). A 4-year old becoming hospitalised and separated from his parents is likely to be differently affected to a 14-year old. If a teenager is traumatised, it affects the brain in different ways than if the same trauma occurred to a 50-year old. However, this guideline should not override the *context* in which the trauma occurred, the possibilities of multiple traumas and how the trauma history may be obfuscated in adult life.

Case example

Take the case of a boarding child, say a boy who is poorly attached. He may already appear an isolate in the social setting of a boarding school. Bowlby suggested that: 'after a very long or repeated separation during the first three years of life detachment can persist indefinitely' (Bowlby, 1975, p. 31). However, even then he will still suffer the trials of homesickness when first sent away, because he has no one to protect him – even though he may have long ago given up on the public expression of such feelings. He will be likely to adapt less well than one who is well attached. If this boy is slow to erect a competent survival personality his peers will most likely bully him. If he is an attractive child who is isolated and vulnerable he may be groomed and sexually abused by a teacher or elder pupil.

Compound traumatic events take their toll. To make things worse, they may be later overlaid by how they are presented in adult ex-boarders, according to how they survived. The Crushed type boarding school survivors may well have such compound traumas hidden by multiple coexisting problems as drug dependency and so on, while the Complier types may have buried themselves in work and institutionalisation.

Therapists have their work cut out picking through the narrative over many years, pre-school, at school and post-school to arrive at a full picture, as well as in helping the client to accept and establish at what point the traumatic history had the most impact.

In general, however, the developmental context and timescale is the most pertinent determining factor on the effects on the brain, as Siegel explains:

> Age affects the impact of trauma on the brain in a huge way. The general developmental neuroscience rule is those regions that are developing have the most vulnerability if there is a trauma at the time of the window of development. Neglect and or abuse are the two forms of trauma that are called *developmental trauma*.
>
> (Siegel, 2014, p. 6)

This newly emerging designation of 'developmental trauma' is of great relevance. In 2007 the US National Child Traumatic Stress Network reported that many children were being frequently misdiagnosed and thereby incorrectly treated. To fill the gap, according to Tori DeAngelis:

> The group is proposing a diagnosis called 'developmental trauma disorder' or DTD, to capture what members see as central realities of life for these children: exposure to multiple, chronic traumas, usually of an

interpersonal nature; a unique set of symptoms that differs from those of post-traumatic stress disorder (PTSD) and a variety of other labels often applied to such children; and the fact that these traumas affect children differently depending on their stage of development.

(DeAngelis, 2007, p. 32)

Bessel van der Kolk of Boston University explains:

> While PTSD is a good definition for acute trauma in adults, it doesn't apply well to children, who are often traumatized in the context of relationships. Because children's brains are still developing, trauma has a much more pervasive and long-range influence on their self-concept, on their sense of the world and on their ability to regulate themselves.
>
> (DeAngelis, 2007, p. 32)

'Developmental trauma' may therefore prove the most useful designation of trauma applying to ex-boarders. In the British case, however, the picture is obscured by the social aspects of class, disguised by familiar expectations on working culture and on our governing elite, not to mention the normalisation of character traits such as the 'stiff upper lip', all militating against its recognition.

Furthermore, neither developmental psychology nor somatic therapy (which is inevitably developmental) has proved very popular here – an additional factor to explain why Boarding School Syndrome has remained unrecognised for so long by the mental health professions in Britain. Here the home-grown disciplines of Object Relations and Attachment Theory have dominated. With the focus firmly on the infant caregiver dyad, developmental psychology, even the psychoanalytic life-stage theories of Erik Erikson and Karen Horney have never really taken root, presumably because they involve the embarrassing business of sexuality. However, even if historically many children were sent away to board even younger, the boarder's attachment rupture and adaptation imperative occurs in the developmental context of latency, puberty and adolescence.

Trauma and the brain

Science has a rather perverse way of studying human functioning. What we know about how the brain operates has been increasingly systematised by observing physical trauma such as brain injuries and strokes, where areas of neural matter are permanently or temporarily disabled. Equally, researchers understand the effects of traumatisation on the brain with reference to healthy brain functioning. Siegel offers this succinct assessment: 'When you are *not* traumatised, you are differentiating and linking your brain in the present moment – it is integrated in creating a flexible, adaptive, and coherent flow that is energised and stable over time' (Siegel, 2014, p. 4). So in a person who has suffered trauma what we are likely to see is:

> The brain will stop being adaptive – it will become maladaptive. Instead of being coherent, it will be incoherent. Instead of being energized, it could be depleted or excessively aroused – not functioning with an optimal amount of energy.
>
> (Siegel, 2014, p. 5)

A further important problem in ex-boarders is Pollecoff's 'personality accommodated to the wound', which is what Siegel goes on to describe: 'In terms of stability, it can have a strange instability (repeating patterns that are recurrently dysfunctional), which from the outside looks stable, but the 'stability' is recurrent dysfunction' (Siegel, 2014, p. 5).

Over the past 40 years ideas about the brain have been transformed, and over the past two decades this process has accelerated. This is partly due to new technology, especially functional magnetic resonance imagers, commonly known as MRI scanners. These devices can detect which parts of the brain are active when someone is thinking a particular thought or performing a specific action, effectively allowing areas of the brain to become mapped. The brain is no longer seen simply as a command and control centre but as a network of interrelating pathways for energy, information and chemical messages, not just within the skull, but encompassing the entire nervous system and extending to the sense receptors, including the skin. In the last decade, moreover, neuroscientists have established that the hippocampus, the corpus callosum and the prefrontal cortex are the three main integrative regions of the brain, with extensive circuits that link widely separate areas.

The new knowledge supports the earlier hypothesis that developmental trauma impairs the brain's integrative growth and functioning. Harvard researcher Martin Teicher scanned the brains of people with documented developmental trauma and established that if the trauma happened during the development of any one of the integrative periods, these brain areas could be blocked in their growth or suffer chemical damage to their neurons (Siegel, 2014, p. 9). He also demonstrated that, depending on the timing, neglect was just as negatively impactful as overt abuse, if not more. As a society we tend to overlook the impact of neglect, which usually happens over extended time periods, as Camila Batmanghelidjh affirms: 'Abuse, however awful, has a beginning, a middle, and an end; for a child, neglect goes on forever' (Batmanghelidjh, 2014).

The over-excited brain

Ex-boarders have clearly suffered neglect in traumatic dimensions and in some cases abuse is piled on top of this, so while they were undoubtedly exposed to intensive education in terms of the rational development of their minds, their *brains* may have been impaired in ways that we are only beginning to understand.

Among the difficulties experienced within the traumatised brain and the entire nervous system are hyperarousal, neurotoxicity, memory flood, traumatic memory, flashbacks, somatisation and pain management problems. *Hyperarousal* is where the trauma sufferer regularly predicts danger where there may be no realistic reason and, in order to stay out of trouble, puts the entire system on stress alert. Stress, especially when it becomes chronic as it does in trauma sufferers, leads to two massive and predictable chemical reactions in the nervous system.

The first is the acute secretion of the stress hormone cortisol, which can engender *neurotoxicity*; the second is the acute release of high levels of adrenalin, which has a direct impact on the processing of one of the most complex functions of the brain – memory. Siegel explains what happens:

> Cortisol, in the acute phase, can lead to a blockage of the activity of the part of the brain called the hippocampus, which is very integrative of memory. Cortisol, with extended periods of release, is neurotoxic. Neurotoxicity, in the developing brain, means that the regions trying to grow and establish synaptic connections may be inhibited in their growth. Cortisol secreted for long periods of time can not only be growth-inhibitory, but also neurotoxic, which means that it can destroy synapses that have already been established and kill *existing* neurons. That can happen especially during the developmental period, but it can also happen in the brains of combat soldiers. The hippocampus becomes smaller. Neurotoxicity, even in an adult, or at least in an older adolescent, can lead to damage to this brain region.
>
> (Siegel, 2014, p. 7)

The second chemical problem concerns the highly complex memory systems in the brain. While adrenalin functions as a natural stimulant of self-preservation and 'get up and go', when excess secretion becomes chronic, as in trauma, it has very notable effects on the complicated ways in which memory is processed within the brain. It especially impacts on what is known as 'encoding' of *implicit memory*.

Implicit memory supports action without consciousness of previous experiences, usually in the form of *procedural memory*, allowing us to remember how to repeat activities without thinking, like riding a bicycle. *Explicit memory* is the intentional recollection of previous experiences and information. We use explicit memory throughout the day, remembering the time of an appointment or recollecting events from years ago. Explicit memory involves conscious recollection, such as remembering a *specific* bike ride; but improved riding skill is a result of implicit memory. Siegel explains what can happen:

Adrenalin increases the encoding of implicit memory, which includes *emotional memory* – the fear of a dog that is attacking me, *perceptual memory* – the imprinting of the perception of the dog that is attacking me, and *procedural memory* – the memory for action, trying or wanting to run but not being able to take that action. Trauma impairs the brain's memory systems by blocking the integrative role of the hippocampus to take implicit puzzle pieces and weave them together into *explicit memory*.

(Siegel, 2014, pp. 7–8)

Memory dysfunctions greatly impact the way that trauma sufferers remain locked into a worldview that unconsciously recapitulates the traumatic situation. Events and images become encoded into implicit memory through non-focal attention, that is to say, without consciousness. Our brains constantly record streams of information flow without paying conscious attention, and these become encoded into implicit memory.

Memories retrieved from implicit memory no longer have the feeling of coming from the past as they come into awareness: they feel clear and present. And when a person's brain has been affected by abuse or developmental trauma at a vulnerable formative time they can become imprisoned in memories that keep repeating rather than getting stored away. The locus of these problems in the brain is complicated, but the point to remember is that they can become global, particularly affecting the hippocampus, because of its importance to survival, conditioning further aspects of *factual* and *episodic* memory on both sides of the brain.

This is what causes the trauma sufferer who has not relied on dissociation to become flooded with memories. The memory function has become maladaptive: events in the past are no longer harmless because they are over but can re-traumatise in the present. So in extreme cases, as in severe child sexual abuse, a person can experience what are known as 'flashbacks' where memories reappear as current experience often with a nightmarish quality. When there has been severe neglect, a sense of perpetual or further neglect, of the imperative to survive utterly alone, can dominate the mind – as real as if it were current.

The social brain

Recently, increased attention has been given to the areas that were formerly thought less significant, such as the *afferent* nervous system, primarily the vagus nerve system, which sends information *towards* the brain from such organs as the heart and the gut. The role of the vagus is to inform the brain and regulate the entire system of the body, including all biological processes like digestion, and especially the nervous system.

This new view of the brain, as part of a very complex system of response to the environment, is increasingly holistic and begins to align with Oriental concepts. It is linked to the whole body, with heart, lungs, intestines, endocrine and the immune system as an interconnected responsive and regulating network. No longer is it possible to say that the body serves the brain, or that mind and brain are identical, or that the Platonic or Cartesian view of the separation of mind and body remain tenable. The mind is clearly part of a wide-ranging relational field and it makes sense that the brain is 'designed' to serve this. Siegel again: 'The mind is a self-organizing, emergent, embodied and relational process that is regulating energy information flow both within the whole body, including the brain, and also between us and the whole world' (Siegel, 2014, p. 19).

The evolution of the entire human nervous system to emotional experience and expression, vocal communication and congruent social behaviour has been set out in Stephen Porges' *The Polyvagal Theory* (Porges, 2011). Porges suggests that, over time, a special connection evolved between the human brain and the enormous quantity of nerve tissue that links the heart and facial muscles used for signalling safety or aggression. This brain-face-heart connection provides the structures for what Porges calls the *Social Engagement System* linking our bodily feelings with facial expression, vocal intonation and gesture; it is critical for the self-regulation of the autonomic nervous system (ANS). Humans are therefore uniquely primed towards precision functioning in emotional bonding situations, within intimate pairings and social groups.

Porges' lab research provides many insights into symptoms observed in several behavioural, psychiatric and physical disorders, but what is most important for us is his understanding of what happens when a person does not feel safe. Under circumstances of threat or stress, we automatically fire the sympathetic branch of the ANS and shut down the activation of the afferent vagal system's messages to the brain, adopting the 'fight or flight' response, for which a huge boost of chemical energy is needed. But in response to an *extreme* threat of annihilation we can shut our whole system down and conserve energy, like a mouse playing dead. For this we use the parasympathetic ANS response to take up the collapsed characteristics of a 'freeze' or *immobilisation* state, trapped within the confines of much earlier, so-called 'reptilian' defences. In immobilisation we are incapable of reading another person's facial signals or of sending the relevant signals in return.

In trauma sufferers this state can become chronic, preventing them taking realistic readings of safety or danger in their social interactions. It frequently causes somatisation (translating into numerous medical problems) in the lower diaphragm (Porges, 2014, p. 6). These discoveries have huge significance when applied to ex-boarders with a long-term but unconscious sense of not being safe. The effect of being eternally strategic, chronically on stress alert, unable to read facial signals or send friendly messages, explains why ex-boarder clients frequently report difficulties in distinguishing intimate approaches from imagined threats. In consequence, they interpret all approaches as danger, just to be on the safe side, which compounds their habitual strategic loneliness and affects the entire social world in which they live.

The final aspect of the new science that we must mention is the new field of *epigenetics*, in which research suggests that the traumatic adaptations of ancestors can affect descendants' DNA sequencing with inbuilt post-traumatic type symptoms. Combined with the research showing how good attachments can foster optimal epigenetic regulation of the stress response, the transgenerational problems of boarding may yet be greater than we have imagined or are able to measure.

Healing the traumatised brain

We now arrive at a crucial question: is it possible to heal a person's brain, especially if they experienced developmental trauma at times of maximum neural growth?

In *Attachment and Loss*, Bowlby pointed in the direction of what he called the 'critical period' and, using terminology drawn from ethology such as 'imprinting', he saw how animals could be subject to 'irreversibility' (Bowlby, 1969, pp. 208–9). But we now know much more about *neuroplasticity*, the ability of the brain to grow new matter and make new connections, even after serious damage, as experienced in strokes. This seems to offer much more evidence for optimism, for as Siegel says, 'Re-integration is what repairs the brain' (Siegel, 2014, p. 5).

Psychiatrist Norman Doidge reports astonishing new advances of neuroplasticity in improving – and even curing – many prevalent brain problems previously thought to be incurable or irreversible. In *The Brain's Way of Healing* (Doidge, 2015) he describes a series of remarkable recoveries using non-invasive techniques, such as sounds played into the ear successfully to treat autism, learning disorders and attention-deficit disorder in children. Gentle electrical stimulation on the tongue has been used to reverse symptoms of multiple sclerosis and Parkinson's; other simple methods have been shown to reduce the risk of dementia.

One of the early proponents of developmental trauma, Bessel van der Kolk, suggests that some of the new 'energy psychologies' seem promising adjuncts in respect of individual post-traumatic work in his latest writing (Van der Kolk, 2014). If memories can be re-stored into the past where they belong, rather than remaining ever present 'in the now', the client can experience and feel that the trauma is 'over', and Eye Movement Desensitisation and Reprocessing (EMDR) can help integrate memories of a traumatic event. EMDR appears to be less helpful when trauma has occurred repeatedly in childhood, presumably because the trauma has impacted during one of the periods of intense brain development.

Working with trauma

What are the implications of our brief overview of emerging ideas about trauma for therapists working with the trauma of ex-boarders?

Once the work has been reframed as trauma work, the first principle that can guide the therapist is that of the crucial need for safety, a generally accepted norm in psychotherapeutic practice. Accordingly, the principle of safety with trauma sufferers, whether they are identified with it or not – and especially at the beginning of the work –has to be very present in the therapist's mind. Accepting that a client has been traumatised can put safety back on the agenda in a way that perhaps has previously been taken for granted or even ignored. Some of the ways in which trauma sufferers remain on constant alert has been revealed by the new knowledge from neuroscience.

For example, the chronic trauma sufferer automatically and intensely scans for low-frequency sounds indicating danger signals, in a way that a non-trauma sufferer has not experienced nor would be expecting, because they regularly develop oversensitivity in the ear due to an archaic brain-sense receptor mechanism that puts the body on red alert. Stephen Porges suggests that consulting rooms should therefore be free from ambient sounds such as traffic noise or ventilation fans:

> We want the rooms to be quiet because the nervous system is going to be detecting these low-frequency sounds as if there is impending doom – as if something bad is going to happen. If you want the clues to this, just look at the masters of the classic symphonies where they basically relax the audience with the first movement by using lullabies – the voice of violins, the mother's voice.
>
> (Porges, 2014, p. 18)

For us, working with trauma is still subject to our overarching model of Recognition, Acceptance and Change. For ex-boarders to recognise that they have been forced into traumatic circumstances that were not recognised, and in which there was no possibility of help, can be incredibly supportive. It may also release a huge well of feelings ranging from anger to grief. Next, ex-boarders face the need to accept themselves for who they have unwittingly become, because of the adaptation imperative and due to the construction of their survival personality. Their psyches have been very wise, even if there has been a cost.

Acceptance also brings responsibility. It means that ex-boarders on the road to healing must practise both self-compassion and reality testing. It may also mean accepting that they, in their turn, have unwittingly caused harm in their current families or intimate relationships. Here, the authors are no better placed than any other ex-boarders in having to accept that – even as so-called experts – they have at times allowed themselves to be overwhelmed by their own post-traumatic emotional disruptions in a way that prevented them from responding 'properly to the reasonable needs and expectations of others' (Bancroft and Patrissi 2011, p. 61).

The acceptance stage is not necessarily easy or happy. Sometimes acceptance means an unusually intense combination of honesty, grief, self-compassion and remorse; it will need to be consistent and practised as a long-term discipline. If this can happen, the change stage becomes a natural and self-facilitating response to the soul work of acceptance.

Therapists, too, may find it surprising to have to identify this kind of work as trauma work, especially where an ex-boarder is presented as a malign player in a relationship situation, or where the client's material circumstances or high functioning may still be concealing it. Since empathic responses – and in particular empathic *interpretations* – are necessary to work well with the split ex-boarder client, it may sometimes be a challenge for therapists to find them, if an ex-boarder client presents with a deep but unconscious sense of entitlement. In *Wounded Leaders* these entitled attitudes were reframed as a compensation for the loss of belonging at home, of love, of spontaneity, of emotions – of the natural child itself (Duffell, 2014).

This compensation can only be maintained by dissociation, so the therapist will need to get beyond the client's outer behaviour to have contact with the abandoned child inside. We must stress that, in such a case, this is not the place for attempting the kind of explicit inner-child work outlined in the previous chapter, involving the client in identification or dis-identification exercises, but for the therapist to fully accept the role of parent or authority. Whether this transference is in either a positive or negative phase, the therapist must fully accept the objectification and speak always to the child's reality within the client. Attempts by therapists to be seen as real persons or with analogous personal experiences will either fall flat, or be overexciting, and act against the therapeutic alliance.

Often various kinds of 'acting out' around apparently practical administrative issues such us place, time, fees or breaks make sense when looked at from the perspective that the trauma client has a view of the world as being fundamentally unsafe. With this in mind, therapists can empathetically interpret such behaviour and gradually make the world they are setting up together with their clients as safe as possible. But overcaring therapists must beware: they will need to establish this safe, maturational environment without forfeiting the powerful leverage needed to get beyond the client's defences and protection of their strategic survival personality. This is one of the reasons why we said at the beginning of this book that therapists would need a very comprehensive theoretical understanding and a large toolkit to work with this client group.

It may also be that the amount of new information about trauma work – especially the science – can overwhelm the therapist, who then starts to feel inadequate. It is good to remember that it is only in very recent times that a greater emphasis has been put on what happens to a person's brain as a result of trauma. Happily, in general, these findings mostly confirm the methodologies that most psychotherapists have instinctively put into practice, rather than the opposite. Applying new insights from neuroscience to practice is still in its early days, with few examples of this being done in work with ex-boarders. Nevertheless, this is an area that we, alongside other interested colleagues, are actively pursuing.

Holistic approaches to trauma work

Van der Kolk recommends a very broad and holistic approach, using a variety of inputs that are tailored to the client's specific needs (Van der Kolk, 2014). When talking about traumatised clients treading the road to recovery, his general key points are:

- There is a need to help restore the proper balance between their rational and emotive brains.
- When somebody is hyper-aroused or extremely shut down, they cannot learn; therefore they cannot heal.
- There is a need to look at the interplay between thoughts and physical sensations; mindfulness and body awareness can assist.
- Naming issues is helpful and it is therapeutic for people to tell their story (narrative) and also *feel* their story (emotive).
- The client should be in the driving seat and own their process of recovery.

Van der Kolk advises clients to choose therapists who can help them stabilise, reduce anxiety, lay their memories to rest and, additionally, reconnect with others. He acknowledges that healing takes time and can involve a variety of approaches including individual therapy and small group work, as well as involvements within the family and wider community, where appropriate.

There are some therapeutic approaches that either involve other members of a family or close friends. Internal Family Systems Therapy encourages clients to see their minds like a family, with members at different levels of maturity, excitability, wisdom and pain: some members have been exiled, others are protectors or managers or fire fighters. The task is to separate different members (sub-personalities) so they become just parts of the self, so that the central self can conduct them like different parts of an orchestra. This is a similar concept to psychosynthesis notions of the 'I' or aware ego and could accompany the ex-boarder's work on the strategic survival personality.

Creating new mentalised structures through somatic approaches like Pesso's Psychomotor Therapy and Poppeliers' Sexual Grounding Therapy can promote an embodied, three-dimensional reality to key issues. Using both real and actual parents alongside ideal and hoped-for parents can create virtual presences to live side by side with painful memories – warm, sensory experiences as antidotes. Van der Kolk extols the virtues of yoga for making links between the body and emotions. Although progress can be slow, and traumatised clients may have difficulty with some poses, learning to breathe and be mindful as part of the practice of yoga helps trust and grounding in the life of the body become re-established.

Sometimes speaking out about why boarding is traumatic for children can help 'lost for words' ex-boarders find their voice. With the frequent interest our programmes receive from the media, we find that asking selected clients if it would be helpful in the current point of their recovery – that is key – for them to share some of their experiences and feelings as illustrations of the problem, when an article is being written or a programme made, can be a major step forward. Of course, supporting clients to expose themselves at the wrong moment can be catastrophic. But Van der Kolk (2014) also reminds us that stories can be told through art, music, dance or community theatre projects. Hence, they can also begin to experience sensory integration through music and rhythm.

Trauma and technology

The other development that is beginning to have encouraging results with trauma sufferers involves the use of biofeedback machines, adapted from healthcare monitoring devices. The use of biofeedback in therapy and self-development was pioneered some years ago by therapists Elmer and Alyce Green, but the digital revolution has vastly improved the applicability, accessibility and affordability of such technology. Using biofeedback to the neuronal activity of the brain, clients can practise techniques such as alpha and theta wave training to learn how to change patterns caused by trauma and its aftermath.

In a webinar series on the emerging understanding of trauma, Ruth Buczynski, President of the National Institute for the Clinical Application of Behavioral Medicine, introduced listeners to neurofeedback practitioner Sebern Fisher. Fisher described the technology that she uses, which involves guiding trauma sufferers, whom she calls 'trainees', to familiarise themselves with the device through exercises – like computer games with body sensors attached. 'Home-training' versions of such systems are available, and Fisher (Fisher 2014) shares a number of examples in which clients have apparently experienced life-changing results from this intervention.

The Institute of HeartMath, based in California, is one of a new kind of company that combines original scientific research with product marketing. HeartMath have been focusing on heart–brain interactions. Their research is based on understanding the nature of heart-rate variability and heart-rhythm coherence, which they claim to be the key to understanding the physiology of optimal learning and performance. The HeartMath Research Center pursues research into 'emotional physiology, optimal function, resilience and stress-management research, psychophysiology, neurocardiology and biophysics, and outcome studies in clinical, workplace, educational and military settings' (HeartMath, 2015).

Their biofeedback device is a hand-held sensor unit that provides input via lights and sound to an interface display on a personal computer. Practitioners learn to cultivate heart-rhythm coherence, a state of synchronisation between the heart, brain and nervous system. In effect, users train to learn how to consciously encourage the parasympathetic branch of the autonomic nervous system. This may prove extremely useful for trauma sufferers and those supporting a strategic survival personality, because the effect of chronic long-term and normalised anxious stress states is that the body can lose its aptitude for firing the 'rest and repair system'. Coherence, claim the manufacturers of the device, encourages 'a simultaneous state of relaxation, readiness and revitalization, improves performance, health and emotional well-being'.

Conclusion

Clearly, such technical solutions will need to be accepted by the therapeutic community and will require extensive testing. But they may prove increasingly popular and potentially effective now that the obsession, within the wider mental health culture, with medication as the only 'cure' begins to decline. Whilst medication cannot cure trauma and has been overused, this is not say that it may not be helpful in small doses under certain circumstances. Similarly, the UK's current obsession, backed by a money-conscious government, with short-term outcome-focused solutions such as Cognitive Behavioural Therapy may not, on their own, prove helpful or effective. In respect to trauma, a process of management is necessary, but de-sensitisation can become be re-traumatising.

Van der Kolk's (2014) idea of a broad-spectrum way of working built on a thorough understanding of the effect of trauma on memory, brain chemistry and behaviour, supported by a variety of approaches – including depth psychotherapy and the use of biofeedback technology – may well be the future of trauma work.

Exercise 8: accepting the trauma

Ask your client to reflect and write on the following questions – noting which cause them to have the most feelings.

How do you feel identifying yourself as a trauma sufferer?
What helps about thinking in this way? What rankles?
Who in your life/circle/family would be most affected by your beginning to think of yourself in this way?
What are the situations when you tend to get overwhelmed by your own anxiety or your own emotions?
What does it look like when you panic or get overwhelmed by what is happening inside you?
Who in your life/circle/family is most affected by your overwhelm?
What could you do differently to stay calm and focused?

References

Bancroft, L. and Patrissi, J. (2011) *Should I Stay or Should I Go? A Guide to Knowing if Your Relationship Can – and Should – Be Saved*, New York: Berkeley.

Batmanghelidjh, C. (2014) Personal correspondence with Simon Partridge.

Bowlby, J. (1969) *Attachment and Loss*, Volume 1, London: Pelican.

Bowlby, J. (1975) *Attachment and Loss*, Volume 2, London: Pelican.

DeAngelis, T. (2007) 'A New Diagnosis for Childhood Trauma?', *Journal of the American Psychology Association*, 38, 3, retrieved from http://www.apa.org/monitor/mar07/diagnosis.aspx.

Doidge, N. (2015) *The Brain's Way of Healing: Stories of Remarkable Recoveries and Discoveries*, London: Allen Lane.

Duffell, N. (2014) *Wounded Leaders: British Elitism and the Entitlement Illusion*, London: Lone Arrow Press.

Fisher, S. (2014) *Neurofeedback in the Treatment of Developmental Trauma: Calming the Fear-Driven Brain*, New York: W.W. Norton.

Grier, F. (2013) 'The Hidden Traumas of the Young Boarding School Child as Seen through the Lens of Adult Couple Therapy', in McGinley, E. and Varchevker, A (eds), *Enduring Trauma through the Life Cycle*, London: Karnac.

HeartMath (2015) http://www.heartmath.org.

Khan, M. (1963) 'The Concept of Cumulative Trauma', *Psychoanalytic Study of the Child*, 18, pp. 288–306.

Pollecoff, M. (2009) in *Self and Society*, Autumn and www.thelongboathome.co.uk.

Porges, S. (2011) *The Polyvagal Theory: Neurophysiological Foundations of Emotions, Attachment, Communication, and Self-Regulation*, New York: W.W. Norton.

Porges, S. (2014) Transcript of *Beyond the Brain: Using Polyvagal Theory to Help Patients 'Reset' the Nervous System after Trauma*, webinar session broadcast 17 October, interviewed by Ruth Buczynski, National Institute for the Clinical Application of Behavioral Medicine.

Siegel, D. (2014) Transcript of *The Neurobiology of Trauma Treatment: How Brain Science Can Lead to More Targeted Interventions for Patients Healing from Trauma*, webinar session broadcast 14 November, interviewed by Ruth Buczynski, National Institute for the Clinical Application of Behavioral Medicine.

Van der Kolk, B. (2014) *The Body Keeps the Score: Brain, Mind and Body in the Healing of Trauma*, New York: Viking.

Chapter 9

Sex

Puberty, gender and abuse

> Anything to do with sex was inevitably linked to shame, ignorance and confusion.
>
> (Email from male ex-boarder)

Key points of chapter

- Boarding schools are not known for their realistic or caring attitudes to sexuality.
- Latency is a preparation for a *differentiated but not separated* life, grounded in belonging and emotion.
- At puberty children need *parenting* – unavailable at boarding school.
- Boarding schools are based on a patriarchal system, underpinned by a culture of misogyny and homophobia, which creates problems for both girls and boys and the adults they become.
- Group workshops can assist ex-boarders in recognising and accepting their personal sexual legacy of boarding.
- Sexual abuse is the ultimate betrayal of the child at boarding school.
- Individual therapy, based on safety and trust, is essential for ex-boarders who have been sexually abused.

Our sexual origins

Human beings come into the world through sex: we are sexual beings. The arising and expression of sexuality, the seeking of identity, as well as the search for loving, sexual relationships are our destiny. All developmental steps on our process of living, loving and dying can be seen as events on a sexual developmental continuum. As the only animals to have consciousness of these processes, we can also think, feel, fantasise and worry about them. We have the freedom to decide whether or not to reproduce, to choose our sexual orientation and – to some extent – even our gender identity.

Because we have sexual awareness, older and wiser cultures than ours have positioned the sexual life as psychically central to the individual and the community. They built this understanding into their social and spiritual cultures. This is why, for example, the extraordinary Hindu and Buddhist sexual iconography remain as luminous teachers; why Native American tribes placed sexuality at the centre of the sacred wheel of human life, the hub around which everything revolved. To the Western mind, conditioned over centuries of sexual fear and repression, such attitudes seem foreign and profoundly challenging.

Since we are social animals, our sexual development takes place socially. None of it can be managed entirely on our own, and there are many things that can go wrong. And because sexuality is so central to human life, a lack of proper recognition and response in childhood from others affects the developing self-concept very deeply. Because sexuality is at our core, sexual abuse or rape impacts on a young person like a powerful but bewildering blow to the core. Sexual wounding affects *all* aspects – sexual, emotional, physical, mental and spiritual – and requires much dedicated effort from both survivor and therapist to heal.

All of society, including the mental health professions, is affected by our cultural sexual heritage. Not all therapists understand what is needed to help repair earlier sexual wounding, either from abuse, or from the even less known topic of *sexual neglect*, meaning the failure to guide the sexual development in a child. In Britain, this is partly due, as we mentioned earlier, to theoretical tendencies towards the mother-infant dyad and away from developmental contexts. Consequently, the distinct developmental issues belonging to latency, puberty and adolescence – precisely those periods of boarding – are often not understood in context and tend to be ignored by therapists, even if anecdotally people often retain many memories about the difficulties of those days.

Before we consider what it means to grow up in a boarding school, we should outline our ideas of what human beings innately expect to go through, regardless of what culture or environment they find themselves in. An overall developmental schema for sexuality – or rather, for establishing a grounded sexual self-concept – would go something like the following, even though this is a gross simplification.

---

1. We first need to ATTACH.
2. Then we need to establish an IDENTITY.
3. We are attracted into RELATIONSHIPS.
4. We EXPRESS ourselves.
5. Then we nurture others and help them EXPRESS and REGULATE their own sexuality.

Sexual development at boarding school

When we come to the problems of sexual awakening within residential education we are no longer focused on boarders' early adaptation. Instead, we must consider their whole developmental period, through *latency* (7–11), *puberty* (12–15) and *early adolescence* (16–18). The ages given are approximate, but these stages are when all human beings prepare for and then become demonstrably and unavoidably subject to the arising of *sexual generative potential* in their bodies and its awareness in their minds. Developmentally, the child starting boarding is usually situated either in the latency or puberty period.

The latency child is above all things an *emotional* being, a developing individual, rooted, as Rudolf Steiner suggested, in *feeling*. In latency a child is not trying to be separate, but to *differentiate* – on the point of entering the world, trying out its emerging sense of self, to become a self in the world that belongs *in* a family but not *to* a family. It attempts to bring the loving emotional foundations of its parental couple into the world, so that its sexual development comes into the container of emotion and belonging. Obviously, by its nature, boarding mitigates against healthy development in this phase.

Next, puberty changes everything, signalling the unavoidable arrival of procreative potential in a child's body. The changes it brings in its wake are profound. Flooded with hormones, the body grows with alarming rapidity and begins to secrete sexual fluids – menses and semen. Aroused by becoming newly visible and by new inner sensations, children become obsessed with how they look, about their appeal to others, about what their peer group is wearing, saying, thinking, listening to. Internally, they are often very confused and in need of guidance. As they move through puberty and into adolescence, children need help from their parents in understanding, embodying and regulating these experiences.

Learning to regulate sexuality cannot be done on one's own; it has to be guided and, what is less known, *mirrored*. Adults who desert them or fail to engage with them truthfully are immediately discounted. The way they conduct their own intimate relationships is under constant scrutiny. Cleary, boarders lose out here, too, because if children do not have loving support in having their sexuality mirrored and regulated they turn to each other. Then, at best, confusion reigns. Whether they know it or not, ex-boarders will look to their therapists to take up the job that was not done.

Boarding children have difficulty maturing sexually; sometimes there is abuse, which makes it much worse. They frequently experience great difficulty embodying healthy identities of gender. The boarding system's starting point is patriarchal, which means that girl boarders suffer a double problem. In addition to losing their family, they are also separated from what is closest to them – their feminine nature. This initially wounds a girl in her *identity* development, which, in a patriarchy, is arguably where women tend to need the most support and encouragement. Female ex-boarders may need help in getting in touch with their anger, often greatest towards their mothers, or in believing in their inner authority, but therapists should not underestimate the wound to the feminine self-concept or identity.

Male boarders, on the other hand, receive an overdose of stereotypical maleness and rationality. In the absence of loving mothers, an overall resentment at their dependence on women is unconsciously fostered. This initially wounds a boy in his *relationship* development, which is where, classically, all men have the steepest learning curve.

In general, our experience tells us that male ex-boarders need help to get in touch with their grief, sometimes considered part of their feminine side, so heavily denied, and, like the vulnerable boy, tainted with repudiated feminine weakness so subtly and continuously reinforced at school. The advent of sexual awakening in the hothouse confinement of boarding, rooted in 'Muscular Christianity' and the cult of boy worship, exceeds anything that the children or even the authorities can manage. It is an educational catastrophe.

Boarding school attitudes to sexuality

The British boarding school system is predicated on what early Scottish theorist Ian Suttie called the 'taboo on tenderness' (Suttie, 1935, p. 67). Going hand in hand with the rediscovery of Attachment Theory, the discipline of Relational Psychoanalysis has inspired many practitioners to rediscover Suttie. Analyst Colin Kirkwood proposes that:

> The process of repressing tenderness . . . has its cultural origins in the stoicism which has pervaded British culture, and British Christianity, for a very long time. Both parents, and the child's older siblings, will already be intolerant of tenderness, to a great or lesser extent, reflecting the degree of stoicism in their own upbringing. The process is reinforced beyond the family, particularly among men and boys. The taboo on tenderness is expressed by upper-class parents who send their sons away from home to attend private single-sex boarding schools.
>
> (Kirkwood, 2005, pp. 28–9)

Self-reliance in childhood is a very dangerous myth, affecting dispatched daughters as well as sons. At puberty, one clear and present danger lurks: children cannot be expected to distinguish between the needed *sexual mirroring* from adults and paedophilic grooming. While homophobic hysteria is pervasive, they cannot know what counts as sexual abuse or affection, nor tease out the difference between homosexuality and age-appropriate sexual experimentation. We will return to all these items in this chapter.

Education should be a preparation for life, and in adults the embodied life is social, relational and sexual. But in the world's most prestigious and expensive institutions, the British boarding school system, where rationality, competitiveness and self-reliance are championed, sex ends up *'inevitably linked to shame, ignorance and confusion'*. Though this view is universally confirmed by countless other writers, its significance continues to be denied. In the meantime, the practice of boarding is normalised and health professionals remain shy of giving useful guidance about children's developmental sexual needs. So the journey into institutional sexual confusion remains the norm; the correspondent quoted earlier continues by recounting his own:

> When I was 8, an older boy of about 12, who was our dormitory monitor, used to occasionally get into bed with one or two of us. It was most probably sexual for him but for me, when it was my turn, it involved being woken up, pinched quite a lot and threatened with dire consequences if I told anyone. I was the unlucky one to have him in my bed when Matron came in one night and we were both marched off to see the Head. I waited nervously at the top of the stairs while he was presumably being given a talking-to and then heard the 6 strokes of the cane. Although a bit ashamed, I had some small hope that the Head would show some sympathy for me and listen to my story. As it was, he just said 'I will not have any vulgarity in my school – bend over'. I got 4 strokes of the cane. The monitor was moved and we got a new one who left us alone to sleep.
>
> (Email from a male ex-boarder)

Traditionally, instead of sexual guidance, boarders inherited an ever present paranoia about sexual exploration with self or others from the nineteenth century, culminating in the risible and delayed sex instruction usually known as the 'leavers' talk' – a ritual of mutual embarrassment that enlightened no one. Our informant continues:

> Some years later, when I was 13, the Head gave me his usual 'leavers' sex talk', which consisted of (1) When you see a bull mount a cow in a field that is what they do to have a baby and (2) Women have periods when they bleed, so when you get married make sure you don't book the honeymoon during such a period.

This story comes from a man who boarded in the 1950s and 1960s. One would hope that attitudes to sexuality had changed by the twenty-first century, and yet, the default position of avoidance, leaving children to work it out for themselves, is still the favoured approach. How can children make sense of life in an institution where the activities of older children and staff are incomprehensible to them? Even when they are at home, children need loving parents to help make sense of sexuality. Here is a recent letter from a workshop participant expressing his own sexual confusion:

I too at prep school had my share of pre-pubescent exploration with one particular boy who was some years older but I can't recall how many years. I can't recall how long it carried on but I must have got something out of it because it carried on for a while. I'm no longer sure if this was an abusive relationship or not but the other boy was older and then one term he never came back, so we couldn't have really been friends. However, other boys started to called me gay, bent, queer, 'batty-boy' – words that meant something cruel, horrible and wounding, but ones which I did not understand, save as to say that I knew there wasn't anything wrong with me except that maybe there was because how did they know something I did not?

(Email from a male ex-boarder)

Without parents to go to, sexual confusion can drive a final wedge between boarding child and parent. Readers will note how this correspondent ends, referring to his abandoned disconnection from his parents:

I don't remember whether this was before I met this boy or after or indeed whether the events were connected. Once this name-calling started it carried on by a particular group of boys and I spent almost the entire 5 years at prep school in abject fear of both the name-calling, of other boys finding out and of the psychological bullying spreading. It really was a life of sheer terror. I was terrified of what they were saying and terrified of telling my parents, but of course I couldn't anyway, they were too far away and if it were true, whatever the words meant then they too would reject me – except of course they already had.

Puberty

With the arrival of puberty, everything changes for a child. Going through puberty in a single-gender institution is not easy. By now the boarder may have become used to the separation, but at puberty children need more than just parents – they need *parenting*. And parenting means that parents have to *do* something; it is not enough for them just to be there, even if they are. Now the tasks for parents are more complicated than before, more hands-on. This demands a level of reality: virtual parenting, however good the technology, just won't work. The boarder has no parents available, either to argue with or to confide in, to approach the complications of gender, relationships and sexuality. They are just not around, by definition. So, later on, in therapy, the therapist will have to stand in for them and may have much leftover repair work to do.

At this point, therapists do well to remember their primary job description: *rent-a-mum* and *rent-a-dad*. They must avoid both psychoanalytic coolness and existential chic, because leftover puberty sexual issues do not require 'not doing'. Humanistic therapists must avoid making the other person the same and equal: in the rent-a-parent role they are not, and clients now need *re-parenting*.

By understanding precisely what children need their parents to *do* at this time, therapists can get a sense of the task.

- As their children become more autonomous, with lives that increasingly encompass both the outside world and home, parents need to be setting realistic boundaries. Sometimes this means getting into conflict.
- They need to engage fully with their children about life: relationships, values, society, religion, etc. Sometimes this means getting into disputes.
- But most of all – and this is vital and irreplaceable – parents have to support their children in becoming sexual human beings, for that is precisely what is happening inside their bodies, whether they like it or not, whether they are prepared for it or not.
- The 'good news' is that this does not mean having a BIG TALK. The 'bad news' is that parents have to authentically put themselves on the line as real people. Teenagers ask real questions and will not accept untruthful parenting.
- Parents have to mirror the child's transition into adult sexuality as a good and wanted event.
- Parents need to give their child supportive feedback about this change, that they are becoming attractive, all the while making their actions about and for the child, not about themselves.

According to UNICEF, Britain has one of the lowest general health and satisfaction levels amongst her youth in the developed world (UNICEF, 2007). But in the Netherlands, one of the high scorers, developmental psychologists like Dr Willem Poppeliers have pioneered an understanding of the needs of teenagers. Poppeliers' somatic sexual psychotherapy, *Sexual Grounding Therapy*, is still little known in Britain, but specialises in the therapeutic repair of adults' unmet childhood sexual developmental needs. He believes that parents play an indispensable role in supporting the sexual development of their children in a grounded and healthy way.

If they get proper *sexual mirroring*, Poppeliers proposes, teenagers are not so driven to have sexual activities early, which he sees as compensation for the lack of parental response (Poppeliers and Broesterhuizen, 2007, pp. 35–42). Crucial implications for therapists from Poppeliers' work are that all children need a sexual *response* from adults. Boarding girls in particular miss out on the sexual response from their fathers, as the boys do from their mothers. These get replayed in what psychoanalysis calls *erotic countertransference* and frequently are misunderstood. Let us be clear: a sexual *response* from adults is required; it is not the same as being involved in *sex acts* with adults.

How much teenagers should be expressing themselves sexually in sex acts is a discussion outside our remit here. But since teenage life is dominated by the impulse to experience oneself as a sexual being this will involve the impulse towards sexual acts. Where children remain unmirrored, they become *overexcited*. Moreover, in a single-sex institution – which effectively includes those boys' schools that have tried to modernise by the inclusion of a handful of unfortunate girls – there are few options but to practise amongst each other. This raises further questions about what can be regarded as teenage experimentation, where the boundaries of sexual abuse begin and end, and whether homosexuality is implicitly encouraged.

Boarding's sexual legacy

In place of living boundaries, on reaching puberty, the boarding child has the enormous and incomprehensible edifice of the public school rulebook. This, according to researcher Alisdare Hickson, was chiefly evolved to protect children from having mutual sexual contact. 'For the last 150 years', he proposes:

> it has been the fear of homosexuality, more than any concerns about children's education or health, which has shaped the experience of boarding school life. It was reflected in the regulations and taboos that grew up around friendships between boys of disparate ages, it swayed decisions concerning the content of the curriculum and the Sunday sermon, it spawned modifications to existing school uniforms, it was the *raison d'être* of the cold shower and it dictated the acceptable bounds of art classes and dramatic societies.
>
> (Hickson, 1995, p. 79)

All boarding children end up suffering from the relentless overexcitement about sexuality in general, the conscious terror of homosexuality in particular, with internalised misogyny as a common unconscious base. These have been consistent monsters in the history of private boarding, raising very real questions for survivors and those who attempt to assist in their recovery, let alone educators and legislators. The most potent impact is on girls and boys trying to embody a healthy gender identity.

Perhaps the most fundamental question is how can girls navigate an education designed for male soldiers and colonial administrators and emerge as real women? Is it possible without sacrificing femininity in service of rationality? In Chapter 1 we quoted Drusilla Modjeska's account of ex-boarders lamenting the loss of their 'Un-English, feminine waywardness' (Modjeska, 1995, p. 235). Revisiting her boarding school as an adult, the main character in her novel is surprised to find that a pupil, a peer from her school days, is now headmistress. They chat, but without real connection:

> The view of the school she offered, based on good standing and tradition, was, by any other standard, as empty of meaning as our conversation. But that, I suppose, is the role of the headmistress: to patrol the split between body and mind that our culture avows; to deny the messy and difficult terrain of the body and its wild desires.
>
> (Modjeska, 1995, p. 200)

Modjeska's resulting question is one that women ex-boarders will inevitably bring to therapy: 'Are we left believing, somewhere, secretly, that we need to tame ourselves in order to harness our capabilities of mind?' (Modjeska, 1995, p. 200) Whatever the answer, female ex-boarders will most likely need to be mirrored by women who have either not had to make such a sacrifice or who have travelled the road back to reclaim an authentic feminine identity.

Psychotherapist Nicola Miller has worked with many women on Boarding School Survivors workshops. She reflects on the difficulties of girls adapting to an institution based on patriarchal values and wonders what they end up internalising about their identity on their way to becoming women. Mothers come in for a lot of blame and are often experienced as having betrayed their natural instincts. This creates a profound anxiety, frequently expressed as an inner misogyny, or a deep mistrust of other women, as Miller explains:

> Working with BSS [Boarding School Survivors] women we see that many of us are terrorised by the internalised projection of the destructive, uncontrolled power of our sexuality. Misogyny in women is a terrifying, destructive force, and groups of BSS women have to dig deep into their reserves of courage and life-affirming nature in order to sit in the room together, the perceived danger can be so intense. Girls' school values have patriarchal and biblical roots – there is an implicit condemnation of women's sexuality. Our bleeding is 'the curse' and we deal with it in secret and in shame.
>
> (Miller, 2009)

In her novel *No Talking after Lights*, Angela Lambert echoes this issue when the leading character Constance realises that her periods have begun while at boarding school, and is overwhelmed with feelings of both embarrassment and panic. There is no one to whom she can turn with her shyness and the overwhelming sense of being embodied in a culture that seems more likely to mirror her mind and leave her feminine self to her own devices (Lambert,

1990, p. 109). In consequence, women ex-boarders frequently need help in reaffirming their identity as women.

Once they go beyond their initial mutual mistrust, the workshops regularly establish a deeply felt and therapeutic sisterhood amongst the participants, as Miller describes:

> This experience also breeds courage, courage to accept what was needed in the past was lost, courage to accept we do not have the power to change our history, and the imperative – we must surrender the constant struggle to recreate what we needed then. So we grieve our female nature, we acknowledge with respect the characters we have become, and we start to really listen for the loving and creative girl who has all the beauty and potential of a woman.
>
> (Miller, 2009)

A band of bereaved misogynists

In 1935 Iain Suttie suggested Freud's taboo on sex was mostly a male displacement of love (Suttie, 1935, pp. 80–96). Misogyny in male boarding school survivors seems rooted in Suttie's 'taboo on tenderness':

> The taboo on tenderness is expressed by upper-class parents who send their sons away from home to attend private single-sex boarding schools, and by the gang of boys who idealise manliness and repudiate any sign of babyishness and girlishness. Suttie characterises their state of mind as involving a reaction against the sentiments related to mother and the nursery, and describes these boys as a band of brothers united by a common bereavement.
>
> (Kirkwood, 2005, pp. 28–9)

This idea of 'a band of brothers' (here Suttie makes a reference to a term used by Freud) 'united by common bereavement' explains much of the attitudes of male ex-boarders, especially in those who survive by being 'Compliers'. It can be seen in their gender-based *esprit de corps*, in their unconscious misogyny, and again in their fond remembrance of 'the best days of your life'. These may well have been enlivened by real friendships formed under duress, but even these were to be wickedly exploited at the start of the senseless First World War. Then, hardly out of public school, boys were encouraged to troop off to war in the fantasy that it was some kind of inter-house rugby match in which their duty was to 'play the game', never mind the cost.

The word 'bereavement' is crucial, too. Therapists may understand the adult world as based on healthy inter-dependence constructed on bonds of love and empathy, but in the male ex-boarder's psyche all of this has had to be repudiated. The 'bereaved' boarder has had to create distance from love, tainted by the forbidden realm of mother, *well before* going into the adult world.

Darrel Hunneybell, an experienced Men's Boarding School Survivors workshop facilitator, describes how a boy learns to survive by over-identifying with the masculine school environment, putting to one side all that is nurturing and feminine, splitting off the grief of separation and loss. At the workshops men may be afraid to let their defences down, worrying that if they really start to talk they will start crying and never stop:

> Such deep grief, hidden from view, kept in his pocket like a cherished object, a secret that cannot be shared. Over time this grief gets buried deeper and deeper, over time it becomes harder to take it seriously and it becomes less and less available. In order to survive, the boy pushes this weakness further and further away until he can get on without it. It appears that for many participants at the workshops the way in which they managed the trauma of abandonment is by splitting off the boy at home from the boy who went to school – present in the workshop is the man who I am now and the boy who was sent away. They bring both of them to the workshop but they are not conscious of each other.
>
> (Hunneybell, 2009)

Another way to frame this loss, as it affects the males' gender identity, is in terms of loss of *the Feminine*:

> The classic pattern for boarding school survivors remains one of achieving a pseudo-independence at the expense of belonging needs. We may suggest that they embrace a partial and immature masculinity, due to the loss of home, security, and everything connected to 'the Feminine'.
>
> (Duffell, 2000, p. 247)

In adult life this loss may be expressed in many different ways, which therapists will need to unpick. Sexual compensation is one: for many young men, lots of freely given sex seems the ideal answer. This solution was creatively portrayed in Lindsay Anderson's 1968 public school fantasy movie *If*, where embattled boarders escape to a café in the town, whose pretty young female attendant offers them playful sex. The scene shows how male ex-boarders can stay stuck in their sexual development in an adolescent phase. Seeing women as fantasy sex goddesses keeps them as objects of entitlement – simply the other side of looking for a full-time mother rather than a real-life partner.

Male ex-boarders may also express the loss of the Feminine in their attitude to self, in the lack of self-care, and especially in their relationship to the women in their lives, who stand for all the mothering of which they have not had enough. This enormously compromises their relational and sexual behaviour:

Many wives have told us how their husbands, who had been dragged away from their mothers from an early age, would behave like little boys in relation to them.

(Duffell, 2000, p. 247)

When such issues emerge, therapists have the job of reality testing, and they must not be afraid to examine any sexual transference phenomena occurring in the room. When such events are seen as arising from the failure of appropriate sexual developmental needs and are related to the correct age, much repair work can be done.

Homophobia

Filling the place of loss, boarding substitutes sexual overexcitement, misogyny and homophobia. These three poisonous elements of the legacy of boarding affect all pupils, and therefore ex-boarders, but in different ways.

Marcus Gottlieb runs therapeutic workshops for gay male boarding school survivors including men who did and who did not identify as gay while at school, as well as those with 'a dim awareness of their gayness':

Some are still uncertain of their sexual orientation. Some had sexual relations at school, which was not always consenting. All were at single-sex boarding schools, and all experienced these as profoundly homophobic environments. Their parents, in some cases disappointed by their failure to align with male gender norms, had sometimes sent them away, in part, to 'make a man of them'. They went to a place where silence around gayness suggested a real sense of dread. Sex was punishable by expulsion – the threat of a second exile – and only took place under pretence of machismo and coldness.

(Gottlieb, 2005)

Gottlieb describes the double standards and invariable sexual confusion that arise out of those 'repressive, austere, joyless institutions from which everything tactile, sensual or voluptuous was excluded', and yet:

Ironically, there was plenty of sex in the Latin poetry that was force-fed to us, one man pointed out. 'But I kept myself safely emasculated and ignorant of what it really meant. *Amo* [I love] was just a verb to be conjugated.' Masculinity was policed from the outside and self-policed. 'If you were identified as a "cock watcher" or a "perv", at the very least you were derided and threatened.' Some attempted to keep themselves safe by adopting an exaggeratedly firm handshake and doing whatever else they could to pass themselves off as heterosexual.

Actor Benedict Cumberbatch confirmed this homophobic culture in recounting an incident at his public school, in which two boys discovered in bed together were chased by a group of others, shouting homophobic abuse (Alexander 2014). For those who imagine that such experiences belong to a bygone era, Olly Hudson, a 16-year-old pupil at boarding school, shows such attitudes still abound at modern boarding schools, erroneously imagined as:

> Hives of latent homosexuality, places where boys, frustrated only in the company of other boys, inevitably turn to one another to experiment sexually, gay or not. It's something widely caricatured in popular culture, though let me assure you, a load of nonsense. So conscious are most of the boys in my school of the abundance of males (and rarity of females), not to mention the homosexual stereotype, that they go over and above to assert their masculinity, an apparently quintessential aspect of which is to see whose 'banter' can descend to the deepest depths of homophobic, inane, misogynistic abuse. In any other context, namely one in which women are present – i.e. real life – this would be abuse, though they refuse to see it as such, for who in an all boys' school could possibly be offended or hurt in any way by this loutishness, when nobody who it affects is seemingly there to hear it?
>
> That is of course, forgetting the gay guys. There aren't many of us, though naturally, there are more than you might think, though we are forced to sit there in silence, and endure an endless torrent of homophobic abuse, most of which is invariably ignored by male teachers. Would they continue if we outed ourselves? Who knows, but who are we to turn round and counter a class full of rowdy, senseless boys on a testosterone high? If we did, goodness knows the onslaught of abuse that would result.
>
> (Hudson, 2013)

Hudson illustrates the toxic combination of homophobia and misogyny emanating from a culture where, in the perverse pursuit of creating 'gentlemen', young men are trained to live in an unreal world where all gentleness and emotion are frowned upon. Yet, in his therapy practice and workshops, Marcus Gottlieb helps repair this deficit by providing a safe place where gay ex-boarder men find they are not alone:

> I have been forcibly struck by participants' truthfulness, their strong appetite for contact and connection, and their evident delight in finding a safe place to share their stories, feelings and reflections on the ways in which boarding has impacted on their adult lives. The feedback has been that they have felt lighter, liberated, relieved of a burden, unblocked, stronger, and much more in touch with their own sadness and gentleness.
>
> (Gottlieb, 2005)

Working with sexual abuse

When parents are not on hand to provide mirroring then the sexual parenting function is devolved to the peer group or to the staff. Either way, this abrogation is problematic: the peer group is patently incapable of fulfilling a role of genuine guidance since it is composed of the uninitiated. The teachers may ignore such *in loco parentis* responsibility. Worse, some may exploit the unmet child by grooming and sexually abusing, for, as Evelyn Waugh wrote in his unfinished autobiography, published just two years before his death, 'Some liked little boys too little and some too much' (Waugh, 1964).

It is one thing suffering from the loss of being abandoned by your parents at a young age but another thing altogether when a teacher trespasses into the inevitable gap left by the parents. This is not to argue that teachers in boarding schools are all paedophiles – far from it; the vast majority of teachers consider sexual abuse of children to be a terrible betrayal of trust. Nevertheless, paedophiles are inevitably drawn to working in institutions with access to young children deprived of both maternal and paternal love, and where they can be in a position to step into this void.

However heavily regulated by Ofsted, these 24/7 institutions are impossible to police. In 1990, ChildLine put on a 6-month experimental helpline targeted at boarding schools and received over 10,000 calls – and this in pre-mobile days when phone access for boarders was still heavily restricted. More than half these calls concerned abuse allegations. Today, the pressure on boarding schools to continually attract paying parents and the eagerness of the media to create new scandals may mean that the incentive to discover sexual impropriety is further discouraged.

Sexual abuse recovery work is always lengthy and subject to highs and lows. We will not reinvent the wheel here, since there is much useful teaching material in print. A good start is the classic *The Courage to Heal* (Bass and Davis, 1988). In general, therapists must be patient and prepared to weather the storms of the Drama Triangle – more in the next chapter – and be seen as persecutory. Because sexual abuse is a core wounding, numerous aspects of the psyche will have been damaged and be compensating. Detective work may be needed: symptoms may be disguised by many other problems, especially hidden under alcohol and drug abuse, and the first defence against the trauma of abuse will be dissociation and normalisation.

Therapists must be both mum and dad, prepared to be outraged, but also patiently linking and naming: 'Yes, it is because you were abused that you feel this'. Linking cause to symptom may seem boring, repetitive work at first, before its compassionate efficacy is understood. It should not, as in the practice of one specialist agency that we came across, be avoided in order to spare the sufferer more labelling! This is an example of therapists putting their own sentiments before those of the client, and thereby replicating the original exploitation.

The sexually abused ex-boarder regularly suffers from deep confusion and shame. The therapist's job is to persistently affirm that the shame belongs to the manipulative, uncaring abuser and has been dumped on the client. A great deal of grooming in the form of giving treats and making the child feel special may have taken place as a prelude to the abuse. This specialness is as toxic as the shame. As an up-to-date account of grooming and abuse at boarding school, comedian Billy Connolly has recommended that the film Chosen, aired on television in 2008, is shown in every school in Britain (2008).

Every child has the right to feel genuinely special, but the boarder forfeits this and may get abused in the bargain. The abused child is chosen, used and then thrown away; so specialness here has pathological dimensions. Sometimes unconsciously it is clung to, and sometimes replicated in the therapy situation. It creates deep confusion, as in the case of 'Henry', who reluctantly seeks therapeutic help aged 32.

Case example: Henry

Henry's partner from a two-year relationship has given him an ultimatum that if he doesn't seek help for his issues their relationship will have to end. She finds his use of alcohol and drugs too much: 'When everyone else has stopped, he just keeps going'. Henry is reluctant to talk about anything and isolates himself when she tries to help or get closer to him. She is at her wits' end with him, but loves him and wants to stay with him.

In therapy, Henry spends a lot of time talking about the good feeling he gets from alcohol and cocaine. When he tries to give up or cut down, he tends to become nervous and withdrawn, whereas with these substances he feels good and can even be 'the life and soul of the party'. He can't imagine life without them. He loves his partner but quickly becomes irritated with her when she stops 'being fun' and 'gets all serious'. He doesn't want to talk about his childhood, which he describes as uneventful and quite happy.

Henry boarded from the age of 8 at the same schools as his father. Most of his friends had similar educational experiences. The therapist tries to get him to remember some of his experiences at boarding school and, under the facade of emotional blankness, detects a kind of covert anger whenever this topic arises. After six months of weekly therapy, suddenly, and without warning, Henry terminates the arrangement, stating that his partner has now left him and that clearly the therapy has not worked. The therapist is unable to get him to come for any closing sessions.

Eleven years later, Henry starts therapy again with a different therapist. In the meantime he has married a woman he met nine years previously. They have a son, who is now 6 years old. He still drinks a lot and takes recreational drugs. It is not a problem, he says, as regards his work in advertising, but it impacts badly on his relationship with his wife. He tells the therapist that he tried therapy once before and it did not work.

Henry brings up an issue with his wife over the education of their son. Henry wants him to go to boarding school but she doesn't. 'She's Swedish, so of course is against what she sees as a stupid and neglectful British habit.' Tradition will have to be broken anyway, as Henry announces that his prep school is now closed – 'Just as well', he says 'as most of the teachers were filthy perverts.' He gets quite angry when recounting this and the therapist asks him for more details. It transpires that the school closed in the 1990s and that two teachers from the past have been given prison sentences for sexual abuse with one teacher having offences at more than one school. 'Luckily I managed to avoid all that', he says, but the therapist is not convinced.

A few months later, Henry arrives for a session in quite a state. He is angry and a bit hungover. There has been a spate of news reports and newspaper articles about child sexual abuse recently, some of it connected to boarding school. He now agrees with his wife that their son must not be sent away. He now talks about a teacher who befriended him at school, giving him sweets and once cooking him a special meal. They used to play tickling games. The teacher also tried hypnosis on him. One thing led to another and 'he touched me where he shouldn't'. Over a number of sessions, the story emerges of regular meetings laced with treats and abuse.

Henry feels very ashamed about the whole thing and says he probably encouraged the teacher. He tried to tell his parents in a rather indirect way to avoid any blame for himself or the teacher and because the headmaster had told them all on more than one occasion that 'what happens in school stays in school' – there being nothing worse than a pupil who tells tales out of school. Henry's father, a very remote and unemotional man, would have none of it and seemed to think that 'these sorts of things' were just part of the school experience. Henry's mother said nothing. It all ended within a year of it starting, when Henry returned to the school to find the teacher had left. There were rumours about him having to leave because 'he was a dirty perv'.

Over several years, with the help of this therapist, Henry moves slowly from believing he was the cause of his own abuse to recognising that he was the victim. In time, he is able to come to terms with what had happened in the past, to praise himself for having the courage to tell his parents what he was enduring and to partially forgive them for not taking action. Next, he tries to track down the abusive teacher and finds out that he retired from teaching quite early and then died of a heart attack.

Henry finds he is gradually able to share all his experiences, both past and present, with his wife and their relationship improves. He is proud that he was able to save his son from potentially the same fate as himself. He thinks about reporting the abuse he experienced to the police but decides not to do this.

Henry's second therapist is able to establish a therapeutic alliance within which Henry begins to feel safe. The therapist is able to notice gradual changes in how Henry relates to her. For example, she notices a shift from the default position of anger and defensiveness at even the smallest of challenges to a less guarded, more open way of presenting himself. With the therapist's gentle but firm boundaries and an emphasis on acceptance and safety, Henry very slowly starts to let go and to take more risks in terms of disclosure. The therapist then notices Henry's willingness to explore the part of him that survived the trauma. Eventually, Henry begins to see that this part of him is not all he is, and in doing so, can begin to let go of the burden of shame that was put upon him by his abuser.

Henry's early prevarication hid his profound need for safety, but reveals why building up trust with a therapist is paramount. Such a client needs time and gentle encouragement to learn to unlearn his trauma response, to turn on his parasympathetic nervous system, to believe that trusting someone does not involve further abuse. Working through such issues requires long-term commitment, but the therapist's reward comes when such a client claims the chance to live rather than just survive.

Exercise 9: sex and boarding

Ask your client to consider the following questions:

- What was the overall attitude to sex in your boarding school/s?
- What do you remember about your sexual education?
- Did anything untoward, confusing, abusive happen to you there?
- How would you describe the general attitude towards sexuality, including homosexuality?
- When you left school, how well were you prepared for your future sexual life?
- Are you still living your life sexually on the premise of those days?

References

Alexander, A. (2014) 'Benedict Cumberbatch on the Incredible Homophobia Suffered by Boys at His School', *Independent*, 9 September.

Bass, E. and Davis, L. (1988) *The Courage to Heal*, New York: Harper and Row.

Chosen (2008) Film directed by Brian Woods, UK: True Vision Productions and Channel 4 BRITDOC Foundation, http://chosen.org.uk/watch_film/.

Duffell, N. (2000) *The Making of Them: The British Attitude to Children and the Boarding School System*, London: Lone Arrow Press.

Gottlieb, M. (2005) 'Working with Gay Boarding School Survivors', *Self and Society*, 33, 3, pp. 16–23.

Hickson, A. (1995) *The Poisoned Bowl: Sex Repression and the Public School System*, Constable: London.

Hudson, O. (2013) *Pink News*, retrieved from http://www.pinknews.co.uk/2013/01/10/comment-the-truth-about-being-a-gay-16-year-old-at-an-all-boys-boarding-school/ on 3 March 2015.

Hunneybell, D. (2009) 'Some Thoughts on the Men's Boarding School Survivor Workshops'. Paper given to Boarding Concern Conference, 14 November. Retrieved from www.boardingconcern.org.uk.

Kirkwood, C. (2005) 'The Person's in-Relation Perspective', in Scharff, J. and Scharff, D. (eds), *The Legacy of Fairbairn and Sutherland: Psychotherapeutic Applications*, Hove: Routledge.

Lambert, A. (1990) *No Talking after Lights*, London: Hamish Hamilton.

Miller, N. (2009) 'Some Issues that Arise for Women Attending Boarding School Survivor Workshops'. Paper given to Boarding Concern Conference, 14 November. Retrieved from http://www.boardingconcern.org.uk.

Modjeska, D. (1995) *The Orchard*, London: Pan Macmillan.

Poppeliers, W. and Broesterhuizen, M. (2007) *Sexual Grounding Therapy*, Breda, The Netherlands: Protocol Media Productions. For details about Sexual Grounding Therapy, see also www.sexualgrounding.com and for training and CPD events www.genderpsychology.com.

Suttie, I. (1935) *The Origins of Love and Hate*, London: Free Association Books.

UNICEF (2007) 'An Overview of Child Well-being in Rich Countries', www.unicef.org/media/files/ChildPovertyReport.pdf.

Waugh, E. (1964) *A Little Learning*, London: Chapman and Hall.

Part III

Change

Chapter 10

The healing process

All things change, nothing is extinguished. There is nothing in the whole world which is permanent.

(Ovid, 43 BC–AD 17)

In discussing an approach to bringing about positive change within oneself, learning is only the first step. There are other factors as well: conviction, determination, action and effort. *So, the next step is developing conviction.* Learning and education are important because they help one develop conviction of the need to change, and help increase one's commitment. *This conviction to change then develops into determination. Next, one transforms determination into action* – the strong determination to change enables one to make a sustained effort to implement the actual changes. *This final factor of effort is critical.*

(HH Dalai Lama, with Cutler, 1998, p. 185)

The therapist with a need-to-cure and a patient with a need-to-fail establish one of the most stable and enduring and unchanging pairs in the civilised world.

(Herbert Gross, quoted in Johnson, 1994, p. 221)

Key points of chapter

- Healing involves recognition, acceptance and commitment to change.
- Ex-boarders can move from *survival* to *living* through an intentional process of change.
- There are various models of change.
- The change process has potential when the hidden pay-offs for staying the same are known and the need for the benefits of change outweigh any losses.
- Therapists must be curious and skilful in the presence of the will *not* to change.

Challenging change

Recognising boarding issues must be thorough to become a precursor to the acceptance that heralds change.

British culture is a complex beast. People often refer to boarding school experiences without necessarily acknowledging the impact and oddly making them somehow 'normal' again. Somewhere buried deep in their minds, there perhaps lurks a sense that the experience has had a negative impact. Alternatively, a close friend, partner or spouse may point it out to them, without them really accepting the importance of it. Sometimes a newspaper will point out that there has been a whiff of public school bullying in parliament. Nothing much changes – in the individual or in society.

There are many examples in literature and the media of a rather grudging recognition. Below, a well-respected and highly competent neurosurgeon, Henry Marsh, makes an almost passing comment about being frequently at odds with management in an account of his working life. Summoned to meet the Chief Executive of the NHS Trust where he works, Marsh writes:

> I may appear to others to be brave and outspoken but I have a deep fear of authority, even of NHS managers, despite the fact that I have no respect for them. I suppose this fear was ingrained in me by an expensive English private education fifty years ago, as was a simultaneous disdain for managers. I was filled with ignominious dread at the thought of being summoned to meet the Chief Executive.
>
> (Marsh, 2014, p. 160)

Marsh's comment illustrates the ex-boarder's complex attitude to authority: a lack of respect for the managers who represent authority combined with an inappropriate fear, probably linked to a pathological terror of the prospects of being found out.

British media regularly interviews celebrities and singles out a juicy story about boarding school, only to drop it again as if it is something everyone takes for granted and is not to be taken seriously. Former captain of England rugby, Will Carling, earned a certain reputation about perfectionism and anger. In February 2015, Carling told *The Sunday Times*: 'I was full of anger. I just wanted to be loved.' But where did this anger come from, wonders the reporter; the sportsman replies:

> It's not something I want to go into in huge detail but my mother, who was a very bright, very intelligent woman, would not have been the most maternal. I was sent away to school at seven and part of me was like, *I will look after myself here*, and I became selfish. I missed that love massively. I wanted to be loved but you sent me away at seven. I crave to be

regarded as worthy by my teammates because I didn't feel I was worthy to my mum. She had sent me away.

(Walsh, 2015)

Carling's account has a familiar style to how boarding issues can trickle out in therapy. A client may begin unwittingly to reveal something, before it is quickly packed away again. Super-packed with meaning and emotion, Carling's revelation is destined only to explain his grit and determination, as the interviewer subsequently steers away from naming the privileged abandonment that Britain normalises. But it does highlight one of the reasons that therapists do not have to be ex-boarders themselves. Ex-boarder clients frequently ask for this, imagining that they will be better empathised with. But sometimes an observer from 'outside the box' has a much better chance of avoiding colluding with the dangerous process of normalisation. Sometimes it is better if the therapist is not even British.

Normalisation is much underrated as a defence mechanism and amounts to what the psychoanalyst Wilfred Bion called an 'attack on linking', and thereby a hindrance to the change process (Bion, 1959, pp. 93–109). And in this context it has a long history and serious implications:

Normalisation, from a psychohistorical perspective, is a very powerful defence mechanism, operating on a systemic, and therefore social, rather than individual, level – although individuals participate. Psychotherapy can get bogged down in the myth of individualism, running from the political to hide in the private, morbidly afraid of generalisations, systemic perspectives, national characteristics. Such attitudes affect how we see our clients and their issues, and in a class-ridden society like Britain are irresponsible, I think.

(Duffell, 2015)

Back to the rugby. This interview is fruitful ground for the would-be ex-boarder therapist. It is more likely that a non-British therapist would pick up Carling's euphemism that his mother 'would not have been the *most* maternal', for this is the kind of phrase that people in the UK often use when talking to each other. His interviewer did not come back to him on it, yet we may imagine that this understatement disguises profound rage. The psychologically minded reader may have noted that with even the slightest attention from a sympathetic interviewer Carling drifts into a reverie, using the pronoun 'you', when telling his story: 'I wanted to be loved but *you* sent me away at seven.'

With the extreme disowning of feelings that a boarding child is forced into, ex-boarders are frequently dripping with emotion, and it can leak out everywhere. First-time correspondents to the Boarding School Survivors website often write lengthy emails, pouring their hearts out to an unknown stranger,

while probably not sharing with their partners. Taking account of this neces-
sitated a steep learning curve for the administrative staff!

The ex-boarder therapist must be alert to all the ways hidden feelings are
conveyed and re-concealed. It is a crucial step for ex-boarders both to get in
touch with their feelings and begin to make sense of them, and the therapist
has a major role here:

> In my profession, we tend to ask the 'What are you feeling?' question
> rather a lot, and many ex-boarders simply do not have an answer. They
> are not, in this case, being duplicitous. Frequently they have dissociated
> from their feelings; they have successfully split them off and are really
> not sure of them anymore. Often they will say 'Just let me think about it
> a moment'.
>
> (Duffell, 2014, p. 261)

Acceptance of these feelings means accepting loss and grief, repressed early
on in the boarding experience. It involves ex-boarders forgiving themselves;
and then forgiving others, such as parents. It means letting go of shame and
having empathy for self and then others – this is the high road to change.

The long and winding road

There may be many false starts on the road to change, as the client gradually
discovers how crippling boarding has been. It can be a testing journey for
the therapist too; those whom the client deems not to be up to the job will be
discarded. Below, Jane Barclay, herself a therapist, recounts her therapeutic
journey to the point where she embraces her process of change:

> 'I've come to work on endings', I stated to my new therapist, Jan.
> My first therapist had been Sam, my 'third-time-lucky-dad'. The sec-
> ond, a woman I saw briefly and she in turn recommended Jan. By this
> time, I had recognised that the way I had ended with Sam, after seeing
> him twice weekly for six years, had repeated my self-protective pattern of
> 'refusing to talk about it', of 'refusing to mind'. But I still didn't under-
> stand just how strongly I 'minded' in the aftermath; how pining, far from
> easing, actually increased to the point of knowing nothing else to do but
> cut off my prime source of support as well – anything to obliterate feel-
> ings of raw longing for what was not available. I didn't know, either, that
> I was projecting my pain directly onto my partner, whom I brutally ban-
> ished. All I felt was relief.
> My previous therapist had been a 'lay-by' on my journey, a safe pull-in
> but not a place to dig in, since I knew from the outset she was retiring in a
> few months. (Perhaps unconsciously I chose her for this). But Jan – here

was the 'mother' I needed, bosomy and pretty and assuring me she wasn't going anywhere.

I told Jan all I knew to tell about my nanny leaving (at 18 months); my father leaving (at the age of 5); my stepfather trampling my hopes for cosy cuddles, his touch subtly sexualised. I told her about my child-terrors during the time I lived alone after I left my husband of 20 years. I told her how I'd said goodbye to Sam, giving six months' notice and then avoiding any mention of the date that loomed. I attached to Jan, mostly via the soft-furred black panther that lived on her futon; I came to trust her, and learned a lot about being feminine, about the mix of gentleness and strength.

(Barclay, 2015)

So far, so good. For the therapist to embark on a process of change with an ex-boarder means digging deep into one's self, making room for everything that the client can throw, acknowledging the complexity of the client's wish for – and dread of – dependence. But then, sometimes, life intervenes. In our example it's the therapist's life, as Barclay continues:

But then came the cut-off point: two years in, Jan told me she would be taking a sabbatical. Not for another year, but that was irrelevant to me. I nodded, said that was 'fine', talked with her about how to prepare, about making space for anger. And proceeded to go through the motions. Yes, I sensed a waft of anger. Yes, I felt a lump in my throat as I stroked Panther for the last time. But . . . but . . .

Cutting off drew me back into a state I was familiar with of 'what's the point', the only way I can describe the grey place of chronic disconnection when nothing much matters – replicating the dreary trudge of day-to-day boarding school life that contaminated holidays too. Packing for a week in France, visiting chateaux, dining deliciously – low-level nausea persisted, enjoyment inaccessible.

As Joy Schaverien recounts, endings and breaks are particularly fraught moments for ex-boarders and will put the therapists on the spot, but they are also portals for entering into forbidden territory, which can initiate the letting go of blocks and facilitate the process of change (Schaverien, 1997). Barclay again:

So I began my search for a therapist again. No recommendations this time, I chose Anne from her photograph: younger than me, she was more likely to last me out. After two years of testing boundaries, I came to trust her reliability, understanding and compassion enough to take the next step – from my own initiative this time. 'I want to do this differently. Not like leaving Sam. I'm not "giving notice"; I'm needing to find a way of keeping ending in awareness, of joining up being here to not being here.' And so we talked about what to look out for, both familiar and new means I might come up with to escape.

First up? Recognising the need for help and hating having to ask. Irritation and apology – from my child-self to whom leaving meant 'fend for yourself', to whom 'go it alone' had been automatic (when asked by my first counselling tutor about what support I had, I'd answered 'I don't understand'). Next, I experienced acute anxiety in the form of the possibility of losing my home. Such was the strength of my defence against the madness of being sent away from home to live at school. I had minded that my mother made plans to see friends during term-time; it was easier to mind her not-missing me than to know that she did; as it was easier for her to believe me happy rather than missing her.

Barclay's change process involves a central plank of telling her own story, and in that she has much in common with other survivors. But it is her process around telling it in the relational encounter of the consulting room that throws up so many feelings, both recognised and unrecognised, which can either derail the therapy or lead it towards change:

> Which brings me up to date, about to tell my own narrative, in full, and be heard, fully. One piece at a time, with pause to *feel* my fear, anger, grief, to welcome these home and be welcomed. I'm glad to be here, excited even, at the prospect. Resourced a-plenty, I'm ready to venture into the depths, to embark on journeys to heal the wounds that reached my soul.

The change process

If, phenomenologically, change is inevitable, trying to intentionally change the self is not. It is a mysterious, complex process, beset with hard work, with highs and lows, gains and setbacks, and surprising reserves of undiscovered inertia. It invariably takes the aspirant back to the Acceptance stage of our RAC model, reprised below. This involves a profound shift in emphasis – away from *survival* and towards *living*.

RAC: the process of change

1. Recognition of the wound, which has three sub-stages:
   a. acknowledging being wounded;
   b. experiencing feelings about being sent away;
   c. recognising survival behaviours.

2. Acceptance: accepting the wound and realising that in developing a strategic survival personality, boarding school survivors did the very best they could to protect themselves at a time when they were unprotected.
3. Change: beginning to substitute healthier behaviour patterns because the cost of continuing merely to survive is too high.

Seeing the process unfold in phases or stages can be useful for the sake of orientation for both therapist and client; it is crucial that the therapist is able to keep track of the process. If helpful, the schema can be visualised as steps on a stairway back to life.

1. The first step is *acknowledging being wounded*. Those who have come to therapy or who attend workshops because of boarding know that they have been. They have begun to recognise some of the symptoms of this wounding. There are probably many more who have not yet dared admit it, neither to others nor to themselves. It may be that their partners have a sense of the woundedness not yet nameable by the survivors. Or it may be that the acknowledgement is being unconsciously avoided. Ways of avoiding that knowledge may include sending their own children off to board, and employing the well-normalised rationalisation 'It never did me any harm.'

2. The second step is *experiencing and accepting feelings about being sent away*, and about what happened at school. These feelings will most likely include anger or rage about abandonment, neglect or abuse – sometimes all three. The difficulty is that those to whom the anger is addressed may not in reality be able to receive it properly without retaliating or feeling blamed. Here the help of the therapist is essential to guide the expression of feelings and to bear witness. There is a further reason why such a helper is useful: boarding school survivors have survived principally through splitting off their emotions, so it can be extremely bewildering when these return to consciousness and are felt in the body. Therapists can help survivors understand what happened to them so that, during the process of rebuilding the self, the feelings are held in some container.

3. The third step is *seeing that they have survived their wounding*, and understanding how they did it. This can be hard work, for it means recognising what kind of person they have become, exactly what patterns of behaviour they have employed to survive, or what sub-personalities they developed in order to adapt to the conditions they found themselves in. They will need to acknowledge how many of these survival patterns still operate in current life, despite the fact that they are no longer children

and no longer at school. In making this examination of their strategic survival personalities they will have had to look closely into the issue of *needs*. They will have to see how they compensated for those which were not met in the family home, and how being sent to an environment where certain needs were impossible to meet, meant that they either developed entirely new ways to adapt themselves – or as is more likely – they refined the styles already learned at home – creating a defensive suit of armour that is now very difficult to remove.

4. The fourth step is one of *acceptance*. In developing their strategic survival personalities they did the very best they could to protect themselves at a time when they were unprotected. In designing their strategic survival personalities they inadvertently betrayed themselves. If they can truly forgive themselves for this, and have compassion for themselves, and make amends to those whom they may have harmed while surviving, then they will be able to move on.

5. Finally, they will have to take on a lengthy process of monitoring their strategic survival personalities and *beginning to substitute more healthy behaviour patterns*. The extent to which they have truly accepted and forgiven themselves will influence how successful they are at changing.

Change involves re-owning the split-off parts of one's personality and integrating new ways of being into life. It means becoming more authentic and true to oneself. Clients need to use their will: conviction, determination, action and effort will be needed (HH Dalai Lama and Cutler, 1998). This is not a 'quick fix'. It requires a good therapeutic alliance, based on trust. Therapists need to be very patient, tolerating the full spectrum of the client's projections, sometimes feeling ineffectual in the client's presence. Patience, presence and non-attachment to outcomes are the key to the therapist's stance.

One way to try to cut through the difficulties of the change process is to assess it extremely practically – almost economically. In the change process there must be a positive balance for a client whereby the perceived benefits of change outweigh the perceived costs of changing. Remaining with the 'status quo' and continuing with life 'as it is' is an easier option, but if the cost of continuing to survive is realistically assessed then not changing becomes less attractive.

And yet the opposite may also hold true: inviting change also evokes inertia. This too is a universal and existential force, of which we shall say more below. Therapists must remain on their toes also, curious and willing to challenge assumptions. The 'pay-off' for not changing, that drives the inertia, the swings and slides of progress, may then become revealed.

Models of change

In the early days of psychotherapy there was little understanding of the change process, but much wonder at the fact that symptoms and behaviour could express themselves in different realms, known as *conversion* or *somatisation*, and that change could occur through talking and having insight. The first change theories were mainly confined to what was known as the patient's *resistance*. This was seminal work for later modelling, but in retrospect it was tainted by the power dynamics, then not understood: the 'competent' Doctor worked on the 'incompetent' patient.

Dynamic models of change really took off in the 1960s with systems theory, based on cybernetics, and anthropology, in particular the work of Gregory Bateson. Systems, including individuals, were said to be seeking *homeostasis*, a state of balance first proposed by nineteenth-century French physician Claude Bernard as the *milieu intérieur*. Polarity between the dynamic forces of maintenance and change worked like a seesaw and moved in a complex dance: increase pressure and resistance would increase; make an opening and something would fill it. Everything was interrelated. The impulse to change sometimes responded to paradox, which we discuss in the next section.

Systems theory inspired one of the most radical breakthroughs in psychotherapy, Systemic Family Therapy, which took off in Italy and in the USA in the 1970s. Rather than using consciousness or insight, systemic family therapists attempted to harness the process of change (and inertia) as the *medium* for change. Change could be either superficial, *first order*, or fundamental *second order*. Systemic therapists developed many novel methodologies. They worked in pairs or groups, they designed strategies to outwit resistance and projection, especially the use of paradox, and they turned hierarchies on their heads by getting supervision from their students.

Systems theory also influenced many philosophers. Inspired by anthropologists' misunderstandings of Native Americans, Robert Pirsig reasoned that the essence of the world, which he calls *Quality*, is a direct experience prior to intellect, consisting of the inter-play between *Static* and *Dynamic Patterns of Value* (Pirsig, 1992). Individuals, societies or ideas lose Quality when they become too static, or overidentified. They resist penetration by Dynamic Quality, which then has the tendency – the moral authority, even – to overturn the known order. Finally, after a struggle and the death of the old pattern, there is surrender: a new more balanced static pattern results.

Pirsig's work is most applicable to the psychological change process, explaining resistance, breakdowns and breakthroughs, as is the work of transpersonal philosopher Ken Wilber. Also influenced by systems theory, Wilber argues that organic change happens not by abandoning levels of context when a new stasis is reached, but by what he calls *Holism* – the tendency to *transcend and include* (Wilber, 1995). Importantly, this is differentiated from pseudo-change, or first order change, called *translation*, which moves horizontally along levels rather than vertically, thereby avoiding transformation. Change sought by *translation* is the speciality of the false self, of the New Age, according to Wilber; it avoids the hard road of psychological and relational work.

Currently, the most popular models of change come from the addiction field and are more pragmatic than philosophic. The 'stages of change' – *pre-contemplation, contemplation, preparation, action, lapse/relapse* and *maintenance* (Prochaska et al. 1992) – are usually represented in a cyclical form. Lapse and relapse are included, as people often go through these stages a number of times. Maintenance is a crucial phase as this is how changes are sustained; whilst it may be short-lived on occasions, the ultimate aim is for it to last a lifetime. Miller and Rollnick champion *Motivational Interviewing*, which has five basic principles: *developing discrepancy, expressing empathy, avoiding augmentation, rolling with resistance* and *supporting self-sufficiency* (Miller and Rollnick, 2002). Here it is important that clients start the ball rolling by wanting to change out of a discrepancy between how their present life is panning out and their goals for the future.

In work with ex-boarders, a potential client may become aware of such a discrepancy, often through a personal crisis, and want to take at least a first step towards what they hope will be a better and more fulfilling life. It is an important departure point when an ex-boarder recognises and is able to say that they have *survived* boarding school. There is something very empowering about moving from a position of feeling a victim to being able to acknowledge that the trauma of boarding has somehow been survived. The young child did what they had to do to survive and get by – their ingenuity and resilience can be honoured. However, both acknowledging survival and identifying as a survivor are not sufficient on their own for moving on to a more full life. In order to move from survival to living, the survival personality needs to be recognised, accepted and then *integrated* into life as a functioning part amongst others.

Roberto Assagioli's Psychosynthesis, which he called 'a psychology of will', is interested in how the personality responds to different aspects of will, from striving to surrender (Assagioli, 1974). For our RAC model we owe him a debt. As a principle methodology, Psychosynthesis uses work with discrete fragmentations of the self, called *sub-personalities*, often compared to an internal orchestra. Sub-personality work has been much developed by Assagioli's successors, James Vargiu and others. Diana Whitmore (2000) presents a strategy for working with sub-personalities in three stages – *recognition, acceptance* and *integration*. Firman and Gila (2002) also employ a similar four-stage model of *recognition, acceptance, inclusion* and *synthesis*.

Early on in our work, it became clear that while the boarding school strategic survival personality operated like Winnicott's 'False Self' or family therapist Murray Bowen's 'Pseudo-self' (Bowen, 1993), it could also be thought of as a dominating sub-personality. Fundamental to work with sub-personalities is the dialogue between the part and that which is aware of it, framed in the notion of *identifying in order to then dis-identify*. Success is seen as integrating the survival personality as a member of the orchestra rather than the conductor. This is only possible, however, when the client is no longer practising severe dissociation. True recognition and acceptance involves full acknowledgement of what was previously split off and dissociated and, importantly, what was put in its place. Only then can the client put some psychic distance between him or herself and the strategic survival personality. One cannot truly move away from that which one has never been up close to. This is what takes time.

There are many things that motivated boarding school survivors can do to encourage the process of change. Therapy is usually essential, but it benefits from being supported on a family and wider community level, by practising mindfulness, and from a wide variety of useful approaches as championed by Van der Kolk (2014). But when applying any concepts of the process of change, Herbert Gross' health warning should be borne in mind: 'The therapist with a need-to-cure and a patient with a need-to-fail establish one of the most stable and enduring and unchanging pairs in the civilised world' (Johnson, 1994, p. 221). The hopeful humanistic therapist may always be foiled if they are not sufficiently aware of the client's ability to dissociate, or if they forget that what Bowen (1993) called the will *not* to change may be stronger than the will to change, which is where we must now turn.

The will not to change

As we saw in Chapter 8, there is a human tendency to hang on to the scenario of trauma or wounding in an internal narrative that may or may not be conscious. New information on the brain and neuro-emotional studies are making it increasingly clear that this has to do with narrative and visual imagery that stimulates the flight/fight or freeze responses at pre-cognitive regulatory levels. Having to create new ways of surviving the same problem gives you tremendous cognitive dissonance; it also means having to create new pathways in the brain. So humans universally try to conserve psychophysical energy by hanging on to the known way. The connections in the brain between emotional and self-reflective cognitive brains that have to be made to inform survival and begin at attachment levels with the mother; they are refined in the narrative world of the family of origin and form a base pattern for further survival. A child's stance towards emotional reality is formed very early on and is hard to re-make.

Even as therapists have to accept that the most frustrating and perverse internal resistances are perfectly normal and energy-saving, they need also to understand, as systemic therapist Harriet Lerner suggests, the many forces that work against change even in those clients who apparently seek it (Lerner, 1989). In the cognitive work we do in Boarding School Survivors groups we call the tendency to survive in specific ways the Survival Pattern.

The developmental problem is that it is a pseudo-adult solution, because it was created by a child during a time of unsupported dependency, and is by nature maladaptive over time. In *The Making of Them* this solution finder was called 'the Architect of the Survival Pattern' (Duffell, 2000, p. 225). Consuming the child's learned experience and creativity, it clings to safety in the form of a known solution at the expense of a self-betrayal, excluding spontaneity, expression or responsibility-taking.

A personality organised in such a way will certainly defeat all cognitive attack. Addicted to solitude, not being loved, not getting 'caught', and not being vulnerable, the boarding school survivor can be a leading exponent of surviving by a kind of self-defeat, cutting of the nose to save the face. Some theorists see this tendency, sometimes known as *self-defeating personality disorder*, as a central structure in the psyche, rather like a dominating sub-personality. The Scottish analyst W.R.D. Fairbairn called it an *anti-libidinal object* (Fairbairn, 1974).

Fairbairn hated his own boarding school and became a renowned agoraphobic. But Fairbairn's remarkable work explains how a bad object is internalised, how this splits into both good and bad parts and also how identification with an aggressor operates. With an internalised bad object one is lonely, but never *alone* – better a bad object than none at all. There always remains a possibility of salvation, to which the masochistic response is always 'Yes, but'.

Popular psychology has taken up Fairbairn's idea, referring to the syndrome as the *internal saboteur*, probably knowing who first conceived of that designation. But popular psychology frequently minimises the syndrome, reducing it to a sub-personality. It is much more than this, and should not be underestimated. Characterological therapists know the strength of this negative attachment and dependency and identify it as *moral*, or *social masochism*.

Social masochism

Psychological (as opposed to sexual) masochism rests on finding a solution to a problem scenario and sticking to it, by apparently losing. It embodies the most amazing creativity of the human spirit, but it is also a disease of the will, for this creativity is turned against the self for the sake of survival.

In response to how their environment failed to respond to them kindly, masochists have had to organise their will against unmoveable forces, which could only be beaten passively, by predicting punishment, or by snatching defeat from the jaws of victory. The environment, in the form of parental and/or school authority, was far too big to control, so the control has to be secretly turned onto the self. Here we may recall Alice Miller's revelation of what she called *poisonous pedagogy* (Miller, 1983, pp. 8–91) – the deliberate application of the breaking of a child's will in order to socialise it, which, in *The Making of Them*, was posited as a conceptual foundation stone of the boarding school system (Duffell, 2000, pp. 91–2).

Stephen Johnson, a psychotherapist rooted in developmental theory, incorporating Reichian as well as psychoanalytic perspectives, acknowledges his debt to Miller and bases his understanding of the psychodynamics of the syndrome on Fairbairn's work. In his masterful and humane manual on personality styles and disorders, *Character Styles*, he compassionately names this syndrome *The Defeated Child* after the conditions existing for the child in the adult who developed it (Johnson, 1994). Space does not permit us here to go far into the specifics of masochism – besides, it would be much better for the reader to study the richness of Johnson's chapter 9, *The Defeated Child: Social Masochism and the Patterns of Self-Defeat*, and better still the entire book. We will confine ourselves here to some remarks on boarding school survival from Johnson's defeated child perspective.

An ex-boarder whose survival personality is based on social masochism can never experience genuine pleasure but will take delight in defeating any authority figure, including a therapist, since it is a perverse way of winning through losing. Johnson is exceptionally clear in describing this complex syndrome and explaining how the masochist's adjustment to abuse 'represents self-defeat and *simultaneously* reproduces and preserves the bad object ties while expressing resistance, rebellion, and retaliation against that object' (Johnson, 1994, p. 201).

Masochists often present as quite 'normal', and all three boarding school survivor types can be masochistic. The Crushed are the most obvious, while Compliers' masochism may disappear into the backdrop of normalised attitudes in society: 'You just get on with things . . . no point going back to the past'. Compliers like to preserve their image of a good childhood and excellent parents. They are highly socialised: shoulder to the wheel, they embody the heart of Middle England, the backbone of Protestant society. As Johnson adds: 'Those displaying the masochistic style are the perfect servants for hierarchical bureaucracies wherever they may be found' (Johnson, 1994, p. 202). Rebel types present more difficulties because of the concealed nature of their masochism. There is integrity in the Rebel's stance, which can embody a refusal to be totally socialised, the unwillingness to surrender to a bad regime. But the masochistic Rebel's war against bad authorities – as in the earlier example of Henry Marsh – often extends to throwing the baby out with the bathwater in a perverse refusal to embody the slightest quality associated with authority. External anger preserves the values that are defended: 'self-defeat preserves pride', as Johnson remarks (p. 212).

In the Rebel, repressive lids are visible, but the splits are often underneath. Rebels can be full of self-sacrifice, pleasing, good at getting and doing what they want without naming it. Unable to fulfil their potential, they want someone – usually the partner or therapist – to feel bad about this. The masochist's aggressive drive is concealed, passive: under totalitarianism, sabotage or passive resistance is the only way to resist (Johnson, 1994, p. 194). Passive aggression may be a deniable type, but it harms. Masquerading as innocence, it can become a way of life, and close partnerships, including those in therapy, can become poisoned. It is most likely that others will find themselves getting angry first.

Skilled in the tendency to self-sabotage, the masochist part of an ex-boarder may seek out difficult environments or poorly rewarded work. Underneath may lurk an inability to accept love, frequently expressed as an inability to care for the self, masking an unconscious entitlement to be cared for. Such complex attitudes get expressed in apparently innocent everyday patterns. For example, one of the authors had to recognise that his unwillingness as an adult to make his bed in the morning had to do with ten years of enforced bed-making as a boarder. While paying the price of sleeping in an unmade bed, he had been harbouring the secret expectation that someone else should do it for him now!

The defeated child in the ex-boarder adult

Working with masochistic boarding school survivor Rebel types is complex.

The Object Relations aspects are challenging: Fairbairn's anti-libidinal object is an internalisation of a *real* external bad object, or better the gross neglect by those *in loco parentis* was a reality. But while it remains firmly projected out onto the world, onto all authorities, it detracts from the internalised problem and the regressive behaviours of the sufferer. By being busy with bad objects, both perceived and projected out in the world, the masochistic defence maintains false hope but also expresses contempt for it at the same time. Fairbairn proposed that the bad object is split into parts – good and bad – and in the good part, kept alive, is the expected hope of having the 'entitled hopes and innate expectations for gratification with which the human being is instilled at birth' finally met (Johnson, 1994, p. 203).

This is understandable: it is pro-life – libidinal – but the problem in the present moment is that these unconscious expectations are *utterly unrealistic*: there may not now be anyone available to take you home from school, to make the bed, etc. The reality is that understanding and remorse from parents, from the school, from the whole of the Establishment even, just isn't going to happen. Consequently, these things have to get acted out, named and resolved in therapy.

It is most likely the therapist has to cope with being the bad authority for a period; having good sources of support is vital. The psychoanalytical model is the *transference triangle*: the therapist stands in for the objects of the past in order to re-experience and redeem the unfinished business. Traditionally, interpretations are based on this process, with the goal of creating a safe holding and maturational environment, the expression and detoxification of previously banished feelings of rage, and a gradually developing ability to recognise the difference between inner and outer worlds and objects.

However, working with masochistic ex-boarders, the likelihood for the therapist is that the *drama triangle* from Berne's Transactional Analysis (Victim, Rescuer, Persecutor) is the working ground. Therapists invariably start out as rescuer to the client's victim from the persecutory forces of the

past, which are usually re-experienced in the present. When they try to deconstruct the ex-boarder's strategic survival personality, life-long friend, ally and
attachment object, therapists inevitably become perceived as persecutory.
Additionally, if the client is internally busy with bad authorities there is no
way the therapist is not going to become one. If not sufficiently resilient and
aware, the blamed therapist starts now to identify as victim, giving power
away to the client, who then possesses multiple strategic options; persecutor,
by terminating the therapy, or rescuer by becoming 'good' again. Attempts
to shift away from this discomfort are usually regressive and turn into further
movements around the triangle.

It is likely that passive-aggressive and masochistic clients may be running
a similar dance everywhere. Therapists must understand the function of this
game, what it serves and, *when the time is right*, they can go into the *heart of
the matter*. Working with these triangles is different with clients repressing or
dissociating, of course.

Really taking on the defeated child is one of the toughest assignments for
a therapist. The therapeutic objective has to be helping the sufferer to take
responsibility for conscious rage and pleasure, both profoundly disowned in
the strategy of winning by losing. Strategic defence sometimes invites strategic action, but therapists should never be tempted to retaliate, however
dire the provocation is. If they do, the misery wins and the therapy loses. As
Gross warns, therapists must 'respond to the miserable patient rather than the
patient's misery' (Johnson, 1994, p. 224).

Paradoxical interventions

Two therapeutic strategies *may* produce results: cognitive work, looking for
the pay-off for not changing, and paradoxical interventions. The former we
do in group settings with *some* participants, but never with those who are
splitting, because it just won't work. The latter is when the therapist suggests
that change is available but paradoxically adds that the client cannot afford
to embrace it.

In response to provocation the client *may* then get the motivation to defeat
the therapist by choosing change instead of practising more self-defeat. Letting
go of the holding hope is crucial to avoiding being an impotent rescuer, since
the unmet hope is contained in the relationship with the anti-libidinal object.
Instead, working with paradoxical frustration may release rage and therefore
begin to dissolve the complex; at least the fury provoked ends the game of
concealing anger.

Paradox was one the specialities of systemic therapists, who also influenced
Johnson. A specific branch, known as 'strategic therapists', invented the 'Why
Change Paradox' (Watzlawick et al., 1974). In this the therapists would outline all the reasons why the client had already found a solution that worked
and why it was better not to change it. This paradoxical style informs some of

our cognitive work with survival patterns but can be amplified to release the masochistic client's will by frustrating their attempts to outwit the therapist and release long-held rage. But it is not easy.

Unless therapists understand the perversity and become as strong as it, they remain ineffective. Johnson says you then get spite rather than rage, which is masochistic aggression and pleasure combined, and is more of the same (Johnson, 1994, p. 226). 'Yes, but' is the masochist's anthem, and their game, after Eric Berne, is 'I try to be good' – then 'fuck you!' (Berne, 1964).

Together, therapist and client must find a viable alternative or this form of survival will never be relinquished. Self-sabotage means no other means can be conceived of. However hard it is, the therapist should continue to make links, not retaliate, seeing how trust is tested and, above all, not give up, resisting hopelessness, even while saying: 'This does seem hopeless; the therapist part in me is not strong enough; you'll never be able to put your trust in me; it looks like you'll never get well.'

It is not an opportunity to defeat the client, but to motivate them, or indeed to learn from them how to employ the strength, determination and skilful willpower that the Dalai Lama recommended in our opening quote. Nor does it have to be a battle between therapist and client, if 'the therapist doesn't need to help too much', as Johnson warns (1994, p. 226). Healing happens in small – but significant – steps, as Darrel Hunneybell recounts:

> What moves me are the profound steps taken in the BSS workshops. The importance of having a coherent narrative and remembering it, telling the stories, both sides of it, the two sides of the split in relation to each other and held by the emergence of a third position, a more real self, that in us which wants us to be more of who we can be. When he steps from self-betrayal and masochistic neglect into a more real relationship with his Self, in that moment there is the beginning of healing.
>
> (Hunneybell, 2009)

Exercise 10: recognising survival personality limitations

Ask your client the following questions:

1. At school, who or what did you become?
2. How did this serve you then?
3. How did this limit you then?
4. Who or what was betrayed then?
5. How does this limit you now?
6. Who or what is still being betrayed?
7. How does this serve you now?

Examples of what might come up in this exercise:

1. A larger-than-life rebel.
2. I put on a bold front.
3. I was unable to show emotion.
4. A small frightened child.
5. It keeps my real self hidden.
6. My passion and sensitive side.
7. It protects me from others.

References

Assagioli, R. (1974) *The Act of Will*, Wellingborough: Turnstone Press.

Barclay, J. (2015) 'Stepping Closer to Home', a special contribution to this volume with author's permission, adapted from Barclay, J. (2011) *Does Therapy Work?* Exeter: Troutbeck Press.

Berne, E. (1964) *Games People Play*, New York: Grove Press.

Bion, W. (1959) 'Attacks on Linking', *International Journal of Psycho-Analysis*, 40, pp. 308–15; reprinted in *Second Thoughts: Selected Papers on Psycho-Analysis*, London: Heinemann, pp. 93–109.

Bowen, M. (1993) *Family Therapy in Clinical Practice*, New York: Jason Aronson.

Duffell, N. (2000) *The Making of Them: The British Attitude to Children and the Boarding School System*, London: Lone Arrow Press.

Duffell, N. (2014) *Wounded Leaders: British Elitism and the Entitlement Illusion*, London: Lone Arrow Press.

Duffell, N. (2015) 'Odd Bedfellows: Psychotherapy, History and Politics in Britain', *Self and Society*, 43, 3.

Fairbairn, W. (1974) *Psychoanlytic Studies of the Personality*, New York: Routledge, Chapman and Hall (original work published 1952).

Firman, J. and Gila, A. (2002) *Psychosynthesis: A Psychology of the Spirit*, New York: State University of New York Press.

HH Dalai Lama and Cutler, H.C. (1998) *The Art of Happiness: A Handbook For Living*, London: Hodder and Stoughton.

Hunneybell, D. (2009) 'Some Thoughts on the Men's Boarding School Survivor Workshops'. Paper given to Boarding Concern Conference, 14 November. Retrieved from www.boardingconcern.org.uk.

Johnson, S.M. (1994) *Character Styles*, New York: W.W. Norton.

Lerner, H. (1989) *The Dance of Intimacy*, London: Thorsons.

Marsh, H. (2014) *Do No Harm: Stories of Life, Death and Brain Surgery*, London: Phoenix.

Miller, A. (1983) *For Your Own Good: The Roots of Violence in Child Rearing*, London: Virago.

Miller, W. and Rollnick, S. (2002) *Motivational Interviewing, Preparing People for Change*, New York: Guildford Press.

Ovid (43 BC–AD 17) Pythagoras's Teachings: The Eternal Flux, Book XV: 176–8, *Metamorphoses*.

Pirsig, R.M. (1992) *Lila: An Enquiry into Morals*, London: Black Swan.

Prochaska, J., DiClemente, C., and Norcross, J. (1992) 'In Search of How People Change: Applications to Addictive Behaviours', *American Psychologist*, 47, 9, pp. 1102–14.

Schaverien, J. (1997) 'Men who Leave too Soon: Further Reflections on the Erotic Transference and Countertransference', *British Journal of Psychotherapy*, 14, 1, pp. 3–17.

Van der Kolk, B. (2014) *The Body Keeps the Score: Brain, Mind and Body in the Healing of Trauma*, New York: Viking.

Walsh, D. (2015) 'I Was full of Anger. I Just Wanted to Be Loved: Former International, Will Carling Is far Happier as a Family Man than He Was as Fired-up Captain of England', *The Sunday Times*, 8 February.

Watzlawick, P., Weakland, J., and Fisch, R. (1974). *Change: Principles of Problem Formation and Problem Resolution*, New York: W.W. Norton.

Whitmore, D. (2000) *Psychosynthesis Counselling in Action,* Second Edition, London: Sage.

Wilber, K. (1995) *Sex Ecology and Spirit: The Spirit of Evolution*, Boston, MA: Shambhala.

Chapter 11

Unmasking survival patterns

People don't relinquish survival patterns, which have worked, until they have better survival patterns, which work just as well.

(Johnson, 1994, p. 226)

An adapted personality can last for life and is hard to change, for we tend to act as if we are entirely that personality and nothing else. But in reality it is as if we have made a mask and put it on, and have forgotten how to take it off.

(Duffell, 2000, p. 239)

I had a white mask which revealed an inkjet black skin.

(Matovu, 2010, p. 16)

Key points of chapter

- The Strategic Survival Personality was designed by a child and may not last for life.
- To effect a process of change, ex-boarders need to be able to identify the survival patterns in their behaviour.
- Tracing how they survived at school, they can recognise how old survival patterns are still operating.
- Fronting up the patterns of behaviour is often a mask, which was put on long ago and is hard to take off.
- Therapists and clients should review children's developmental needs and the compensations for them not being met.

The central role of survival

This chapter outlines some of the methodology designed to assist the change process that we have employed in working with boarding school survivors. The most critical therapeutic work is the weakening of the ex-boarder's reliance on the Strategic Survival Personality. It cannot be overstated how important this concept is in recovery work with ex-boarders.

Many of the problems associated with boarding can be understood from an Attachment perspective; but this alone is not sufficient to get behind the dissociated and strategic way of life of ex-boarders. Again, some therapists may imagine that the well-attached boarder will cope well enough with boarding. We must signal extreme caution about therapists' assumptions in general and about such a view in particular. It may be due to not appreciating what it is like to be in a hostile environment 24 hours a day, unsupported by parents, subject to potential bullying and abuse. It can skip over the developmental needs of children at puberty. It may risk colluding with the excuses of the proponents of boarding, who regularly suggest that 'some children aren't cut out for boarding'; in other words, boarding sorts out the wheat from the chaff and vulnerability is once more pathologised. Crucially, it overlooks the boarder's survival imperative and may delay the recovery process, which, for us, is based on recognising the survival self and *unlearning* survival patterns.

Prioritising early attachments over the boarding trauma also goes counter to the evidence. In the workshops we regularly hear from people who were sufficiently well attached before they boarded and happy at home, but for whom the shock of the school environment and its survival imperative was catastrophic. One man recently told us with pride about his warm mother and happy family and having been well prepared to go to school; but his experience when he got there was completely overwhelming. Of course good attachments are important, and what affects a child is a complex mix of circumstances and tendencies; however, all we can predict for sure is that the *poorly attached* boarding child is likely to fare badly and that very early boarding will affect brain functioning.

As we explained earlier, with the rupture of attachments boarders cleave to their internal protector – the survival personality – with a limpet-like attachment. And it is not only a problem for the very youngest: just at the time when children should be completing the internalisation of their parental imagoes their real parents are absent. The lack of active parenting in the puberty-adolescent phase strengthens this internal self-reliance; the values of the school system support it.

This attachment to and reliance on the solution achieved in childhood is accompanied by the traumatic profile we described earlier and is not to be underestimated. It is highly unlikely, therefore, that a therapist or a concerned spouse has the power to break the ex-boarder's compensatory attachment and reliance on the survival personality. There are strong emotional pressures to stay in a state of dependency on the created solution, for it inevitably forbids higher feeling that would hinder strategic functioning. The wider society largely normalises and supports such limitations to the personality. Feminist philosophers and psychologists, such as Carol Gilligan, have long argued that patriarchal systems want soldiers and mothers as the basic role types (Gilligan, 2003). Boarding does turn out little soldiers, and what use to a soldier is empathy, grief or compassion?

Moreover, a powerful internal loyalty conflict arises when attempting to jettison the survival personality. Therapists may be very clear with their clients that stepping out of habitual short-term survival, to avoid the shame of admitting they are wrong or out of order, is a necessary way to bring about the demise of the strategic survival personality's command over the ex-boarder's psyche. But they need also to remember that in pushing for these vital steps of change they have to contradict a long-held internal logic: how could you betray the little architect of behaviour who has kept you safe until now? This conflict has to be set next to its current regressive stance and undermined with self-compassion, therapeutic persistence and subtlety.

A final caution: the wish to enter therapy is not always what it seems: some ex-boarders come into therapy from a false-self strengthening perspective, for example, simply to cope better with the crisis rather than get underneath it; or alternatively sometimes seeking to become trainee therapists.

Running out of strategies

In fact, what usually happens is that life intervenes and, one way or another, the ex-boarder starts to run out of strategies and either panics or begins a process of self-enquiry. It is at those sorts of moments that the ex-boarder will present for therapy and may be ready for work.

One man who attended a workshop described his family of origin as supporting and his school experiences as 'not especially traumatic'. However, 'when my kids came along my coping mechanisms fell apart', he told us. Or it could be that someone recognises that trouble with a boss at work that is not getting any better or getting them into constant trouble is based on a consistent problem with authority. What often happens is the psyche of the ex-boarder responds to changing life events by a kind of breakdown in strategic functioning. It is hardly surprising that it might not last forever. The survival personality was designed by a child and therefore bound to become maladaptive sometime in adult life. Such a crisis feels like a breakdown at the time; but, with luck, attention, effort and support, it can develop into a breakthrough.

Breakthroughs will most likely be built on the gradual dismantling of the hold that the Strategic Survival Personality (SSP) has on the client's life. Our Strategic Survival Personality flowchart (Figure 11.1) is offered here to help therapists see the pattern of its inevitable construction, how it fights for its life, and how it may finally run out of strategies.

The flowchart starts by showing that both family and school are in a systemic relationship, so that blaming either may in the end be fruitless. The child has already developed some ways of being in the family, in terms of

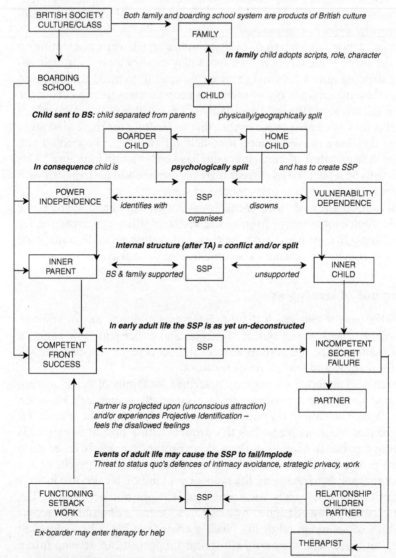

Figure 11.1 Strategic Survival Personality flowchart

roles or scripts or character, and these behavioural tendencies usually form the raw material for the construction of the strategic survival personality. In separating the child from home, boarding splits the child: first physically and eventually psychically. With only short visits back home, the child is unable to 'stay home' psychologically: boarding school is where the child now lives. Here survival is a matter of psychological life and death, so there is no option but to create a survival personality; and since the boarding world cannot be shared with parents, the child builds this into a secret, private realm.

Because the foundation of this structure is the necessary renouncing of all vulnerability it generally resembles a self-reliant, autonomous, competent, confident, successful character that the school ethos supports, that the family has invested in, and is perceived by society as a winner. Alternatively, it may be defensively formed to be compliant and integrated into the mass of middle-class society without drawing too much attention, hiding behind the clichés associated with sensible Middle England.

However, achieved at the expense of love, belonging and safety – genuine human needs that ought to be self-evident to children's carers – it is a personality on the run, under stress and brittle. Its creator frequently has many traumatic systems such as not managing its own stress well and the misreading of 'social engagement' signals (Porges, 2011). In adult life this personality uses dissociation and projection and frequently seeks out a spouse to carry the disowned vulnerable parts that it was unable to integrate.

Eventually some setback may bring about the failure of strategic functioning – it could be that the partner refuses any longer to carry the disowned psychic material – and the ex-boarder may enter therapy. Here, struggling for its life, the unheard words of the survival personality scream, as it were: 'Help me but don't you dare take away my lifelong *modus operandi!*' Attacks on the therapist, especially the threat of leaving and the projection of uselessness and incompetence, now abound, as the slippery fish that is the ex-boarder's survival self flaps wildly for breath on the deck of the practitioner's boat.

Spotting the pattern

There can be no set format for therapeutic work with boarding school survivors: it all depends on the individual, their story and the therapist's style. But once ex-boarder clients have recognised and accepted both the inevitability and the cost of surviving boarding school, therapists can re-focus them on precisely *how* they survived. Again, this is hugely individual, but having a very simple general theoretical overview that can be shared at this point helps clients get a context for their survival and recovery.

Boarders 'go forth with well-developed bodies, fairly developed minds and undeveloped hearts', as E.M. Forster put it, and so too much mental understanding might be unhelpful to those whose minds are already defensively set (Forster, 1964, p. 15). There is a balance between having sufficient understanding so that the client gets a perspective on the work and too much didactic material that might interfere with the relational aspects. But Forster continued: 'An undeveloped heart – not a cold one. The difference is important.' As new feelings arise to inform the development of the survivor's heart, the mind can actually provide a containing function, so a little theory is not to be despised.

Figure 11.2 presents such a simple schema. Diagram 1 represents how we humans come into the world very vulnerable, expecting to be protected and cared for by adult caregivers over a very long period. Our primary impulse is to survive and for this we need protection. Whenever this protection begins to let us down we attempt to control the caregivers, for example, when a hungry or distressed baby screams to attract attention or nurturing. As we grow, we attempt to control the environment we find ourselves in by organising it in a way that serves our protection, as in Diagram 2. But whenever we find ourselves, in an environment that is far too big, powerful, bewildering or hostile to control – a boarding school, for example – this control is turned back against the self as a form of self-protection to serve survival as in Diagram 3. Such control involves various forms of self-negation, primarily to protect our vulnerability, such as dissociation. In terms of survival it may work, but it has a cost and is a form of self-betrayal, because it involves the cutting off of parts of the self in order to survive.

Once the inevitability of this story has been established as a shared context in the consulting room, therapy can begin to move into the next phase: the identification of the patterns of behaviour that are still rooted in past trauma. The survival personality adopted was born out of the trauma of separation and abandonment in a hostile institution, but may retain many elements of the character developed before school. These patterns of behaviour now form a protective layer, or 'carapace' as one ex-boarder described it, to assert some control over the environment – primarily the peer group and the teaching staff – but also the parents (as in Diagram 4). This is why children at boarding school rarely look distressed: they are wearing their 'happy masks'.

At the same time, survivors are controlling their personalities, shaping the self by hiding away all the unwanted aspects of their self such as vulnerability, although in some perverse cases also success. According to the disposition, skills, backgrounds, tendencies and the particular nature of the environment needing control, boarders reinvent themselves in an astonishing variety of ways to get their needs partially met through behaviour patterns. The survival personality may have several incarnations or roles that it plays, which can be identified by careful self-observation in all the different environments in which the ex-boarder operates. First, in looking at the past at school: in the common rooms, on the games fields, in the classrooms. Such roles include the Clown, the Isolate, the Rebel, the Nice Guy, the Bully, the Swot and so on (as in Diagram 5).

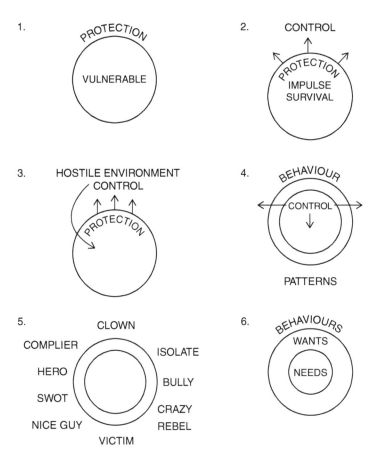

Figure 11.2 Survival patterns

Next, the client needs to see which of these are still operating in current life, and which have been most prominent in adult life – at work, in leisure, amongst friends, at home or in intimate relationships. Many different aspects of the self may be active, but sometimes it is just one principal self. Sometimes it can be helpful to name these patterns, for example: 'Mr Nice Guy', 'Belinda the Bully', 'Dennis the Doormat' or 'Crazy Karen'. In realising what sort of person they have become, ex-boarders can also see how behaviour patterns learned at school are still operating. These roles have their own identities, which can be very convincing, but are still outward-facing aspects of the survival carapace. Eventually, having identified them, clients may choose to substitute 'better survival patterns', or more appropriate adult behaviours.

The dynamics and techniques of working with such parts of the personality have been well described in the psychological literature, in Voice Dialogue work or Jungian Active Imagination, and we are not proposing to reinvent the wheel here. A description of the operation of ex-boarders' survival masks is detailed in *The Making of Them* (Duffell, 2000, pp. 236–49). The chief principle is that by increasing awareness of survival patterns the client is helped to sever the unconscious identification with the role. By becoming increasingly aware, for example, that 'I am not a Clown, but I have used this style as a way of surviving, having a role, avoiding anxiety, getting liked and so on', the client develops more choice about how to behave and present in the various relational encounters of their life.

Earlier we warned that the usefulness of sub-personality work is subject to the client not dissociating. For this reason more psychodynamically oriented therapists have traditionally avoided such approaches. However, sometimes clients themselves may spontaneously resort to seeing such patterns themselves.

Joy Schaverien, who is a psychoanalyst and also an art psychotherapist, describes powerful work with an ex-boarder client who used drawing to come into relationship with parts of his psyche that had been driving him (Schaverien, 2015, p. 100). In one session he produced an image of what he called 'The Controller', representing an aspect of his strategic survival personality that was keeping him safe by keeping him buttoned up (Schaverien, 2015, figure 7.3). In another drawing he illustrated a further aspect of his survival self by representing a tortoise, an animal which he knew well because he kept them as pets. Next he showed the beautiful garden his wife and he had made and where the tortoises lived. This meticulous plotting of the elements of the survival self bring the psyche's activity into consciousness, assisting the client to move away from their unconscious control. By looking at the drawings, Schaverien was able to speculate on which were created by his child self and which by his adult self, adding a further layer of awareness to the picture and another step on the road to healing.

Taking off the mask

Adopting a survival personality can be similar to putting on a mask. This personality problem is not confined to boarders but is universal: in fact in Greek the word for mask is *persona*. But the intensity of institutional abandonment encourages the boarding child to hide behind a mask at great speed, and sometimes the mask deceives even the wearer. Ex-boarders use their facility in this level of self-presentation and self-invention to become very competent spies, actors, comedians and politicians. But when the mask becomes an identity without which the wearer becomes helpless, authentic relationships become impossible.

The ex-boarder's mask can prove tricky for the therapist to see behind, due to the complex defence mechanisms the survivor can employ. *Reaction formation*, which reduces anxiety by taking up the opposite feeling, impulse or behaviour, can sometimes confuse the picture. Similarly, employing *identification with the aggressor* or *Stockholm Syndrome*, Compliers can minimise their distress by appearing competent and supportive of the system. When such a mask slips, the ensuing crisis may bring them to therapy for help in putting it back on. Even more complicated are those Rebels who have to face that some of their behaviours, to their partners or towards parts of their own self, operate like the Establishment.

Sometimes there are added circumstances that mean that the boarder's mask has to be extra concealing or extra incongruent. As one of only two black boarders, Rovianne Matovu, who boarded from the age of 4, eloquently describes the mask she had to put on at her school:

> I was the only black boarder in my house and as I got older one of just two black girls in the whole school of about 300 pupils. We had an almost tribal thing – the acknowledging wink in the Victorian school corridor when we saw each other from a distance amongst the sea of red and grey uniformed girls. The silent black salute of solidarity. We were alone on our own small island of alienation.
>
> I did suffer from racism, even though it was tacit and non-violent. Comments were made of the peculiarities of my African physique but I did win them over with my enviably chocolate-coloured silky skin. My natural athleticism, musicality, aptitude for drama and mimickery (in class and in the dorm!) gained me popularity but it still did not compensate for the obvious fact that I looked very different from my Caucasian female peers.
>
> The worst thing was, I could not fight back intellectually about the pros of Africa or being African. I had no knowledge of my country and roots. I was kept in the dark. I did not even proudly speak my own mother tongue: Luganda or Swahili. There were, of course, no black teachers and no warm maternal black matrons.
>
> Our history lessons did not help. The famous European Scramble for Africa just humiliated me even more – pictures of mud huts and half-clothed natives were not going to make me feel empowered. The collective black inferiority complex that Franz Fanon (1952) talks about was firmly planted in those formative years. I had no role models. I had no reason to be black and proud. There were no black pupils with their names glittering in gold as ex-Head girls or ex-School captains or who had won prestigious scholarships carrying the torch, having gone before me and so making it easier for the next aspiring black generation. Back then Barack Obama was just a fantastical dream and Nelson Mandela was incarcerated on Robben Island.

Education is a prized commodity in Africa. Parents make huge sacrifices. You owe it to them to do well; and I had the extra black woman's burden to represent the whole race, continent and family and prove that black people and indeed, black women, can make it and sit at the same high table as the privileged whites. So I suffered from a double homesickness: a deep longing for my country, home and family; and especially my mother.

I had a white mask which revealed an inkjet black skin. I could not scrub that off. My colour betrayed my aping of a white upper-middle-class persona. I had the accent but not the inheritance.

(Matovu, 2010, pp. 15–16)

Discovering needs

A potent way to look at the boarding experience is to get back to the basics of what children need. One of the exercises at the end of this chapter, which was developed in the group sessions, explains a simple way to do this. Clients can see that most of their self-evident needs, which they have now linked to children in general, were not met. In consequence, they recognise that their behavioural patterns were unsurprisingly compensatory.

Children cannot articulate what their needs are, so their unconscious and unmet needs drive their behaviour. This is perhaps the most fundamental psychic law. Figure 11.2 unpacks the carapace of survival behaviours: underneath the pattern is a motivation, and beneath that a need. For example, the Clown wants to make people laugh, but there is a need underneath what the mask wants to achieve; in this case, probably to belong. By focusing on needs in this way, ex-boarders begin to address the whole issue of their adult needs, especially how they may have unvoiced needs partly met through manipulative behaviour or by expressing the absence of need by means of masochistic patterns of low self-care.

Therapists can help raise awareness of needs in the same persistent way they may have to do with feelings. They must remind themselves how many ex-boarders do not know what they feel, let alone what they want or what they need. However, this apparent blank does not mean that the therapist should not persevere with such questions. Interpretations can also be useful here – especially when the therapist gets it wrong, because the client may be better able to say 'No, that is not what I feel, that is not want I want', and thereby may finally arrive at the need.

How others deal with their needs also now starts to become forefront, and much of this may be expressed in transference arising in the consulting room. It may be that awareness of these patterns only emerges in the dealings related to the practical matters of therapy. Therapists should always be attentive here, knowing, for example, that apparent administrative issues such as times, dates, breaks, room changes and especially fees are all areas where unconscious controlling needs may emerge into the light.

The 'Pump' - A Hierarchy of Needs © The Centre for Gender Psychology 2006
looking at psychic development from a post-Maslovian frame

The table should be read from the bottom up. It applies to individuals, systems and groups; it applies to all interactions at any age, and is key for workers' role-response.

MOTHER, Attachment, Security, Love Safety or Depth, Receptive Energy, Static patterns of value; symbol = Bowl	FATHER, Separation-Individuation, Autonomy, Will, Freedom, Penetrative Energy, Dynamic patterns of value; symbol = Sword

6. SURRENDER
Elder needs. Fully recognising interdependence and developing the art of Becoming Nobody.

5. EXPRESSION
Adult needs. Doing one's work, making one's mark, being creative, speaking out, making a contribution to the world, acting from recognised autonomy as an accountable being.

4. RECOGNITION
Adolescent needs. Being seen, being approved of, understood, acknowledge for self-worth, getting positive feedback, being valued, being in right relationship.

3. AUTONOMY
Toddler needs. Achieving a sense of autonomy, status, independence, feeling powerful, effective, have one's own thoughts, be individual, sense of agency and self-worth.

2. BELONGING
Infant needs. The Matrix: making strong attachments, safety, love, security, acceptance, belonging, bonding, nurture, care, basic positive affirmation.
PLUS - The Matrix and psychosis; splitting good and bad, persecutory Object relations. The two pre-Oedipal tasks: self and other, inner and outer.

1. SURVIVAL
Organismic needs. Basic provision of food, shelter, clothing, warmth; then stimulus. Prerequisite for psychic growth. Failure in 1 means annihilation. Failure in 2 means threat of annihilation compensated by stressful return to 1. Firing sympathetic nervous system. Fight or flight and/or splitting.

Figure 11.3 The 'Pump'

Next, therapists can assist their clients to get a hold of the pattern of their corresponding compensations for needs. Figure 11.3 shows a schema of inter-relating needs in a developmental framework of interdependence.

Readers may be familiar with Abraham Maslow's 'Hierarchy of Needs', the first version of which appeared in the journal *Psychology Review* (Maslow,

1943). Maslow's model has been adapted to work with boarding school survivors and was first introduced as a map of psychic development in *The Making of Them* (Duffell 2000, p. 244). *The Pump* is a useful framework for therapeutic work at this stage, organised to show the tension between safety, acceptance and belonging and autonomy and self-expression – the need to be contained and the need of being in the world as an individual. Healthy development involves a consistent zigzag movement up the model, establishing a healthy self-concept, rooted in belonging, and seeing the world as an interdependent universe.

When built over unmet needs, however, development tends to be compensatory; it lacks resilience and authenticity. Here again, unmet needs compromise developmental achievements because of their unconscious domination. In many ex-boarders the need for autonomy, and the behaviour built around it, were often built at the expense of the need to belong, feel safe and wanted, since they had to cut off from their home and their attachments to their parents and siblings. Safety and belonging are critical to the development of authentic autonomy. Sufficient belonging allows a child a degree of autonomy; when this is achieved a genuine expression made out of realistic individuality is possible. But a boarding child who tries to develop self-reliant independence built over insufficient belonging is compensating and will build a personality that is brittle. Genuine expression can be compromised by the constant need for recognition, which is another level of acceptance or belonging.

Using this scale, ex-boarders who have done sufficient Acceptance work can be guided by their therapists to see where issues of unmet needs and compensations are active in their life, keeping them still stuck, and still encouraging dependence on their survival personality. One of the crucial skills that can be practised, within and without the therapy is the voicing of needs. It is wise to start this work in a very limited and contained way; it is not about helping clients say: 'I need a career change.' Often even the slightest ability to express wants has been disowned, because wanting and desiring makes you vulnerable. Therapists can best help their clients who have disowned their needs by practising in small steps, with very small wants and desires, such as being able to voice: 'I want to sleep', or 'I want to eat something' or even 'I want the last piece of chocolate.'

Exercise 11: what children need

Ask your client to come up with a list of things that children need in order to have a happy and secure life. Below are some examples, taken from a workshop exercise, of what might come up in this exercise:

> safety; validation; love; play; recognition; food; fresh air;
> cuddles; exercise; education; mum; dad; compassion; nurture;
> boundaries; acceptance; fun; protection; role models;
> family; support; friends; care; encouragement; privacy

Exercise 12: patterns of survival

First set the scene by asking your client, in their imagination, to go back into their school – to see all the places and people they can remember. Ask them to notice how they feel.
Then ask:

How did you behave in these different situations?
Can you see any patterns emerging?

Ask them to make notes listing their behaviour patterns – seeing how many different styles they adopted or whether there was just one central one.
Ask them to return to their reflections and now see themselves at home in the family, when they were a young child and then a teenager and then an adult.
Ask them about their behaviour patterns:

Are they the same or different to the ones you adopted at school?

Ask them to see themselves in different situations as an adult in their family, at work, with their friends, in their relationships, in their most intimate relationship.

Which patterns still operate?

Ask them to make a list of all the patterns they can spot and to note the correlations between then and now.
Ask them to prioritise the two most important survival patterns and make a choice to be no longer governed by them, perhaps giving a name or an image to each pattern and asking them to think what the overall aim of each pattern was.
Then take time to draw out and work with these questions:

1. How did this pattern serve you in the past?
2. How did this pattern limit you in the past?
3. How does this pattern limit you now?
4. How does this pattern serve you now?

The third question is probably the easiest, since usually clients come into therapy because something is no longer working in their lives. The final question is the most difficult because therein may lie the payoff for not changing. It may need time and reflection or the therapist's skill with paradox to help draw this out.

References

Duffell, N. (2000) *The Making of Them: The British Attitude to Children and the Boarding School System*, London: Lone Arrow Press.

Fanon, F. (1952) *Black Skin, White Masks*, London: Pluto Press.

Forster, E.M. (1964) *Abinger Harvest*, New York: Harvest/Harcourt, Brace and World.

Gilligan, C. (2003) *The Birth of Pleasure*, London: Vintage.

Johnson, S.M. (1994) *Character Styles*, New York: W.W. Norton.

Maslow, A.H. (1943) 'A Theory of Human Motivation', *Psychology Review*, 50, 4, 370–96.

Matovu, R. (2010) 'Boarding with a Difference'. Boarding Concern newsletter, Summer, retrieved from www.boardingconcern.org.uk.

Porges, S. (2011) *The Polyvagal Theory: Neurophysiological Foundations of Emotions, Attachment, Communication, and Self-Regulation*, New York: W.W. Norton.

Schaverien, J. (2015) *Boarding School Syndrome: The Psychological Trauma of the 'Privileged' Child*, London and New York: Routledge.

Chapter 12

Homecoming

I set the book down, getting up to pee,
And in the window spy some towering bore
With shelves of books in ranks and rows behind
Me, stooping, thin, refined, towards the door.

My parents sent me off, as they were taught,
To boarding school, which formed me in their place.
The years of work and family now past,
I'm whittled back to what at core I was.

'Now settle down,' I turn to face the books,
Covered up, facing me like boys.
'Today we learn the Classical ideal:
To master passions, first control the joys.'

I close the door, certain there will be
No loose looks behind me, and no noise.
　　　　　(*In Loco Parentis*, by Andrew Morrison,
　　　　　　with kind permission of the author)

Key points of chapter

- Change may involve elements of forgiveness from ex-boarders towards their parents for sending them away.
- Therapists can facilitate ex-boarders telling their story: a powerful way to address the self-betrayal of the past and celebrate the ability to survive.
- Current research may soon assist therapists in their work.
- Persistence helps therapists support their clients through recognition to acceptance and then change.

Resolution and reparation

The boarder's deep longing to come home has to be suppressed at school but can last a lifetime in the psyche.

In some ex-boarder clients it can fuel motivation to recover, to become more at home in oneself, and to make amends for any harm unwittingly caused by the imperative to survive. For others it may facilitate coming to terms with who they have become: acknowledging their loss, their mistakes and their woundedness. It is less a question of 'moving on', as some suggest, since that runs perilously close to repression again, rather of deep acceptance, of integration, grieving and embracing life. Nor is it a question of provocative isolationism saying: 'This is who I am – like it or leave it.' Coming home is more of a state of awareness of who I am, how I had to become like this, and how I now choose to live.

> Being at home in ourselves implies a certain self-sufficiency, deriving from pleasure in a self which is not an island, not based on an empty shell that needs filling. It offers the prospect of completion, not a retreat into privacy out of fear, but an ability to be content with one's self, perhaps augmented by nature, or pleasant companions.
>
> (Duffell, 2000, p. 275)

For some ex-boarder clients it may be that coming home means that they have done the work to recover their natural self, to re-member their emotional self, to reinhabit their humanity that had to be compromised as a child and may have been compensated for with a cloak of entitlement. In others, the longing to come home is preserved as a wish for resolution with parents. Coming to terms with boarding is a difficult topic, and how clients want to handle this varies according to the individual. Some ex-boarders are able to talk things over with their parents and reach some sort of resolution.

Case example: Stephanie

A woman in her sixties plucked up the courage to discuss her boarding experience with her mother, who was in her nineties. After her brief first few statements about the harm she felt it had caused her, she was surprised when her mother said that she had always regretted sending her away and that it was a mistake she wished she had never made. This spontaneous apology from the heart had a great healing effect and improved their relationship in the final years of her mother's life. Stephanie was left wishing she had had this conversation a bit earlier.

Ex-boarders are exiles in a way, so appreciating the value of now having a home may also constitute a homecoming. Sometimes it may mean returning to their original home, in reality or the imagination, allowing themselves to let their love for the place have a special room in their psyche. Therapists can encourage clients to write a letter to the place that had to be forsaken in favour of the new life at school. Sometimes a letter or a poem can express what still may be unable to be spoken in ordinary words. Steve Potter, a Cognitive Analytic therapist who trusts the power of voicing feelings of loss, abandonment or exile and understands the issues involved for boarders, helped set up a website (www.dearhomeland.com) for the explicit purpose of receiving and publishing such heartfelt letters focused on place.

We have already discussed in this book how ex-boarders can write an imaginary letter to their parents about how they really felt at school as opposed to the rather bland letters that were usually sent when they were at school. This letter, or some other up-to-date communication with their parents, need not be shared: it can be composed but not delivered, as a therapeutic exercise. Sometimes it is better *not* to share the letter but to use it simply as a healing tool within therapy.

Many ex-boarders long for their parents to acknowledge their mistake by apologising for sending them away, and hearing what effect it has had. Others feel there is little point raising the issue with parents who would not be receptive, or may only feel blamed, which would create further alienation. And yet closure cannot take place without some element of forgiveness. This may come in the form of an understanding that the parents were only doing what they thought was right and best. Resolution is often complicated by a strange role reversal that can occur when parents become old and frail.

Case example: Susan

Susan's mother has dementia and then after breaking her hip in a fall becomes hospitalised. In hospital her dementia gets much worse; since her own home is now quite unsuitable to return to, she is admitted to a care home on discharge.

Susan accompanies her mother to the care home where all the residents have dementia. It seems a very alien and scary place in which to leave her mother and she finds it hard to leave, especially when her mother says: 'Don't leave me here – I want to go home.'

Eventually Susan just has to leave. That first night she worries about her mother. She feels very guilty for leaving her in such an alien place, even though the staff had seemed kind and friendly and some of the residents had also tried to be welcoming to her mother.

While Susan sits and worries it suddenly comes to her that her mother had done the same thing to her when she was a child, leaving her in a strange institution – her first boarding school. And now, almost 60 years later, a reversal of roles has occurred. Over time, Susan was able to forgive her mother for sending her away to board. Now, thinking back, she begins to feel some empathy for her mother about how she must have felt when leaving Susan for the first time.

> Some weeks later Susan is pleasantly surprised by her mother's accept-
> ance of the care home and its ordered life and routines. She wonders if her
> mother's ability to fit in is rooted in her experience of being sent away to
> boarding school many years ago when she was a young girl.

Susan's story contains some element of resolution and reparation. There is
a natural rhythm to it – the rhythm of life over generations.

Story telling

Often referred to as using a 'narrative approach', story telling has become
increasingly accepted as part and parcel of qualitative research across a number of professions and fields of study. Donald Polkinghorne (1988) led the
way with an emphasis on what he calls 'narrative knowing'.

In the broader field of mental health, people with lived experience of mental health issues have come to see telling their stories and being heard as an
essential part of recovery. Researcher and writer Alison Faulkner says:

> I have always believed in the value of telling our stories. One of the most
> powerful things we can encounter within mental health services is some-
> one willing to listen to our distress and come alongside us as we try to
> make sense of it. Unfortunately this doesn't often happen. Psychiatry's
> need to diagnose and treat often closes us down and prevents us from
> story telling, a process that can in itself cause more damage.
>
> Finding a way to tell our stories is not always easy. Some people may
> have been actively silenced as the result of trauma and abuse, and some
> may need considerable time and space to learn how to tell their stories.
> It isn't always easy to put things into words for the first time, to believe
> that someone is really interested to hear your words. My first experience
> of therapy was revelatory in this respect; I actually found my inner world
> more interesting as a result of learning how to speak about it.
>
> (Faulkner, 2014)

In a similar vein, Jayasree Kalathil reports on narratives of recovery and resilience among African, Afro-Caribbean and South Asian women. She finds
that people's understandings of their recovery from mental distress are rooted
in the ways in which they make sense of their mental distress often through
telling their story:

> Sometimes you can't make sense of what has happened in your life unless
> you are actually telling somebody the story, you know, so re-living the

story for me is always a healing experience. Even though I might feel that I am completely healed, you heal a bit more every time you tell the story.

(Kalathil, 2011, p. 20)

Story telling forms a key part of the individual and group therapeutic experience for ex-boarders: indeed, we have used many such stories to illustrate key points in this book. The relief in the psyches of ex-boarders when stories that have been secret for many years are heard, honoured and met by other stories has become the bedrock of method in Boarding School Survivors therapeutic group sessions.

In individual therapy, when narrative is used within the context of deconstructing the survival personality, it has the added bonus of providing an overview of the whole journey from survival to living. It can best be done by reference to the hierarchy of needs, the behavioural pattern work, or the general change process model described earlier. Below, Richard recounts his journey towards recovery, in which he both told his story and revisited his prep school. His journey is laid out within the RAC framework:

Richard's path to recovery

Richard boarded between the ages of 8 and 18 in the 1950s and 1960s. He married in his early twenties and had two children. There was never any question of them going to boarding school. In his late thirties his marriage broke down and he got divorced. He sought help from a therapist and found the experience very beneficial but there was no discussion about his time at boarding school. Richard didn't see it as an issue: he disliked it but had done OK and got by. The therapist looked no further into this and so the topic was left unexplored.

Recognition

Richard married for a second time in his late forties and, encouraged by his new partner, sought the help of a therapist again. This therapist had been a boarder himself and was more comfortable talking about the issue. Richard felt less frightened about revisiting this part of his life.

On advice, Richard read *The Making of Them*, which brought back feelings of loss and abandonment connected to his boarding experience. Imagining he would have little in common with the other participants, he tentatively signed up for the Boarding School Survivors workshop. But the reverse was true, and a very emotional weekend of sharing long-lost sadness took Richard into a different emotional place. Something had shifted in his body, mind and soul.

Acceptance

The second workshop weekend built on the first, and Richard was able to make more sense of his life decisions and choices in the light of his early boarding experiences. He began to understand the sort of person he had become when he was forced to abandon childhood and grow up too quickly at boarding school.

Now he became able to bury the hatchet with his mother and tell her he loved her, which greatly improved their relationship in the last years of her life. He was also able to write about his boarding experiences and plucked up the courage to re-visit his prep school, almost 50 years from the day of his first arrival there.

Change

Now Richard became motivated to change what had originally been a very bad experience into a part of his lived experience; he began to put it to good use to help others who had suffered broken attachments through boarding.

Change is a slow process, but over time Richard learned to be less frightened of his emotions and to let the tears flow rather than bite his lip. He still has a long way to go, but with help, assistance and love from his wife, family and friends, he now travels his life journey with a much lighter heart.

In Chapter 11 Rovianne Matovu wrote about her boarding experience. In 2015, she wrote to update us with the story of her own recovery:

> The legacy of boarding has not left me and never will. However, rather than call myself merely a Survivor, I am learning to live rather than to exist. I have my own home, a loving partner and am embarking on a new career. But it has been a long and very painful journey. I have had lots of therapy including Jungian Analysis for over 5 years. I am in recovery with a spiritual 12-step programme. I go to church to replace crippling fear with faith. I do yoga and meditation. Living in multicultural London I am no longer insecure due to the colour of my skin. I am one amongst millions. The heritage of our Continent is so rich. I am so proud of my African Roots. I feel more integrated within myself with all my inherent contradictions and cultural hybridity.
>
> However, it is difficult to disentangle the boarding school experience from the personality and the inherited genes for survival. I am very

grateful for the education, which I did take for granted – especially at my preparatory school. A good education does give you a certain amount of confidence. It gave me the tools to think independently and be critical. But the skills I was not taught were practical and emotional life skills such as how to survive in the outside world, outside of academia, the dormitory and the lacrosse pitch. They didn't teach you how to be a woman and just be a contented ordinary human being. Being institutionalised for so long, cut off from wider perspectives and global issues, gave you no mental and emotional preparation at all, and no defences for failure and disappointment.

Ironically, I am now arranging a slightly premature 50-year reunion of five close girlfriends, from both my schools, who supported me even if they could not understand my feeling of deep difference. I stayed with their families and even after, they have been there for me during my very dark times. So like women in prison, you do make strong life-lasting friends who also survived in their own unique and troubled way.

(Matovu, 2015)

Therapists will realise that the journey towards what Rovianne calls 'learning to live rather than to exist' is far from straightforward. They are likely to be tested, reviled, abandoned and challenged by the many ways that a client will cling to their survival personality. Travel writer and ex-boarder John Stuart Clark, whose cartoons under the name of Brick adorn this book, told us how resistant he was to therapeutic attempts to deconstruct his survival personality:

One thing is certain, I was a crap 'client' for my three therapists. My first was the more sympathetic, maybe because she was a walker and understood my need to be alone and left alone. My last and longest lasting couldn't get her head round that. She came from the standpoint that loners were socially inept if not one step away from serial rapists. But throughout our four years together I must have been hell to work with, sounding as if I was a stuck LP reiterating, 'I don't get why emotions are supposed to be so important' until blue in the face. When cuts in funding stopped our sessions for good, I think her sigh of relief could be heard in the Orkneys!!

(Brick, 2014, personal correspondence)

Brick used his own survival mechanism, a prodigious talent for humour, drawing and story telling, as the specific instrument to map his recovery. In his extraordinary graphic novel, *Depresso* (Brick 2010), he was able to use his experience of boarding and mental health issues to benefit both himself and others. One way he also makes sense of his experience is by helping others to gain understanding as he presents aspects of his life to mental health workers:

I am now in a position to share my grizzly journey with student nurses and practising professionals. I do so in the hope that some of what I disclose rings a bell with sufficient of their own, maybe not so traumatic experiences to reassure them that being bonkers is just part of being human. I do it because what they reveal of themselves sometimes helps me make a little more sense of where the hell I've been, and because many of their patients need a lot more care and understanding than I got.

(Clark, 2010, p. 180)

Current research

Therapists to boarding school survivor clients may sometimes feel powerless – like parents who cannot bring their child back home – in the sense that they cannot ever take away the fact of their having been sent away. They can focus their attention on the feelings evoked in the room; they can name the trauma and highlight that the consequent compensations for the loss of a secure childhood have occurred and are now becoming maladaptive. Nevertheless, with the metaphor of homecoming as a context for the therapeutic journey, therapists can help to guide their clients home by helping them outgrow the habit of drastic and strategic self-protection at any cost to become more at home in themselves.

In this process therapists also need support, particularly to know that they are not alone in the work. We hope that this book is a step in that direction. We are also pleased to say that, while Britain has not yet emerged from the denial and normalisation of boarding, increasingly we are hearing from academics and mature students who are undertaking research or dissertations on the psychological effects of Boarding School Syndrome. In time, therapists may have the benefits of such research endeavours to support their therapeutic efforts with ex-boarders. However, a syndrome that starts at 8 and that may not show symptoms until 40, and whose symptoms are only recognised by a small number of professionals, is notoriously difficult to research. The financial lobby that supports boarding means that funding for such research is very unlikely. Below we report on two projects, which stand out as exceptionally interesting among those that have come to our notice.

Zuzana Kucerova is a Czech national with two young children and a British partner who has lived in the UK for 20 years. As part of her MSc studies at the Institute of Psychiatry, Psychology and Neuroscience at King's College, London, she aims to conduct research that investigates the impact of early boarding on emotional wellbeing in adulthood, in particular to establish whether separation at an early age may affect adult attachment style (Kucerova, 2015). Kucerova's study is informed by literature on experiences associated with early boarding, such as narratives of boarding children, views of psychotherapists based on their clients' accounts, as well as other relevant journal papers. It is underpinned by Attachment Theory plus recent empirical research such as cross-cultural studies, longitudinal studies and neurobiological studies. It is further informed by studies that look into the impact of insecure attachment and bullying on mental health problems.

Findings from longitudinal studies reveal that attachment is subject to change over the lifetime and that secure attachment, as established in infancy, can become insecure as a result of stressful events like attachment-figure separation and divorce. Taking this into consideration, Kucerova's research aims to examine whether ex-boarders' adult attachment style might be predominantly insecure as a result of early separation and potential stress associated with early boarding, for example homesickness, bullying, strict regime, overcompetitiveness and so on. Here's how she describes her methodology:

> The study will employ a quantitative correlational research design, where data obtained from established measures like the *Revised Adult Attachment Scale* and *Parental Bonding Instrument* will reveal participants' adult attachment style and their primary caregivers' parental behaviour, as well as any correlation between childhood and adulthood attachment patterns. Also, the *Traumatic Life Events Scale* will be used to assess traumatic life events and control for traumatic events outside boarding. Furthermore, a *Demographic Questionnaire* with relevant questions about the participants' age of boarding, type of boarding school, caregivers and opinions about early boarding will be given to the participants in order to gain better understanding of what factors might impact on the formation of a particular attachment style. Fifty male and female participants, aged 30+ who boarded before the age of 13, will be recruited mainly through snowball sampling and asked to complete the four questionnaires either online or, if they prefer, in a pen and paper form. Their anonymous data will be analysed using SPSS.
>
> (Kucerova, 2015)

Coming at the issue from an entirely different perspective, Olya Khaleelee, who was the first female director of the Tavistock Leicester Conference, is a corporate psychologist and organisational consultant. Khaleelee did not set out to have anything to do with boarding: for several decades she has been involved with organisations in transition and engaged in psychometric testing for the corporate recruitment of senior managers. Using a variety of tests, including one developed in Sweden in the 1950s to test air force pilots for resilience, flexibility and accurate perception under stress, she discovered that there was an unlooked-for correlation between low scores and those candidates who had boarded as children. Here is how Khaleelee puts it:

In the course of my professional life, I have assessed approximately 2,000 senior managers, 90% of whom were male. Of these, about 400 went to boarding school, many before the age of 11, either because their families were abroad and they were having to make frequent changes of country and school, or because family tradition dictated that sons (and sometimes daughters) should follow in their fathers' or grandfathers' footsteps and attend the same public school as boarders.

The assessment process consists of a number of exercises and discussions followed by feedback. One exercise, the Defence Mechanisms Test, tries to explain in what ways perception of reality is influenced by early experience and the development of defence mechanisms that protect the individual from anxiety and stress. The exercise produces a timeline of emotional development and indicates when particular defence mechanisms are mobilised. These defences include those described by Anna Freud: repression, isolation, projection, introjection, regression, denial, reaction formation, identification with the aggressor and depression (Freud, 1936).

The data suggests that those executives who went to boarding school before they reached 11 years of age almost always show signs of 'regression' at that point in their timeline. This indicates a shock to the system and is usually followed by the development of other defences such as 'isolation', designed to compartmentalise and keep sensitive feelings well separated. Cutting off from their feelings enables these executives to function reasonably well at work so long as they do not have to cope with too much stress, which would make them feel overwhelmed.

(Khaleelee, 2015)

So far this is what we would expect. But, because of a surprising result in the results about resilience in ex-boarders, Khaleelee was intrigued by findings which indicated that boarding did not in fact deliver what is today often called 'grit' and used to be called 'character'. Resilience, a term more used by psychologists than psychotherapists, is an individual's ability to usefully adapt to stress and adversity, whether caused by work or financial stressors, as well as family or relationship or health problems. Resilience is demonstrated when a person can face difficult experiences and rise above them with relative ease. According to Wikipedia, psychological resilience is not a rare gift:

In reality, it is found in the average individual and it can be learned and developed by virtually anyone. Resilience should be considered a process, rather than a trait to be had. There is a common misconception that people who are resilient experience no negative emotions or thoughts and display optimism in all situations. Contrary to this misconception, the reality remains that resiliency is demonstrated within individuals who can effectively and relatively easily navigate their way around crises and utilize effective methods of coping. In other words, people who demonstrate resilience are people with positive emotionality; they are keen to effectively balance negative emotions with positive ones.

(Wikipedia, 2015)

The article then forecasts the optimal environments for developing psychological resilience:

The primary factor in resilience is having positive relationships inside or outside one's family. It is the single most critical means of handling both ordinary and extraordinary levels of stress. These positive relationships include traits such as mutual, reciprocal support and caring. Such relationships aid in bolstering a person's resilience.

In this context, boarders do not seem to have been in the best place to develop it. Here is what Khalalee concluded from analysing the results of the many testing sessions about the ex-boarder candidates she happened to meet:

Often their intellectual capacity is the basis on which they function and they are frequently observed to be out of touch with their feelings or hard to reach. Underlying this are well-hidden difficulties with trusting others. Many executives, when talking of their formative experiences, will state that although boarding school was initially a shock, they felt that it made them self-sufficient at an early age and many use the word 'resilient'. This is in stark contrast to their test results, which indicate that these early experiences have in fact damaged their resilience and have generated a significant imbalance between intellectual capacity and emotional intelligence.

(Khaleelee, 2015)

Khaleelee's conclusions challenge the conventional wisdom that boarding is character building. Boarding can be 'the making of them', but perhaps in the wrong way. Clearly there is much work for interested therapists and campaigners to do in educating the public in the difference between premature self-sufficiency, learned *per force* by the relationship-deprived boarder at an early age, and genuine resilience, which is something rooted in being at home in one's self, one's family and in relationships in general.

Therapeutic persistence

In writing this book, outlining useful approaches and techniques that we have found to bear fruit, we hope that we have contributed to therapists feeling less alone in the difficult work with ex-boarders. As in all therapeutic endeavours, and especially work with boarding school survivors, therapy has its rhythm: it swings up and down, between hope and hopelessness, between apparent success and apparent failure, between alliances and battles. The therapist's main task is not to miss clues and, if possible, to prevent the client from leaving therapy too early. For this, persistence and resilience will be necessary.

We will conclude with two case examples of boarding school survivors who have found their way home through the therapeutic process, albeit by circuitous routes. In these cases, therapeutic persistence and a combination of individual, couple work and group therapeutic approaches have contributed in helping ex-boarders move from survival to living. These cases are set out according to the RAC framework so that readers can see how the process can pan out over time.

Case example: Nigel

Nigel is in his early fifties and comes from a wealthy family in the Midlands and is on the board of the family firm. Boarding is not a subject that receives any degree of censure within his family or circle of friends; it is the assumed destiny of all the male children and many of the girls.

Nigel did not present for therapy because of any recognised boarding issues, but asked for couple therapy, because 'communication had broken down' in his marriage and his wife was becoming estranged from him. His wife was a somewhat reluctant participant, expressing doubt that the marriage could be repaired after many years of her being unhappy and mistreated by Nigel, whom she described as unable to show any emotion apart from anger. Nigel said he was irritated by his wife's constant pleas for more intimacy and he wished she would just leave him alone so he could get on with the various chores of life.

In the first couple of sessions, it was immediately apparent that Nigel would bark at his wife whenever he sensed any disagreement or criticism, to which he seemed allergic. It turned out that this pattern had become the norm, which might account for his wife's withdrawal and the cessation of their sex life. The therapy tried to focus on tracing the history of Nigel's defensiveness and anger. Following the first bout of couple therapy, both Nigel and his wife agreed to seek some individual therapy to address their particular personal issues. Neither of them had done anything like this before.

Recognition

When asked about his childhood in his individual therapy, Nigel imagined that he had needed to make up for his mother's obvious unhappiness about his father's absent, overworking tendencies. His father was an ex-boarder himself, and Nigel went on to attend the same schools. Nigel boarded from the age of 7 and felt that consequently he had failed to adequately support his mother at home. When asked, he felt no anger at this, but some guilt. The therapist wondered why Nigel did not feel angry about this role, which was evidently too big for a boy to carry out. Nigel added that he was now estranged from both his elderly mother and his siblings and that he tended to bury his frustrations in his work.

He did recall that he had developed a habit at his prep school, which he had perfected at his public school, of keeping his head down until he sensed a specific threat from any of his peers. Then he would explode in rage, which seemed to work by keeping him safe. Nigel imagined he had learned this trick from his father, but as a boarder it had become a way of life. He originally didn't recognise, but then – prompted by his therapist – slowly began to see that he was still doing something similar in his current life. Previously he had discounted his wife's protests as her always finding fault and blaming him.

The therapist recommended that he read the book *The Making of Them*. Nigel immediately read it and his reading evoked many unexpected emotions. At his next session, he said he realised that it was 'all about me'. This began a period where Nigel was able to recognise and acknowledge the amount of anxiety and anger he had been sitting on and how this had been polluting his intimate relationship.

Acceptance

As Nigel's work of recognition progressed, Nigel reported that, in talking with his wife, she had said she was pleased that the therapist had not discounted her side of the story. But Nigel now felt he had let his guard down and was taking too much of the blame for their relationship difficulties. The dynamic of each partner wanting to blame the other was a constant hurdle for the therapist to deal with. Nigel found it hard to accept that it was his survival style that was fuelling the marital situation and insisted that things should be more even and fair, since everyone – except apparently his therapist – knew that 'it took two to tango'!

The therapist did not take sides but encouraged Nigel to reflect on his part in the marriage. She also stood firm and insisted boarding to be the worst training for empathy and relationship imaginable. She offered continued support to Nigel in his work of beginning to accept that his strategy for surviving boarding school had stayed with him in adult life and had created a barrier between him and his wife. Nigel began to accept that he had the ability to both understand his situation and make changes to how he contributed to the relationship, for example, by less work and more play.

Change

Although Nigel expressed frustration that the process was taking so long, he made the choice to attend a group workshop. He wanted to find out how other men had experienced the difficulties of relationships when they had been unwittingly committed to surviving boarding school. He found this a most useful experience, in particular as he established some common ground with other participants and felt less alone with his issues.

Over time Nigel's angry outbursts became less; he reported sometimes even catching himself halfway into one of them, before stopping and apologising to his wife for what he *might* have said. He reported that he and his wife were able to be more intimate and that both his and her individual therapy had allowed them to be less defensive with each other and even to sometimes talk about their problems and vulnerabilities in an open and honest way. There was a long way to go but the marriage was beginning to feel less like a battlefield and more like a partnership.

Case example: Pete

Pete boarded between the ages of 9 and 19; his parents were expats living abroad. From his early teens, he knew he was gay and, whilst he did very little sexual experimentation at school, he came out of the closet without much difficulty once he got to university, helped by the relatively more tolerant atmosphere of the late 1970s. Pete has never had a serious intimate relationship – by his own definition one lasting more than three months – and relies heavily on a successful career for his sense of worth. He has few close friends, and they are mostly in other countries. He has a permanent chest pain going back to childhood, and has been having more and more anxious dreams, often set in school exam rooms or dining halls.

Recognition

When he was in his forties a parent died and a lover left him; Pete suffered a depressive breakdown, which frightened and bewildered him and led him to seek out therapy. In the early stages of therapy he had two important insights:

1) The shock of arriving at a cold, damp, formal, English boarding school, and then having to survive in that environment which was essentially hostile (he didn't like sports and wasn't particularly academic), fostered a personality that was exceedingly self-controlled, well-ordered, and skilled at keeping himself safe. He knew exactly when, where and how to hide in the computer room or the art and design school.

2) From the beginning of his life the homophobic attitudes of his parents, and of society at large, had penetrated him. His consequent sense of alienation adversely affected his ability to trust others and even himself, and thereby his capacity for intimacy.

Acceptance

In the course of the therapy, Pete came to accept that from the first day onwards boarding school constituted a trauma to mind, soul and body. His therapist framed this as an example of what somatic therapist Stanley Keleman calls an *insult to form* (Keleman, 1975). In consequence, a very wise part of young Pete protected him by focusing his attention on self-care and safety and by keeping his inner life exceedingly private.

Change

When a major job crisis arose, Pete could see it as an opportunity to become less work-focused, less driven and more human. He handled that well and gained confidence in his ability to direct his own life. The long-term theme of the therapy has been: 'what happens when we allow ourselves to depend on each other?' This involves risky experimentation and occasionally having painful or uncomfortable conversations. Nevertheless, Pete has palpably and visibly warmed and softened; his world is now filled with nurturing and supportive relationships to an extent that it is still sometimes hard for him to appreciate.

Working therapeutically with ex-boarders is not easy, it takes time and a lot of patience, but the rewards are great. The authors sincerely wish good luck to those undertaking the task.

Maybe – just maybe – one day the British themselves will kick the habit of traumatising their young children through early boarding. We can but hope.

References

Brick (2010) *Depresso: or How I Learned to Stop Worrying and Embrace Being Bonkers*, London: Knockabout.

Clark, J.S. (2010) *Walking with Dinosaurs*, in Basset, T. and Stickley, T. (eds), *Voices of Experience: Narratives of Mental Health Survivors*, Chichester: Wiley-Blackwell.

Duffell, N. (2000) *The Making of Them: The British Attitude to Children and the Boarding School System*, London: Lone Arrow Press.

Faulkner, A (2014) 'Outside the Box', *Mental Health Today*, July/August, p. 17.

Freud, A. (1936) *The Ego and Mechanisms of Defence*, London: Hogarth Press and Institute of Psycho-Analysis.

Kalathil, J. (2011) *Recovery and Resilience: African, African-Caribbean and South Asian Women's Narratives of Recovering from Mental Distress*, London: Mental Health Foundation.

Keleman, S. (1975) *Human Ground: Sexuality, Self and Survival*, Berkeley, CA: Center Press.

Khaleelee, O. (2015) 'A Note Regarding the Effect of Boarding School on the Emotional Development of Senior Executives', a dedicated summary for this book.

Kucerova, Z. (2015) '*The Impact of Early Boarding on Emotional Wellbeing in Adulthood*', research project in preparation at the Institute of Psychiatry, King's College, London.

Matovu, R. (2015) 'My Life as an Adult and Learning to Survive: A Phoenix Risen from the Ashes', unpublished account.

Polkinghorne, D. (1988) *Narrative Knowing and the Human Sciences*, Albany, NY: SUNY Press.

Wikipedia (2015) http://en.wikipedia.org/wiki/Psychological_resilience, retrieved 13 May 2015.

Boarding in the twenty-first century

It is often claimed that the evils of boarding life are all in the past, that the schools are much less harsh than they were 50 years ago. Physical punishments, which could be quite brutal, are no more. Outdated practices such as fagging have been stopped. Some schools have even shed the plethora of pointless rules that used to dominate school life. Children now have access to mobile phones, email and social network sites. Dormitories are less bleak with posters on the wall, personal photos and teddy bears. Boarding is sometimes not full time with weekend boarding or flexi-boarding as options in some schools.

However, there are still no parents. The trauma of separation and loss of family is the same. Attachments are still deliberately broken; the 'settling-in period', in which parental contact for the new boarder is discouraged, is frequently still maintained.

To illustrate that boarding is still problematic in current times we end this book with correspondence we received in 2015. These three unsolicited letters have been much shortened. We start with a counsellor employed by a boarding school – right in the thick of it – who wanted to share the case of a child she has been working with:

> Millie is one of the girls I have recently worked with, where the presenting issues pertained to 'homesickness' as schools prefer to describe it. She was 8 when I saw her and had major separation anxiety and on occasions, suffered complete emotional collapse. She would be found by caring staff and pupils, in a huddle in a corner, unable to manage the transition between one activity and the next.
>
> In our initial sessions, she would sit tight, holding onto a teddy or a stretchy toy, fearful of letting go and finding words for what it was like for her. She responded to my attempts to engage her and express my concern for her dilemma by looking at me intently, making me feel that she really needed to know whether she could trust me, wondering perhaps how long I would be around and was it worth investing in this relationship. In the third week, after 24 hours with her dad at the weekend (her parents

were divorced), she burst into the room, shaking and sobbing – words not being able to be found to express the deep sadness that her dad had left her at school again. She needed a parent but wasn't going to get one. I had to accept the inadequacies of what I could offer. We sat together in the despondency of her situation.

In the next session, her eyes were more open to the resources and toys in the room, and courageously she found a way to engage in something immediate by using sand trays and miniature toys. This helped her to identify the anger and confusion towards each parent and the loneliness of her emotional life at school. She was able to describe the business of boarding school life but also how devastated she was by not having the familiarity of her home. She was envious of her younger brother who did. The sessions with me began to offer a secure base and I was told that her 'homesickness' had decreased. She became able to manage the day-to-day routine of the school but she wasn't learning and had become something of a 'class clown'. After 6 terms, our work finished and she was by then experienced by others as a regular pupil, who was performing well enough. I was told that the therapy had been 'successful'.

As with a number of other children I have seen with similar presentations, I question whether helping Millie to cope and develop defences will be effective in the long term. However, I comfort myself that we had a very sustaining relationship and that Millie began to see the connections between her feelings and behaviour and also the value of voicing her needs. She became curious about how other young pupils coped with what she had been through and asked about becoming a 'school buddy' for new pupils.

School counsellors are placed in a very difficult bind; many wonder whether they are colluding with the problem or helping the children. Realistically, only going home can help end a child's suffering at boarding school.

Such confusion about boarding extends also to mothers, who can feel that they have to override their natural instincts to go along with the boarding habit. This is especially true if they are not used to the British scene. Some of the most important testimonials we have received are from people not raised in the UK and therefore not subject to the blanket normalisation or denial that is current here about boarding. Next we hear from the Swiss mother of a 13-year-old boy, who wrote to us in real anguish:

I'm in a difficult situation and usually work most situations out but I'm finding this terribly difficult to work out. I found your contact information online about boarding school survival so I'm hoping you can help.

I'm from Switzerland and came to the UK in the 1990s. I married a conservative Englishman who is a product of the boarding school system and says it's the best experience he's ever had. We had a son and I have raised him very lovingly and taught him to care about his feelings and have empathy to all around him. I admire my son, we have a very close relationship and hug each other and he knows no matter what he does in life, I'm already so proud of him.

Since birth, it was never a question of where he would go to school at 13. We put him in a day prep school closely linked to his future boarding school and I enjoyed taking him every day. When his entrance exam time came, we supported him with tutors, etc. and he got in! One day, he looked at me and said 'are we going to look at any other schools?' And I was horrified to realise we never gave this a thought. The choice was made by my husband, and that was final.

Now he is boarding and suffering greatly. I can't tell you how heart-breaking this process has been. Frequently my son holds on to me begging for me not to leave him, while the matron, housemaster and my husband say for him to stick it out. Every bone in my body is saying to bring him home – this is not a fake cry – it's deep and he's in real pain.

Everyone is saying 'he'll get over it' and he needs to detach, but it's been 6 weeks and he's getting worse, not better. I'm receiving emails and texts of great distress and he says I've just left him, abandoned him, while the staff are telling me to ignore his calls and only speak to him once a day for 5 minutes, then hang up on him.

I desperately need advice! Please give me your opinion on this.

We may wonder what happens to such children if the voice of feminine instinct and reason is not valued? What sort of adults do they grow up to be? Is the current system still producing adults who are emotionally and sexually immature? We will end by hearing from a young European woman married to an English ex-boarder:

Given that I did not grow up in the U.K. and thus did not experience what attending daily versus boarding school meant, I should in theory be unbiased and have a fresh outlook on the British education system. However, I cannot imagine sending my children away for two reasons: firstly, I cannot imagine sending my children away – a) breaking the attachment bond and b) being without them during their formative years. Secondly, I can see in my husband the effects that boarding school can have on adults. Although he would never admit it did him any harm (in fact, he would claim otherwise), my feeling is that he is in denial.

He was sent to a weekly boarding school at age 6 and then to a top rank public school. Sadly, he had lost his mother in an accident even earlier. Bizarrely, he has never learnt anything about her, as it has been a big taboo at home. So, understandably, he had to suppress emotions from a very early age and boarding certainly did not help in this respect. He is a successful banker now, very sociable, extremely confident – somewhat overconfident in my view. He thinks that boarding school was great fun and if it were his choice, he would send our children to boarding schools too.

I have observed one striking similarity between him and his friends who attended boarding school – i.e. that they are not able to talk about feelings or deal with emotions. If I ever talk about emotions, I am met with ridicule and presented with a rational, practical piece of advice.

Appendix: useful organisations

Boarding School Survivors (www.boardingschoolsurvivors.co.uk) provides therapeutic help to ex-boarders and provides specialist training for therapists. They have recently augmented their number of workshops to cope with increasing demand.

Boarding Recovery: Healing the Wounds (www.boardingrecovery.com) is a network of therapists with particular expertise in working with ex-boarders. They have also noticed an increase in referrals in recent times.

Boarding Concern (www.boardingconcern.org.uk) aims to support boarding school survivors and educate the public about the risks of boarding. It also promotes the welfare of children in education.

Boarding School Action (http://boardingschoolaction.wordpress.com) is a campaigning organisation that seeks to challenge the tradition of boarding in Britain.

Index